Photography by Virginia Cangelosi, Allegra Cangelosi, and A. Smith

revealing the
Economic Value
of protecting the
Great Lakes

Project Managers

Allegra Cangelosi (NEMW), Editor

Rodney Weiher (NOAA)

Jessica Taverna (NEMW)

Patricia Cicero (NEMW)

NORTHEAST-MIDWEST INSTITUTE

**NATIONAL OCEANIC AND
ATMOSPHERIC ADMINISTRATION**

ACKNOWLEDGEMENTS

Many hands, hearts, and minds helped in the preparation of this guidebook. The project managers thank the project funders: the Joyce Foundation, the Environmental Protection Agency's Great Lakes National Program Office, the George Gund Foundation, and NOAA Coastal Oceans Program. We are indebted to the authors, who hail from major universities and policy think-tanks throughout the Great Lakes region and Washington, DC. They skillfully adapted their specific expertise to the general needs of the guidebook readership, and waited patiently or the product to come together. In particular, we thank Jay Coggins, the author of several chapters, for carefully describing the fundamentals of resource economics in terms of the Great Lakes. The guidebook benefited greatly from project staff—Jessica Taverna, Carrie Selberg, and Patricia Cicero—who successively carried the guidebook toward publication and so carefully passed the baton—always in excellent condition and with a clear roadmap for the way forward—to the next project steward. We thank the Blue Ribbon Panel of Economists who supported, critiqued, and argued the important principles contained in the guidebook. We are indebted to the Stakeholders Forum Participants and the International Joint Commission's Sediment Priority Action Committee, who corrected our course and enriched our understanding of the issues. Finally, we thank our copy and layout editors: Amy Marks, Lani Sinclair, Merrill Leffler, and Rashne Green.

Table of Contents

Preface: Purpose of the Guidebook 5

PART I. BASIC PRINCIPLES

**Chapter 1. Introduction: Economics, Environmental Protection,
and the Great Lakes** *Allegra Cangelosi* 9
Here Are Some Questions 9
Can Economics Supply the Answers? 10
Tradeoffs and the Environment 10
Valuation and the Great Lakes 12
Grappling with the Gray Area 14
References 17

**Chapter 2. Economics and Environmental Policy:
What Are the Trends?** *Sandra Archibald* 19
Federal Laws, Court Rulings, and Executive Orders 20
    Cost-Benefit Comparisons 20
    Economic Assessment of Natural Resource Damages 22
    Economics for Other Purposes 24
    State Laws 24
Rules of the Game: The Devil's in the Details 25
    Guidance for Cost-Benefit Analysis 26
    Guidance for Conducting Natural Resource Damage Assessments 27
Conclusion 28
References 29

**Chapter 3. The Value of the Great Lakes Environment:
What Do Economists Mean?** *Jay Coggins* 31
Value in the Eyes of the Economist 31
    Economic Value and Willingness to Pay 32
    Goal: A Common Metric to Answer "What If" Questions 33
    Caution: Simplifying Assumptions 34
How Do We Value the Great Lakes? Let Us Count the Ways 34
    Market and Nonmarket Values 37
    Use and Nonuse Values 37

Values from Extractive and In Situ Services 38

Monetizable and Nonmonetizable Benefits 39

Conclusion 39

Chapter 4. Putting Economics to Work in the Real World:
Issues and Options *Jay Coggins* 41

Analytical Challenges 42

Converting Great Lakes Benefits of the Future to Present-Day Value 42

Irreplaceable Amenities and Irreversible Outcomes 45

Accounting for Natural Resource Capital 45

Risk and Uncertainty 46

Sorting Through Benefits from Multiple Projects 48

Accounting for Secondary Impacts 48

Social Justice and Ethical Challenges 49

Distribution of Benefits Across Society 49

Distribution of Benefits Across Generations 51

Placing a Value on Human Life and Health 53

Conclusion 54

References 54

PART II. METHODS

Chapter 5. Models for Great Lakes Environmental Decision-Making *Jay Coggins* . . .57

Cost-Benefit Analysis: Will the Intervention Pay Off? 58

Cost-Effectiveness Analysis: What's the Biggest Bang for the Buck? 61

Natural Resource Damage Assessment: What Did We Lose? 64

Economic Impact Analysis: Does Economic Activity Increase? 65

Value Clarification: Did We Miss Something? 66

Conclusion 66

Chapter 6. Tools of the Trade: Placing a Value on Great Lakes
Environmental Benefits 69

Valuing Environmental Goods and Services Traded in Markets, *Brent Songhen* 70

Changes in Producer and Consumer Surpluses 70

Defensive Expenditures 71

Valuing Nonmarket Environmental Goods and Services 72

Travel-Cost Method, *Frank Lupi* 72

Hedonic Valuation of Environmental Improvements, *John Braden, Sudip Chattopadhay* . . .78

Contingent Valuation Method, *Richard Bishop* 83

Benefits Transfer, *Leroy Hushak* 90

Meta-Analysis 95

References 97

Recommended Reading 97

Chapter 7. Case Studies 101

Case Study of a Market-Based Analysis: Soil Erosion in the Maumee River Basin,
Brent Songhen 102

Case Study of a Travel-Cost Analysis: The Michigan Angling Demand Model,
Frank Lupi 111

Case Study of a Hedonics Analysis: The Benefits of Air Quality Improvement
in the Great Lakes Region, *Sudip Chattopadhyay, John Braden* 120

Case Study of a Contingent Valuation Analysis: The Benefits of Sediment Remediation,
Richard Bishop 130

Case Study of a Benefits Transfer Analysis: Wetlands Restoration in Saginaw Bay,
Leroy Hushak 134

PART III. DISCUSSION

Chapter 8. Designing a Benefits Assessment: Sediment Remediation at Fox River
Richard Bishop 145

Clarifying the Scenario and the Question to Be Asked 145

Scoping the Benefits 147

Selecting the Tool to Answer the Question 152

Conclusion 156

References 156

Chapter 9. Addressing the Analytical Challenges of Valuation:
Aquatic Nuisance Species Control *Alan Randall and Hyma Gollamudi* 157

Background: Controlling the Spread of Aquatic Nuisance Species Between the
Great Lakes and Mississippi River Watersheds 157

Complexities 159

Risk and Uncertainty 162

Magnitude and Geographic Scale 165

Conclusion 165

References 166

Chapter 10. Measuring the Value of Health Improvements from
Great Lakes Cleanup *Dallas Burtraw and Alan Krupnick* 167

Principles of Valuation 168

Techniques for Valuation 170

The Value of a Statistical Life 172

Comparisons Without Valuation 173

Valuation of Potential Health Effects of Pollution in the Great Lakes 174

     Fish Consumption 175

     Air Pathways 182

Equity Considerations in Economic Valuation 185

     Adjusting for Quality of Life and Life Expectancy 185

     Involuntary Exposures 186

     Effects on Sensitive Populations 186

Conclusion 187

References 188

PART IV. APPENDICES

Great Lakes Web Sites and Valuation References 193

Resources for Performing Great Lakes Environmental Valuations 199

Resources for Economic Valuation of Environmental Benefit Studies 205

Project Collaborators 235

Excerpt from Restoration and Compensation Determination Plan:
Lower Fox River/Green Bay Natural Resource Damage Assessment 241

Purpose of
the Guidebook

With major policy decisions for the Great Lakes hanging in the balance, it is crucial that the Great Lakes community explore approaches to and uses of economic assessments in resource management decisions. In an effort to increase understanding and consensus regarding the role of economics in decision-making over Great Lakes environmental issues, the Northeast-Midwest and the National Oceanic and Atmospheric Administration launched a two-year project with support from the George Gund and Joyce Foundations. The project's purposes were to stimulate informed discussion, to forge greater consensus within the Great Lakes region on the appropriate use of economics in Great Lakes environmental decision-making, and to chart and catalyze the best next steps in increasing economic information on Great Lakes environmental amenities.

This guidebook was produced as part of the overall effort to familiarize resource managers and decision-makers for the Great Lakes with the techniques currently available for economic analysis of environmental benefits, including the strengths and limitations of these techniques. Rather than advocate the use of these economic techniques, the guidebook takes an objective look, pointing out caveats and advantages associated with the techniques currently available. This fundamental information is extremely important in the process of building consensus around the use of information these techniques can supply.

The guidebook comprises contributions of a blue ribbon panel of leading resource economists from Great Lakes universities and national nongovernmental research organizations to focus on the application of environmental valuation methods to Great Lakes environmental concerns. The guidebook focuses on techniques that are either well-accepted or increasingly accepted in actual policy applications. Because it is geared to environmental management practitioners, the guidebook describes in less detail cutting-edge theory—for example, that which is emerging from the new field of ecological economics.

The Institute and NOAA convened forums with Great Lakes stakeholders in July 1998 and September 1999 in order to vet the techniques and concepts contained in this guidebook. The project collaborators hope that this guidebook will catalyze more primary economic research on the benefits of Great Lakes environmental protection and restoration. Used properly, this information will further illuminate our options: what we stand to gain, or trade away, in our decisions regarding the protection and restoration of our main source of wealth, the Great Lake ecosystem.

part I:
Basic Principles

Chapter 1

Introduction: Economics, Environmental Protection, and the Great Lakes[1]

HERE ARE SOME QUESTIONS:

■ Sediment rolls down the Maumee River to Maumee Bay of Lake Erie every hour of every day. The material becomes contaminated as it passes leaking landfills, making it expensive to dredge and store. Even clean, it adds maintenance costs to water treatment. Upstream prevention measures could significantly reduce the sediment loads into the harbor, but such initiatives cost money. *How much money would Maumee Bay communities and the Army Corp of Engineers save if sediment loading into the river and bay were reduced? Do these direct savings exceed the direct costs of implementing upland prevention measures?*

■ A wetland area near the Saginaw Bay of Lake Huron is slated for development. But the state of Michigan could purchase the wetland for use by hunters and anglers if it could justify to voters the cost of the land. *What are the economic benefits of conserving the wetland? What value would be lost in development?*

■ In the early part of the twentieth century, the Army Corps of Engineers reversed the flow of the Chicago River and developed canals to facilitate drinking water sanitation for the Chicago area. The Illinois River, as a result, now channels Lake Michigan water into the Mississippi River basin, allowing aquatic organisms to pass relatively freely between the two systems. Aquatic nuisance species invasions speed permanent decline in Great Lakes biological diversity, and they impose new maintenance costs on industrial users of Great Lakes water. Three plans for reducing organism transfers via the Chicago River have been proposed, each more effective — and expensive — than the next. We know that a new invasion via the Chicago River is possible, but we don't know when it might occur or how bad the consequences might be. *How much should we invest in prevention of interbasin transfers of species at the Chicago River? When should the investment be made?*

[1] *Allegra Cangelosi, Senior Policy Analyst, Northeast-Midwest Institute*

■ Contaminated harbor sediments release significant new loads of polychlorinated biphenols (PCBs) into the Great Lakes. Recent research demonstrates that clear negative human health effects result from consuming fish contaminated with PCBs and that populations of children and adults in the basin suffer those effects. Cleanup is possible but expensive. From a moral standpoint, we would want to remove as much PCBs from harbor systems as is physically possible. But complete cleanup of all sediments contaminated with PCBs would severely tax, if not exceed, the combined resources of the United States and Canada for environmental protection of the Great Lakes. Meanwhile, such a cleanup would still not rid the system completely of the contamination because PCBs are also released from leaking disposal sites and old electrical equipment still in use. *How much would society gain in averted health care costs through cleanup of Great Lakes sediment? Where and when should limited cleanup dollars be invested in order to maximize the benefits they may yield?*

CAN ECONOMICS SUPPLY THE ANSWERS?

Can the field of economics answer these environmental policy questions for the Great Lakes region? It depends on the nature and difficulty of the policy problem. The first question (related to Maumee Bay) is a straightforward economic problem about commercially traded goods and is fairly simple to answer with conventional economics. In contrast, the other three questions are more complex, involving environmental goods and services not normally traded in markets, uncertain outcomes, and even social values. Here, economics may not be determinative.

However, even when economics alone will not deliver "the answer," economic information about environmental benefits can help us understand our policy options. In particular, economics can help policymakers define more clearly the economic tradeoffs associated with diverse courses of action — in terms of commercial goods and services and, increasingly, nonmarket values, as well. The challenge for Great Lakes policymakers will be in distinguishing the appropriate role for economic benefits assessment in environmental decision-making — one that neither overrates nor underutilizes the power and quality of that economic information.

TRADEOFFS AND THE ENVIRONMENT

Tradeoffs are a fact of life. We face them in every aspect of our existence, from where we live to what we do for a living. Sometimes we make choices fully aware of what the tradeoffs may imply, but more often we are forced to choose in the dark. The more complex the choice, the more often we must choose among options with incomplete knowledge of the potential outcomes. In these cases, we can be surprised by the consequences of our choices.

Certainly society has faced tremendous surprises as a consequence of its choices with respect to the environment — the most complex system of all. Had society known that the construction of the Welland Canal would lead to a sea lamprey infestation in the Great Lakes, it might have urged investment in a prevention measure at the outset, rather than accept the permanent price of lost fishery resources and chemical lamprey control in the lakes. Many of those who chose before environmental regulations to dispose of factory wastes in Great Lakes rivers and harbors did so because they were unaware of the consequences contaminated sediments would have for the health of Great Lakes anglers and their offspring for generations to come. Had they known, many (though not all) would have handled disposal differently. These oversights may not be relegated only to the past. Members of Great Lakes industries have argued that the benefits of more stringent effluent standards on industrial discharges do not warrant the cost to society of industry meeting them. Instead, control of more diffuse sources of pollution, like urban run-off, would render greater benefits to the environment for the price, they contend. These individuals anticipate that society will later wish it had spent more on control of nonpoint source pollution and less on control of pollution from point sources.

> Had society known that the construction of the Welland Canal would lead to a sea lamprey infestation in the Great Lakes, it might have urged investment in a prevention measure at the outset, rather than accept the permanent price of lost fishery resources and chemical lamprey control in the lakes.

Today, society has better information than ever before on the implications of its decisions for the environment — information it has gleaned from an all too rocky track record. With this information, theoretically, society can understand the tradeoffs it faces and make more informed choices about its use of the environment. What makes understanding these tradeoffs less than straightforward is the strikingly distinct nature of costs and benefits associated with environmental policy decisions. As an example, the cost of preventing new introductions of aquatic nuisance species via the ballast water of ships takes the form of easily monetizable goods, such as equipment installed in ships or ballast exchange at sea. In contrast, many of the benefits of prevention are intangible and not traded directly in markets (such as conservation of biological diversity) or are uncertain (such as the benefits of avoiding a yet-unspecified aquatic nuisance species invasion). The same contrast exists between the nature of costs and benefits associated with other environmental protection actions such as habitat conservation and toxic discharge reductions.

VALUATION AND THE GREAT LAKES

To help make costs and benefits more comparable, resource economists have developed methods by which to quantify changes in the economic value of environmental amenities associated with environmental programs. Surveys to estimate public preference (contingent valuation), statistical analysis of changes in real estate value associated with environmental characteristics (hedonics), and calculation of the amount the public travels to enjoy certain benefits such as fishing (travel-cost analysis) are ingeniously applied to arrive at these estimates. These techniques can estimate the economic benefits of a diverse array of environmental policy initiatives, including whether to implement a wetland conservation project, a new environmental regulation, or a project to clean up contaminated sediment. They apply as well to valuation of losses due to environmental degradation. That is, the proposed intervention could be a new development project, and the question could be: What is the economic value of the environmental amenities that may be lost?

The valuation of environmental benefits comes into play in public policy in a number of ways. The three most common formal policy applications of benefits assessment are cost-benefit comparisons, cost-effectiveness analyses, and natural resource damage assessments (i.e., estimates of the value of lost benefits). These applications usually pertain to a particular project or intervention that may alter the value of environmental amenities.

Cost-benefit analysis is the comparison of any positive (or negative) changes in the value of environmental amenities with the costs (or benefits) of implementing the proposed change. With much of the low-hanging fruit in environmental protection exhausted, today's environmental protection and restoration proposals often carry a high price tag, or produce more subtle improvements. As a result, decision-makers place increasing importance on evaluating environmental pay-backs relative to costs associated with proposed environmental improvements. The assumption that costs and benefits can be estimated to an equivalent extent, allowing meaningful comparison, however, is often questioned. President Clinton issued an Executive Order (12866) in 1993 requiring cost-benefit analysis of any new federal regulations with a pricetag exceeding $100 million. In response to this order, in the Great Lakes region, a major cost-benefit analysis of the Great Lakes Water Quality Initiative was undertaken. The analysis predicted positive net economic benefits for the region.

Cost-effectiveness analysis assumes that the decision to implement an intervention (such as a cleanup) has been made. Normally it is used to determine which among several competing implementation approaches is the least costly. For example, a cost-effectiveness study would help determine the most efficient way to achieve a waste-load reduction allocation pursuant to a Lakewide Management Plan. The cost of prevention approaches necessary to achieve the goal could be weighed against the cost of engineered approaches. In these cases, there is no need to calculate benefits because they are constant. However, the same technique can help determine how to maximize Great Lakes environmental benefits when the cost remains fixed. Such an analysis might reveal to a Remedial Action Planning Committee how best to use a limited sum of cleanup money to yield the greatest environmental benefits for the harbor. In this case, resource valuation techniques would be used to estimate and compare the benefits of various cleanup scenarios.

Natural resource damage assessments, such as those carried out under the Superfund hazardous waste law, help society estimate the amount of money that affected parties should receive in compensation for natural resource damage by a pollution event. Estimates of the value to the public of environmental goods and services that were lost due to a pollution event determine the level of compensation. For example, the Great Lakes Environmental Trust Fund is an outcome of a damage assessment. The fund compensates the state of Michigan and its public for lost fishing benefits caused by an improperly designed water intake on a power plant. It now provides a continuing source of funds for environmental projects that benefit the region.

Benefits assessments also play an informal role in policy making by shining a spotlight on formerly hidden values. In these cases, the benefits assessment may not pertain to a particular project, but to a set of benefits or potential benefits that may have been too little noticed in the past and therefore was poorly stewarded. For example, the International Joint Commission's Sediment Priority Action Committee recently recommended benefits assessments of sediment remediation in Great Lakes harbors in order to help clarify for Great Lakes residents what they could gain by taking on a cleanup project (SedPAC 1997). On a grander scale, in an article published recently in the journal *Nature*, Robert Costanza and coauthors valued the world's natural resources in order to help illustrate the importance of global conservation efforts (Costanza et al, 1997).

GRAPPLING WITH THE GRAY AREA

Society is not always interested in making decisions strictly on the basis of market economics. For example, Dutch research on the cost to society of cigarette smoking revealed that lifetime health care costs for smokers is less than for nonsmokers because the smokers' lives were shorter (Barendregt, et al, 1997). Yet it is unlikely that a national campaign to promote smoking will ensue from this research. In the same way, many environmental advocates argue that market benefits of environmental improvement cannot be the sole deciding factor in environmental policy decisions. For example, even if research cannot show a net economic loss associated with diminished child intelligence quotient (IQ) scores resulting from exposure to contaminants, society should not assume that the diminishment is of no importance.

Part of the challenge is incorporating the value of nonmarket benefits into economic analyses. The field of environmental economics emerged in large part in response to that challenge. Experts in this field fashioned the new generation of valuation techniques to be consistent with formal economics, but to expand its scope to reliably capture more of the values that humans place on environmental and other social amenities. For example, these newer methods would incorporate the value we place on longevity in a cost-benefit analysis of smoking, reflecting in the results society's willingness to pay for the long life of self and loved ones. Such an estimation of general preference likely would yield opposite results from a study based solely on a comparison of medical costs. These techniques are intended to allow more equivalent comparisons between costs and benefits of different qualities.

Resource valuation methods reduce but do not eliminate the gray area between economics and policy. Some of the environmental amenities or services that flow from natural resources are more easily quantified than others, even when economists apply the new generation of valuation methods. Quantification is particularly difficult when the amenities are not based on an observable use, or when the amenities are uncertain. For example, the value of preserving a species (or the cost of its extinction) is difficult to estimate because much of its value to society rests in sheer awareness of its existence. In addition, there is no way to predict the potential for the yet undiscovered market value that the species might have for future generations. Likewise, the value of preventing further global climate change is difficult to gauge because we cannot be sure of all the potential outcomes of no action until these outcomes are upon us and it is no longer possible to prevent them. For this reason, benefits assessments generated by valuation methods have been controversial in some applications, especially legal ones. Industry economists contend that such assessments are likely to overshoot the actual value, whereas environmental advocates express concern that these assessments can only underestimate environmental worth. Meanwhile, social justice advocates point to inherent biases within both basic economic theory and the newer valuation methods that skew results to the detriment of already disadvantaged sectors.

So how do we grapple with the gray area? The answer to this question has implications for the role of economics in decision-making. Some stakeholders, especially within industry, respond to the gray area in environmental valuation by restricting the scope of legitimate economic analysis. These users contend that decisions indeed should be based on cost-benefit comparisons but that values that are not readily monetizable should not be added into the cost-benefit calculation. Using this approach, they argue, the cost-benefit analysis is guaranteed to compare apples with apples, providing the best information to society about the implications of a change in the environment for economic well-being and overall welfare. Some within the environmental community tend to agree with this approach, but only if we recognize that the result of such a study (such as the finding that smokers save society money by dying young) is only a part of the story, in some cases a minor part. This approach recognizes and accepts the limitations of market economics and relegates the non-market considerations to the realm of the unknowable.

So how do we grapple with the gray area? The answer to this question has implications for the role of economics in decision-making.

Meanwhile, experts in the fields of ecological economics and environmental justice are responding to the gray area by designing new theories that correct perceived inherent biases within conventional economic theory toward resource exploitation and the uneven distribution of environmental hazards. These fields no doubt over time will generate important theories directed at improving the accuracy and fairness of environmental benefits assessments.

But what of the resource managers and policymakers who face decisions today on the best ways to spend limited resource protection and restoration dollars? The option of restricting analysis to market goods, such that we must shoot in the dark on all other values, seems irresponsible. But equally irresponsible is the prospect of using the new generation of valuation methods to generate numbers that appear comprehensive but perhaps are not. In either case, the numbers could take on a life of their own in a cost-benefit comparison, regardless of the caveats that a researcher may wish to place on them. These concerns and the urgent information needs of policymakers are driving near-term efforts to (1) establish standards to assure the valuation methods are effectively implemented and (2) develop processes to carefully place economic information — and its limitations — in a proper context in policy decision-making.

Much progress has already been made toward the first objective. In light of the importance of measuring difficult-to-assess values, federal and state governments are seeking criteria and guidelines for the effective use of valuation methods. For example, a Michigan law restricts the use of the contingent valuation method in natural resource damage assessments until guidelines for its appropriate use are developed. A blue ribbon panel convened by the National Oceanic and Atmospheric Administration (NOAA) developed a set of national guidelines for economic valuation, including contingent valuation. We discuss these initiatives in greater detail in Chapter 2.

Less progress has been made toward the second objective of creating a context for economic information in environmental policy decisions. Fortunately, however, there is still an opening for such a decision context to be developed and applied. Executive Order 12866 (and proposed Senate legislation that would codify it), which requires cost-benefit analysis in decisions relating to policies that may cost society more than $100 million, recognizes the limitations of cost-benefit comparisons in environmental policy. While directing that the study take place, Executive Order 12866 does not require adherence to the study outcome, simply consideration of it. Legislative language in the Water Resources Development Act is even clearer in asserting the advisory nature of the economic information associated with sediment cleanup decisions. These applications recognize the importance of benefits assessments and cost-benefit comparisons as spotlights illuminating society tradeoffs, including hidden benefits of environmental quality, but such applications also recognize the limitations of these methods. While requiring the assessments to inform decisions, they do not prescribe their use as strict decision-making formulas.

Participants at a forum on Great Lakes environmental valuation strongly raised the need for a decision-making context that can range beyond straight economics. They agreed that more information about potential changes in the value of environmental amenities generated through resource valuation methods should accompany estimates of direct costs to industry in environmental policy discussions. They also agreed, however, that although valuable, economic information must not be confused with the answers to environmental policy questions. Instead, such information should serve simply as one consideration in a broader decision-making process incorporating noneconomic factors, as well. Moreover, the specific questions that a given economic study does answer should be distinguished carefully from the broader environmental policy issues. This approach to incorporating economics into environmental policy for the Great Lakes — i.e., only very carefully — makes considerable sense given the specialized nature of the questions the various valuation methods may answer.

Taking this second objective a step further and establishing ways to keep economic information and its limitations in perspective in environmental policy discussions will be challenging. There is currently much more agreement about the idea of economic valuation of environmental benefits than about how it is to be carried out and when it is to be used. Yet as cost-benefit analysis in particular gains popularity as a decision-making tool, consensus around approaches and uses of benefits assessment is critical.

References

Barendregt, Jan J., Luc Bonneux, and Paul J. Van Der Maas. 1997. The Health Care Costs of Smoking. *New England Journal of Medicine* 337(15):1052-1057.

Costanza, Robert, Ralph d'Arge, Rudolf de Groot, Stephen Farber, Monica Grasso, Bruce Hannon, Karin Limberg, Shahid Naeem, Robert V. O'Neill, Jose Paruelo, Robert G. Raskin, Paul Sutton, and Marjan van den Belt. 1997. The Value of the World's Ecosystem Services and Natural Capital. *Nature* 387: 253-260.

SedPAC. 1997. *Overcoming Obstacles to Sediment Remediation in the Great Lakes Basin.* White Paper developed by Sediment Priority Action Committee, Great Lakes Water Quality Board, International Joint Commission.

Chapter 2

Economics and Environmental Policy: What are the Trends?[2]

as we described in Chapter 1, economics has come to play an important role in environmental decision-making. In this chapter, we focus on how decision-makers have carved out a formal role for economics in federal and state law. Initially, federal environmental laws and implementing regulations focused on how to control pollution, not on the economics of doing so. The visible levels of air and water pollution made the benefits of investment in pollution control obvious to policymakers and the public. However, as the first round of pollution control came to fruition, investment decisions in further pollution control became more complex, in part because the marginal cost of added controls were much more expensive. Moreover, evidence of the need for added benefits has become increasingly subtle — far less "in the face" of policymakers than in the 1960s and 1970s.

In the 1970s, it cost $.50 per ton to reduce volatile organic compounds in the Los Angeles basin; now it costs $50,000 per ton. (Portney, 1998)

Consequently, economic impacts — benefits and costs — are now at the center of many policy and legislative debates in the Great Lakes region and nationally. Some stakeholders worry that important environmental services may be ignored in these economic analyses. However, these requirements could just as easily draw attention to hidden benefits of pollution prevention and control measures henceforth unrecognized.

In 1995, damages at the Blackbird Mine Site were settled for $60 million to restore salmon to the Salmon River region in central Idaho. The settlement was based in part on an estimate of the lost resource. (Renner, 1998)

---

[2]*Sandra Archibald, Professor of Public Policy, Humphrey Institute of Public Affairs, University of Minnesota, Minneapolis*

FEDERAL LAWS, COURT RULINGS, AND EXECUTIVE ORDERS

Legislative and executive branch policymakers, buoyed by court pressure, have enacted legislation and issued orders requiring that the potential benefits from added environmental improvements be compared to the costs to help determine whether such improvements are economically justified. They also developed legislation to improve cost-effectiveness of pollution control scenarios, and required that affected parties be compensated for natural resource damages.

Cost-Benefit Comparisons

Several environmental statutes have provisions requiring cost-benefit analysis, the formal measurement and comparison of costs and benefits of increased environmental controls. However, these pieces of legislation are not consistent in their application of the cost-benefit tool. For example, of the nine major environmental statutes in effect, the Toxic Substances Control Act requires cost-benefit analysis to assure that regulatory limits do not result in costs disproportionate to benefits. The Clean Air Act (1970) and the Clean Water Act (1972) set standards based on public health criteria and specifically prohibit weighing of benefits and costs in setting these standards (NOAA, 1995). However, this criterion is being challenge in front of the Supreme Court in American Trucking Association v. Browner. Industry groups contend that the EPA should consider the impact of standards on the financial health of the economy, due to the cost of compliance.[3] The 1980 Comprehensive Environmental Response, Compensation and Liability Act (CERCLA) requires natural resource damage assessments (including assessment of lost environmental benefits) and allows natural resource trustees to be compensated for those damages. The National Environmental Policy Act (NEPA) of 1969 requires the use of cost-benefit analysis in the preparation of Environmental Impact Statements. Other of the major laws require that costs be reasonable or that costs be balanced with benefits, but stop short of requiring a formal cost-benefit analysis. Specific details about the requirements under each major law are available from the Environmental Protection Agency. (www.epa.gov/epahome/laws.htm)

In none of these laws is the cost-benefit analysis the decision rule; rather, where it is applied, it is as a tool to advise decision-makers in setting standards and limits. For instance, the 1996 Safe Drinking Water Act Amendments require that whenever the U.S. Environmental Protection Agency (EPA) proposes a national primary drinking water regulation, it must publish a cost-benefit analysis, but EPA need not limit its reg-

---

[3] *On November 7, 2000, the U.S. Supreme Court heard oral arguments in American Trucking Association v. Browner (Docket # 99-1426) and the related Browner V. American Trucking Association (# 99-1257), both of which represent potential challenges to the Clean Air Act. A decision is not expected until the summer.*

ulation to instances in which the benefits outweigh the costs. Amendments to the Federal Insecticide, Fungicide, and Rodenticide Act (1988) require the re-evaluation of specific uses for all pesticides every five years. This law requires the manufacturer to prove that the benefits from a given pesticide outweigh its economic and environmental costs, including damages (lost or foregone benefits) to environmental services.

Over the past decade, Congressional debate over "regulatory reform" has resulted in legislative proposals that would require all federal regulatory agencies dealing with the environment, safety, or health to pay closer attention to the benefits and costs of the regulations they issue. This legislation seeks to enlarge the role of economics and benefit-cost analysis in environmental policy (Portney, 1998). To date, no comprehensive legislation has been enacted, but the debate continues.

Statutory ambivalence in the application of economics to environmental decision-making has spawned a series of court rulings on the role of economics in standard setting and assessment requirements. The courts interpreted some statutes as prohibiting consideration of costs in some cases. Court decisions have held that cost-benefit studies cannot be considered unless the statute expressly authorizes them. A 1989 court ruling found that the cost-balancing test in a Clean Water Act case allows EPA to consider costs but precludes the agency from giving costs primary importance. In other cases, the balancing requirement has been interpreted as restricting the setting of environmental limits when the costs are disproportionate to the benefits.

Table 2.1.
MAJOR ENVIRONMENTAL STATUTES.

- Clean Air Act, 1970 (42 U.S.C. s/s740 et. seq.)
- Clean Water Act, 1977 (33 U.S.C. s/s121 et seq.)
- Safe Drinking Water Act, 1974 (42 U.S.C. s/s 300f et seq.)
- Resource Conservation and Recovery Act, 1976 (42 U.S.C. s/s 321 et seq.)
- Federal Insecticide, Fungicide, and Rodenticide Act, 1972 (7 U.S.C. s/s 135 et seq.)
- Toxic Substances Control Act, 1976 (15 U.S.C. s/s 260 et seq.)
- Comprehensive Environmental Response, Compensation and Liability Act, 1980 (42 U.S.C. s/s 9601 et seq.)
- National Environmental Policy Act, 1969 (42 U.S.C. 4321-4347
- Pollution Prevention Act, 1990 (42 U.S.C. 13101 and 13102 s/s et seq.)

Both Presidents Ford and Carter required federal agencies to conduct some form of economic analysis of major regulations. President Reagan formalized this in 1981 with Executive Order 12291 requiring cabinet level departments to conduct a benefit-cost analysis for major changes in rules. Issued in 1993, President Clinton's Executive Order 12866 requires that a cost-benefit analysis of all major regulations (i.e., those with an expected impact in excess of $100 million) be conducted. The order states that "an attempt should be made to quantify all potential real incremental benefits to society in monetary terms to the maximum extent possible." Any benefits that cannot be valued in monetary terms should be presented and explained. The order does not require that regulations pass a cost-benefit test, but regulations whose costs exceed estimated benefits must be explained. To address issues of environmental justice, the impacts of proposed regulations on various groups must be identified specifically.

Economic Assessment of Natural Resource Damages

Legislative provisions incorporating resource economics into environmental decision-making do not always take the form of cost-benefit requirements. Several federal statutes authorize recovery of damages for the destruction, loss, or injury of natural resources and related services (Table 2.2). These include Section 301(C) of the 1980 Comprehensive Environmental Response, Compensation and Liability Act (CERCLA) (42 U.S.C. 9601 et seq.) and Section 1006 of the 1990 Oil Pollution Act. The National Marine Sanctuary Act Section 312 Title III authorizes the National Oceanic and Atmospheric Administration (NOAA) to recover damages for the destruction, loss, or injury of sanctuary resources in national marine sanctuaries. These statutes require the development of regulations to guide assessment of natural resource damages from oil spills and hazardous substances. This process is referred to as natural resource damage assessment and is watched especially closely because the findings are tied closely to compensation amounts.

The role for economics in natural resource damage assessment is complex. The statutory emphasis is on restoration of resource services to their baseline conditions (i.e., primary restoration), compensation for the loss in value of the injured natural resources from the time of the injury until full recovery (i.e., interim losses), and the costs of damage assessment. The estimation of interim losses in particular requires innovative benefits assessment techniques. The development of natural resource damage assessment regulations was controversial because stakeholders disagreed over what damages would be assessed, how damages would be calculated, and how damages to environmental goods and services not valued in traditional markets would be calculated. Regulations related to Natural Resource Damage Assessment were promulgated

Table 2.2

SELECTED LAWS AND REGULATIONS RELATED TO
NATURAL RESOURCE DAMAGE ASSESSMENT

Law/Regulation	Scope	Responsible Agency*
Anadromous Fish Conservation Act, 16 U.S.C. 757	Requires conservation and restoration of anadromous fish resources and habitat	NMFS, USFWS, state
Clean Water Act, 33 U.S.C. 1251 et seq.	Regulates discharge of dredge and fill material in U.S. waters, protects wetlands	Army Corps of Engineers, EPA
Coastal Zone Management Act, 16 U.S.C. 1451 et seq.	Protects coastal zone; certification by state required	NOAA, state
Comprehensive Environmental Response, Compensation, and Liability Act, 42 U.S.C.9601	Provides authorization and framework for Superfund site remediation and restoration	NOAA, DOI, DOJ, state
Fish and Wildlife Coordination Act, 16 U.S.C. 661	Protects fish and wildlife; applies to federal actions only	USFWS, NMFS
National Environmental Policy Act of 1969, 42 U.S.C. 4321-4370d; 40 CFR 1500-1508	Requires disclosure of environmental impacts of proposed project and evaluation of alternatives; applies to federal actions	Federal lead agency, EPA
National Marine Sanctuaries Act, 33 U.S.C. 1401 et seq.	Prohibits destruction, injury, or loss of sanctuary resources and liability for natural resources damage	NOAA
Oil Pollution Act of 1990, 33 U.S.C. 2701-2761	Establishes liability for damages resulting from oil pollution and a fund for payment of compensation of such damages	NOAA

DOI - Department of the Interior; DOJ - Department of Justice; EPA - U.S. Environmental Protection Agency; NMFS – National Marine Fisheries Service; NOAA - National Oceanic and Atmospheric Administration; USFWS - U.S. Fish and Wildlife Service.

in 1986 (51 Federal Register, 27,674) and revised in 1988 (Federal Register, 5,166). The State of Ohio challenged these regulations in DC District Court. *Ohio v. US Department of Interior* (DC Circ. 1989) invalidated portions of the NRDA regulations. The DOI proposed new regulations in 1991 and 1993, and issued final regulations in 1994 (59 Federal Register, 14,262).

Current rules set out procedures for calculating natural resource damages based on the costs of restoring, rehabilitating, or replacing the equivalent of injured resources. These rules allow for the inclusion of all values that are lost to the public, both use and nonuse. This restoration approach to damage assessment — one that fully compensates the American public for injury to its natural resources — was upheld by the U.S. Court of Appeals in 1997. The Court concluded that natural resource trustees could select their assessment methods on a case-by-case basis. Industry claims that the contingent valuation method was inherently unreliable were rejected. The Court verified that Congress had clearly authorized trustees to recover a range of values from environmental goods and services, including those goods and services not traded in traditional markets.

Economics for Other Purposes

Legislation also requires the use of economics to enhance cost-effectiveness and to aid overall assessment of program impacts. For example, the 1990 Clean Air Act Amendments (Title IV) allow firms with higher sulfur dioxide emissions reduction costs to purchase emissions credits from firms that can reduce emissions at lesser cost (i.e., more economically). This credit trading allows the air quality standards to be met in the most cost-effective manner. Further changes in the Clean Air Act Amendments (Section 812) require EPA to assess periodically the effects of the Clean Air Act on the "public health, economy and the environment of the U.S." as a general assessment rather than as a formal cost-benefit analysis.

> *The cost-effective marketable allowance mechanism for sulfur dioxide emissions from electric power plants under the Clean Air Act Amendments is estimated to have saved ratepayers $240 each in 1990 alone.* (Stavins, 1998)

State Laws

Recently, state governments have enacted legislation requiring cost-benefit analyses for major new regulations. Eight states — including Illinois, Michigan, and Wisconsin — have passed such legislation (Table 2.3). As devolution of responsibility to states continues, we can expect other states to follow.

Table 2.3.
GREAT LAKES STATE LAWS

Illinois Environmental Protection Act (X 27(b))
■ The Department of Commerce and Community Affairs must conduct a study of the economic impact of a proposed rule. The study must address the economic, environmental, and public health benefits that may be achieved through compliance with the rule.

■ Before adopting the rule, the Illinois Pollution Control Board must determine, based on the economic impact study and other evidence, whether the proposed rule has any adverse economic impact.

Michigan Environmental Protection Act (X 324.20104)
■ The Michigan Department of Environmental Quality (DEQ) is restricted from using contingent valuation or other valuation methods to quantify nonuse values in natural resource damage calculations. DEQ will be able to use nonuse valuation methods in the future if they determine that the methods satisfy "principles of scientific and economic validity and reliability" and they promulgate rules for their use.

Natural Resources Chapter of Wisconsin Statute (X 293.65)
■ The Wisconsin Department of Natural Resources will deny a permit for the diversion of surface water for the purposes of metallic mining if the injury to the public exceeds the public benefits generated by the mining.

RULES OF THE GAME: THE DEVIL'S IN THE DETAILS

Congressional legislation, court rulings, and executive orders all now inject economics into environmental decisions. Although cost-benefit analysis has a long history in public investment decision-making, the legal and policy framework is changing over time as new priorities emerge, our information improves, and new valuation techniques and methods evolve. Policy guidance and regulations developed by agencies to implement legislation often specify in detail how environmental values are to be used in decision-making, what environmental values are to be estimated, and even the techniques that can be used to do so. Although some efforts have been made to encourage consistency, approaches to incorporating economics in environmental decision-making often differ significantly from one governmental agency and even program to the next.

The Office of Management and Budget has developed guidance for implementing President Clinton's Executive Order 12866, and agencies charged with implementing environmental statutes and regulations have developed precise standards for the conduct of cost-benefit analysis and methods of measuring economic valuation of natural resource services (Table 2.4). Policy guidance documents are revised more frequently than statutes and implementing regulations, and are not necessarily consistent across agencies, although there is growing pressure to make them consistent. Informal guidance from expert panels, technical documents, and peer-reviewed academic research also influences valuation of environmental benefits.

Guidance for Cost-Benefit Analysis

The Office of Management and Budget's 1996 guidance document "Economic Analysis of Federal Regulations Under Executive Order 12866" provides guidance for cost-benefit analysis of regulations. The document promotes the use of "best economic practices" to standardize assumptions and methods across regulatory programs. It describes principles for valuing, both directly and indirectly, benefits traded in markets, as well as principles for valuing benefits not traded in markets. There is also guidance related to methods for valuing health and safety effects. The document is specific about the conduct of cost-benefit analyses. It lays out how future benefits and costs should be discounted to present values, tells analysts how to account for risk, and

Table 2.4.
SELECTED GUIDANCE DOCUMENTS FOR COST-BENEFIT ANALYSIS AND NATURAL RESOURCE DAMAGE ASSESSMENTS

- Economic Analysis of Federal Regulations Under Executive Order 12866, Office of Management and Budget, January 11, 1996.

- Guidelines for Performing Regulatory Impact Analysis, Environmental Protection Agency, Reissued 1991.

- Circular A-94: Guidelines and Discount Rates for Benefit-Cost Analysis of Federal Programs, Office of Management and Budget, October 20, 1992.

- Economic and Environmental Principles and Guidelines for Water and Related Land Resources Implementation Studies, Chapter ii, National Development Benefit Evaluation Procedures, U. S. Army Corp of Engineers, March 10, 1983.

- The CERCLA Type A Natural Resource Damage Assessment Model for Coastal and Marine Environments (NRDAM/CME), Department of the Interior, 1996.

- The CERCLA Type A Natural Resource Damage Assessment Model for the Great Lakes Environment (NRDAM/GLE), Department of the Interior, 1996.

- Natural Resource Damage Assessment Guidance Document: Specification, Use of NRDAM/CME Version 2.4 to Generate Compensation Formula (Oil Pollution Act of 1990), National Oceanic and Atmospheric Administration, 1996.

specifies the way that benefits and costs should be measured. *Willingness to pay* (or *willingness to accept*) is considered the appropriate measure of benefits, and techniques that measure willingness to pay based on observable behavior deserve the greatest confidence. Other innovative benefit estimates, including contingent valuation methods (see Chapter 6), should be reviewed carefully.

The Office of Management and Budget's "Circular A-94" requires cost-benefit analysis of projects and programs. Benefits are to be monetized, although intangible and tangible benefits not capable of being valued in monetary terms should be recognized. A-94 measures benefits in terms of what consumers are willing to pay for the outcome and relies on consumer surplus as the best measure of the total benefit to society from a government program or project. It requires that cost-benefit analyses should consider situations in which projects have dissimilar impacts in terms of income or other groups affected.

Cost-benefit analysis began with federal water projects, and yet another set of guidelines pertains to these large projects. The "Principles and Guidelines for Federal Water Projects" guides water projects under the authority of the Army Corps of Engineers. The measure of value is willingness to pay for each increment of output from a project or program, and the measure of social benefit is consumer surplus.

To meet the goal of restoring damaged natural resources, agencies must assess the extent of injury, link it to a toxic release, devise a restoration plan, and determine the full value of what the public has lost.

Guidance for Conducting Natural Resource Damage Assessments

As we noted earlier in this chapter, in order to meet the goal of restoring damaged natural resources, agencies must assess the extent of injury, link it to a toxic release, devise a restoration plan, and determine the full value of what the public has lost. Valuation of lost uses has evolved as our economic and scientific understanding has increased. Damage assessments evaluate both restoration of the damaged natural resources (i.e., primary restoration) and compensatory damages. Economics plays a role in both, but is crucial in the determination of compensatory damages to compensate the public for interim losses. Still somewhat controversial is how to determine the value for nonmarket activities such as recreational fishing. More controversial are values for goods and services not measured by traditional market exchange (e.g., existence and other nonuse values).

Cross-agency

cost-benefit

comparisons...

should bring

into focus

inconsistencies

in the role

of economics

or valuation

among

different

agencies.

In 1997 NOAA issued a guidance document on implementing the 1986 natural resource damage assessment regulations. The guidance document changed the focus of the regulations from damages valued solely in monetary terms to the restoration of services. Replacing lost services rests on the assumption that the public is willing to accept a one-to-one tradeoff between a unit of services lost due to injury and a unit of service gained due to restoration. For example, habitat equivalency compares the present discounted value of service increases from restoration to the present discounted value of the interim losses of that same service due to the resource injury. When it is not possible to find equivalent services, value-to-value approaches require placing a value on the service loss caused by the injury and the resource gain realized from the planned compensatory restoration. The goal is a restoration level that produces a gain in value equivalent to the lost value (including nonuse value) caused by the injury.

The value-to-value approach laid out in the NOAA guidance document relies on a variety of economic methods to determine the public's willingness to forego lost services for services provided by compensatory restoration projects. The document allows more experimental methods such as contingent valuation to be used to measure use values alone or use values plus nonuse values. Although the courts also have held that damages can be recovered for the public's lost use and nonuse values, provided those damages can be calculated reliably, controversy continues.

CONCLUSION

There is pressure to expand the scope of cost-benefit analysis in national policymaking. In the last several sessions of Congress, proposals to require federal regulatory agencies dealing with environmental, health and safety regulations to pay greater attention to costs and benefits of legislation have been introduced and debated.

For example, the Regulatory Impact Act of 1997 (S. 981) would have required agencies to compare benefits and costs of regulatory actions. It did not require that costs and benefits be quantified or expressed in monetary terms, but did require a qualitative cost-benefit analysis. Such legislation would add statutory weight to 20 years of executive branch regulatory reform efforts.

There is an emerging focus on cross-agency cost-benefit comparisons to determine which regulations bring the largest benefits. This approach should bring into focus inconsistencies in the role of economics or valuation among different agencies. There also seems to be growing pressure to incorporate nonmonetary values in the economic analyses to be considered in the decision-making process. It seems logical that as more nonmarket values and hard-to-monetize nonmarket values are included — even qualitatively — there will be a surge of interest by economists to develop new methods to do so, and by environmentalists to assure that these values are addressed sufficiently.

References

Portney, Paul. 1998. Counting the Cost: The Growing Role of Economics in Environmental Decision-making. *Environment Magazine* (www.weathervane.rff.org/refdocs/portney-enviro.html.)

Renner, Rebecca. 1998. Calculating the Cost of Natural Resource Damage. *Environmental Science and Technology* 132(3):86A-90A.

Stavins, Robert. 1998. What Can We Learn from the Grand Policy Experiment? Positive and Normative Lessons from SO2 Allowance Trading. *Journal of Economic Perspectives* 12(3):69-88.

Chapter 3

The Value of the Great Lakes Environment: What do Economists Mean?[4]

Clearly, there is a great need to understand the potential benefits and costs of environmental protection and restoration, both to help reveal advantageous environmental programs, and to obey the law. Yet, apples-to-apples comparisons remain elusive in the arena of environmental economics. As a result, it is critical that environmental decision-makers completely understand the capabilities and the limitations of resource economic analysis. This chapter walks the reader through some fundamentals of resource economics, in particular, how economists define value, the goal of economic valuation exercises, and the types of environmental values that resource economists hope to measure.

VALUE IN THE EYES OF THE ECONOMIST

The value of a wetland to a biologist might be its benefit to the reproductive capacity of fish. A hydrologist might measure a wetland's value by its ability to recharge groundwater. The function of the wetland of greatest concern to the economist is similarly specialized to the field. To an economist, a wetland's value relates to the extent to which people benefit from its goods and services. This economic value then likely includes its roles as a nursery for fish and as a groundwater recharge zone, but only to the extent that people realize these benefits.

To measure the economic value of a resource, economists observe human preferences — and, when possible, the behavior resulting from those preferences. What is human preference? Preference is what drives our decisions to select one alternative over another. For example, someone who chooses to buy a house in downtown Chicago over less expensive suburban homes has a preference for the city. The extent of this

---

[4] *Jay Coggins, Associate Professor of Applied Economics, University of Minnesota*

preference is revealed in the amount of time and money that person is willing to give up in return for the preferred living situation.

Similarly, an individual who chooses to drive farther to reach a better fishing site values high-quality fishing experiences. How far the individual is willing to drive for the improvement reveals the strength of the preference. In both cases, the "consumer" makes a decision to give up something — either money or time — for the opportunity to enjoy the preferred experience — either a house in the city or an excellent fishing trip.

Clearly, a focus on human preference and observed behavior directly reflects the interests of only a subset of the parties affected by environmental management decisions. Other species, for example, derive value and welfare from resources like a wetland, but these preferences are not the subject of economic study. The well-being of future generations of humans is also tied to the condition of natural resources, yet economics has few tools to capture these concerns. In addition, economics cannot capture the value of changes in the intrinsic value of natural places. The anthropocentric and current generation focus in economics certainly affects the outcome of valuation exercises, but not as much as one might suspect. Economics does incorporate non-human and intergenerational considerations indirectly if they influence, as they often do, present human attitudes toward proposed changes in the condition of the resource.

Economic Value as Willingness to Pay

To measure value, economists determine the maximum amount an individual would be willing to forego in other goods and services, such as time or money, in order to obtain a preferred good, service, or state of the world. This maximum amount is formally expressed in a concept called willingness to pay. The concept of *willingness to pay* is applicable whether or not the good in question is traded in a market. The gain in value associated with a specific improvement in environmental quality is thus detected by an increase in people's willingness to pay for the environmental good or service.

Willingness to pay may be quite different from price (what one *must* pay). Consider an avid naturalist who is willing to pay up to $40 for a day of quality bird-watching. The naturalist is fortunate, though, to have a superb bird-watching site right out the back door, so the actual cost is only about $1 (the cost of a peanut butter sandwich) for a day of fine birding. The fact that the naturalist is observed "paying" $1 only reveals a willingness to pay at least that amount. An observer interested in measuring the value of the site to the naturalist must estimate the maximum he/she is willing to pay in travel and other expenses for quality bird-watching. Even a fixed market price (e.g., the price of joining a guided tour in a tract of prime bird-watching habitat) may underestimate the true value of the amenity to the consumer.

The difference between $40 (the consumer's willingness to pay) and $1 (the price actually paid) is known as *surplus*, which in the current example refers to the well-being that a single consumer enjoys at being able to bird watch for less than the cost he/she is willing to pay. If a development project eliminated birding at the backdoor site, the birder loses this surplus, represented by $39. The next nearest site is a long drive away and is privately owned. Now the price of birding is $30 (the cost of gas plus the admission fee to use the site), and the surplus is only $10. The value of a birding site to the naturalist remains $40, but now he/she enjoys much less surplus and, therefore, much less satisfaction. The cost to the birder of the change in environmental quality caused by the development is at least the difference between the surplus before and after the change, or $29.

We quantify consumer well-being by adding together the surplus values over time for each experience. For example, the consumer surplus that an angler enjoys from fishing at his/her favorite site is the sum of the surplus values to the angler of each fish caught at the site over a season. This is usually not a strict arithmetic operation. As the number of fish an angler catches increases, his or her willingness to pay for an additional fish usually declines. (Would you expect our angler to be willing to pay as much for the 30th fish in a season as for the first?) If we take one more step and add together the consumer surpluses for all anglers, then we have a measure of the surplus value to all anglers of this fishery. This surplus value for all anglers can be compared against the value likely to result if a proposed change in the environment were carried out. In so doing, we are able to measure some of the change in societal value resulting from the proposed change.

To measure value, economists determine the maximum amount an individual would be willing to forego in other goods and services, such as time or money, in order to obtain a preferred good, service, or state of the world.

Goal: A Common Metric to Answer "What If" Questions

Sometimes economists and others attempt the daunting task of placing an absolute value on the environment or on a portion of it (the Great Lakes, for example). These exercises help highlight our complete dependency on natural resources. They help answer the general question: Do we know what we have? In day-to-day policy applications, however, we often face more specific questions such as, "What are the economic benefits of a 50 percent reduction in mercury loadings into Lake Erie?" For this reason, most resource valuation analyses measure some or all of the changes in consumer well-being attributable to a given or proposed policy intervention.

Resource economists seek to translate environmental values, both quantitative and qualitative, into a common metric. The economic value of amenities, including environmental amenities, is most often measured in dollars. Recently there has been some experimentation with the use of nonmonetary indices to account for natural resource capital (see Chapter 4). Still, we are speaking of a common metric, helping society and decision-makers to clarify tradeoffs.

Caution: Simplifying Assumptions

As with any science, economists use simplifying assumptions to model and explain economic behavior. One of the key economic assumptions is that people husband their resources rationally. That is, they are aware of available options, and both consumers and producers choose among them to maximize their own economic welfare. Economists then would expect a consumer that values the goods and services that the Great Lakes provide to value protection measures. However, often the cost of acquiring information by itself is substantial, and consumers choose in the absence of complete information.

Economists also often assume that people value gains and losses similarly. If they do not in fact do this — for example, if they weigh losses more heavily than gains — there may be a higher value on preserving environmental amenities than the economic estimates indicate.

HOW DO WE VALUE THE GREAT LAKES? LET US COUNT THE WAYS

Economists view the environment as an asset that provides a variety of services. The Great Lakes, for example, provide aesthetic, ecological, recreational, industrial, and life-sustaining services. Indeed, the complexity of the physical and biological processes that comprise the Great Lakes makes the number of ways in which the Great Lakes can provide value to people almost limitless. Table 3.1 lists some specific services provided by the Great Lakes, along with the values affected by them.

The change in services and their associated value due to a given policy intervention can be equally complex. For example, a program to carefully remove or contain con-

Table 3.1.
GREAT LAKES SERVICE FLOWS AND THE AFFECTED VALUES

Service Provided	Affected Value
Potable water for residential use	Availability of potable water Human health and health risk
Landscape and turf irrigation	Cost of maintaining public or private property
Agricultural crop irrigation	Value of crops or production costs
Livestock watering	Value of livestock products
Food product processing	Value of food products Human health and health risk
Other manufacturing processes	Value of manufactured goods Production costs
Water for hydropower plants	Cost of electricity generation
Cooling water for other power plants	Cost of electricity generation
Medium for wastes and other byproducts of human activity	Human health or health risks attributable to changes in water quality
Improved water quality through support for living organisms	Human health or health risks attributable to change in water quality Animal (fish and wildlife) health or health risks attributable to change in water quality Economic output or production costs attributable to use of water resources as "sink" for wastes
Nonuse services (e.g., existence or bequest motivations)	Personal utility
Erosion, flood and storm protection	Value of shoreline property Costs of transportation
Recreational swimming, boating, fishing, hunting, trapping, and plant gathering	Quality or quantity of recreational activities
Commercial fishing, hunting, trapping, and plant gathering	Value of commercial harvest or costs Human health or health risks
Tribal fishing, hunting, trapping, and plant gathering	Quantity or quality of food supplies Other (personal utility)
On-site observation or study of fish, wildlife, and plants for leisure or for educational or scientific study	Quantity or quality of on-site observation or study activity

continued on next page

Table 3.1 (continued from previous page)

Service Provided	Affected Value
Transport and treatment of wastes and other byproducts of human economic activity	Human health or health risks attributable to change in water quality Animal (fish and wildlife) health or health risks attributable to change in water quality or quantity Economic output or production costs attributable to use of wetlands for disposing of wastes
Indirect, off-site fish, wildlife, and plant uses (e.g., viewing wildlife photos)	Quality or quantity of indirect off-site activities
Improved water quality resulting from living organisms	Human health or health risks attributable to change in air quality Value of economic output or production costs attributable to change in air quality
Regulation of climate through support of plants	Human health or health risks attributable to change in climate Animal (fish and wildlife) health or health risks attributable to change in climate Value of economic output or production costs attributable to change in climate
Provision of nonuse services associated with water bodies or wetlands environments or ecosystems	Personal utility

taminated sediment at a Great Lakes harbor could improve the habitat for fish and, consequently, the health of people and wildlife that catch and eat fish from the affected area. But these are just two of many potential linkages between an intervention and its value, all tied to one or more of the services provided by the affected environmental resource. Waterborne cargo tonnage, recreational and housing opportunities may also improve. Parsing the types of economic value that an environmental amenity supplies is a necessary first step to assessing that value.

Economists use a variety of terms to categorize the types of values that environmental amenities provide. Unfortunately, these categories can overlap and be confusing to lay users of economic information. The following sections summarize the fundamental types of benefits that may derive from an environmental intervention. We discuss the techniques used to measure these types of values in Chapter 5.

Market and Nonmarket Values

Perhaps the most fundamental distinction in economic value is between market and nonmarket goods and services. Some environmental goods and services are traded in markets, where their prices can be observed. The commercial fishery is one example in which an environmental good has a market in the same sense that computers or automobiles have a market. Another example is the operation of a harbor on the Great Lakes. In estimating the benefits of such goods or services, economists use the same techniques they would use in measuring the benefits of any market good, such as dairy products or leather jackets.

Other environmental goods and services do not have a market in the usual sense. Recreational anglers incur some costs, in licenses, equipment, boats, fuel, travel, and so on. Although these costs are associated with fishing, the fishing experience itself cannot be bought and sold in a market. The same situation often exists for swimming, wildlife viewing, hunting, and the like. In these cases, users must value the environmental resource, but in using it they do not pay an observable price for it. Estimating the benefits of nonmarket goods and services is one of the primary goals of environmental economics.

Most environmental interventions effect both market and non-market values. An improvement in air quality is a good example. As the level of a harmful pollutant in Gary, Indiana, falls, the location becomes a more desirable place to live, and the market value of nearby houses may rise. But an associated improvement in human health cannot be bought and sold directly and represents a nonmarket good. Similarly, a reduction in the levels of polychlorinated biphenols (PCBs) in Lake Michigan will improve both commercial and recreational fishing opportunities. The former can be measured using direct market techniques; the latter must be measured using indirect techniques which capture non-market value.

Use and Nonuse Values

A second categorization of value relates to the extent that consumers use the benefit. The value accruing to the direct use of a resource is called, not surprisingly, *use value*. It may be a market or a non-market in nature. An angler — commercial or recreational — derives value from the Great Lakes through direct use. Recreational boating and swimming and the use of water for municipal supplies are additional examples.

However, people also derive value from the environment without using it in an observable manner. The ban on DDT use in the United States led to a dramatic resurgence in bald eagle populations in the Great Lakes region. A Great Lakes resident may value the ban for that reason whether or not that individual ever sees a bald eagle first-hand. Evidence of such *nonuse* economic value is readily apparent in the contributions to environmental organizations that people make to protect assets they never expect to visit.

There are many types of nonuse, or passive use, values. Perhaps the contributor believed that some day he or she may choose to experience the environmental resource. The value from maintaining the resource in order to keep the option of visiting open, especially when one is unsure whether or not a visit will ever occur, is called *option value*. On the other hand, the contributor who is certain he/she will never experience the environmental amenity in person may be motivated by *existence value*, or the value one derives from knowing the resource is there and healthy. A concern for the ability of future generations to experience the resource generates *bequest value*.

Values from Extractive and In Situ Services

In addition to categorizing goods and services based on the extent to which they are traded in markets and used directly by consumers, economists divide goods and services based on the nature of the service. Environmental services can be usefully divided into two categories: extractive services and in situ services. An *extractive service* is obtained only through a use that takes part of the resource away. For example, an angler who keeps the catch is extracting the fish from their environment. Likewise, water used for municipal, agricultural, and industrial purposes is an extractive value. An *in situ service* can be obtained while leaving the resource in its original state. The *in situ* services of the Great Lakes include the provision of a venue for recreational activities such as boating and swimming, an infrastructure for commercial navigation, wildlife habitat, and a reservoir of energy for hydropower production.

Some interventions affect the provision of both extractive and in situ services. A reduction in the zebra mussel population in Lake Michigan, for example, would reduce the cost to municipal water users by removing the need to clean intake facilities. This is an extractive service. To the extent that fish populations are improved, it would also improve the in situ services provided to catch-and-release anglers.

Monetizable and Nonmonetizable Benefits

When performing cost-benefit analysis, one attempts to monetize as many of the benefits as possible (see Chapter 4). In the case of a cost-benefit analysis of a new and more stringent PCBs standard for Lake Michigan, one would want to account for the benefits enjoyed by recreational swimmers and anglers, by residential and commercial water users, by bird-watchers, and so on. By accounting for as many of the potential benefits as possible, one makes the comparison of costs and benefits more accurate.

Few people would argue that every benefit can be monetized. Market benefits and use values are most readily converted into monetary values because economists can observe human behavior. Non-market values that are derived from environmental services that do not involve "use", on the other hand, can be particularly challenging to measure. The only way to find out how much a person values this type of amenity is to ask the individual. This approach, known as contingent valuation, may still fail to capture all of the value individuals might place on the amenity because scientific knowledge may be too primitive or too unreliable to provide a basis for an informed response. Benefits of this sort should not be ignored simply because their value cannot be expressed in dollars. They can and should enter the policy process as qualitative variables, which can be compared for policymaking purposes.

CONCLUSION

Economic value is measured in terms of tradeoffs and based on human preferences and, if possible, on human behavior. Such value is added up across individuals to obtain a measure, most often in dollars, of aggregate value represented by consumer well-being.

The Great Lakes supply many services to residents of the region, including those that are readily measured in dollars and those that are not. Resource valuation information can help society to view its diverse values with a common metric. However, we must recognize the influence of economic assumptions on the outcome of these analyses. Economists recognize that variations in assumptions can have profound effects on the outcome of an analysis — in the measurement of costs and benefits. They also recognize that measurement error can introduce bias in statistical estimates and that extrapolation

> Economic value is measured in terms of tradeoffs and based on human preferences and, if possible, on human behavior.

of results from one population to another must rest on sound statistical principles. However, too much can be made of these limitations. Scientific studies confront similar measurement and estimation problems, yet they are considered critical contributions to our knowledge base.

Chapter 4

Putting Economics to Work in the Real World: Issues and Options[5]

S everal "real world" considerations complicate the application of valuation theory to actual environmental problems in the Great Lakes and elsewhere. Some of these considerations are analytical in nature, and others involve questions of social justice and ethics.

Determining the best formula for consolidating ongoing nonmarket benefits into a lump-sum present-day value is one very difficult analytical challenge. Another is factoring in irreversibility and the availability (or not) of substitutes. A third is the need to account for the wealth that improvements to the resource may generate over time (natural resource capitol). A fourth analytical challenge is in accounting for risk and uncertainty regarding the way an intervention will play out for the environment or individuals affected by it. Finally, because an intervention rarely takes place in a void, the economist must differentiate benefits associated with multiple interventions aimed at a common problem.

Social justice and ethical considerations are in play because environmental quality affects quality of life, health, and even longevity. Economics takes a strictly monetary view to relating morbidity and mortality to value, and accordingly, includes methods for placing a monetary value on a human life. Moreover, a simple cost-benefit comparison does not tell whose costs and whose benefits may have been altered, or the relationship of this distribution to ongoing patterns of social injustice. When the benefits span generations, social justice and ethical questions are particularly challenging because key affected populations cannot be surveyed. Other ethical concerns relate to the fact that these interventions alter the natural world, which transcends human needs.

---

[5] *Jay Coggins, Associate Professor of Applied Economics, University of Minnesota*

In this chapter, we provide a brief introduction to these real-world considerations and the ways in which resource economists incorporate these considerations into their analyses of proposed environmental interventions. Although these considerations cannot be segregated entirely, we discuss analytical challenges first, and social justice and ethical concerns second. We discuss some of these challenges in greater depth in Chapters 9 and 10.

ANALYTICAL CHALLENGES

Converting Great Lakes Benefits of the Future to Present-Day Value

Many environmental interventions have effects — both benefits and costs — that play out over many years. The benefits from cleaning up a contaminated site in Lake Michigan, for example, can accrue to anglers each year for several years. Prevention of global warming provides another example. How do we compare the costs today of controlling carbon dioxide emissions in the Great Lakes basin with the benefits that may not begin accruing to the Great Lakes region for several decades?

For many purposes, in environmental planning and elsewhere, one must be clear about whether the value of a given set of services is being estimated as a stock today or as a flow into the future. In economic parlance, a *stock* of some resource is the asset that supplies a flow of services. The population of lake trout in Lake Huron, taken in its entirety, is one example of a stock. Another is a public beach on Lake St. Clair. Each of these resources, however, is experienced by people through the *flow* of services that it provides each year, for example, the number of fishing trips on the lake, fresh fish meals, or days of fun on the beach with the family. The difference between stocks and flows is that a stock is a lump-sum value in today's terms, whereas a flow is a series of values that occur into the future.

Especially in cost-benefit comparisons (see Chapter 5), costs and benefits in future years must be brought into comparable terms. Economists aggregate streams of costs and benefits over time through *discounting*. Discounting reflects the opportunity cost of not having access to money or any other benefit immediately. People typically prefer a dollar today to a dollar in 10 years. This preference is evidenced by the fact that banks must offer interest payments in order to get people to deposit money, thereby foregoing current consumption. Similarly, people may value recreational experience more highly now than if they were promised the same experience 10 years from now.

The discount rate reflects the amount an individual would be willing to forego today in order to have an amenity in the future. Selecting the most appropriate rate is extremely important to the outcome of the analysis and is a good starting point for someone who seeks to understand the assumptions and results of a resource valuation study. If present consumption is preferred to later consumption for any reason, a positive discount rate is appropriate. If later consumption is preferred to current consumption, a negative discount rate is needed.

Although discounting is a widely accepted procedure, debate continues over the appropriate rate to use in evaluating public programs, particularly those involving natural resources and environmental amenities. Dozens of different interest rates are used in society — rates on regular savings accounts, certificates of deposit, bank loans, government bonds, and so on. In many economic problems, the appropriate discount rate is the market rate derived from the interest rate paid on government bonds. The market rate combines information about the supply and demand for capital in society overall. But the market rate may not relate well to public or environmental projects that yield benefits not traded in markets, as is the case in many resource valuation studies. The difference in the value of a restored wetland a year from now versus today may not be at all proportional to the difference in value of a dollar a year from now versus today.

One way economists select a discount rate for a project that provides benefits not traded in markets is through use of the *time-preference approach*. With this approach, one seeks a discount rate that reflects the way people themselves think about the value of a benefit over time. In a specific application, this might require use of a survey aimed at deducing how people value the future benefits of a project in relation to benefits enjoyed today. Unfortunately the approach clearly cannot be used to directly assess preferences of future generations. The lump-sum present-day value is at least partially reflected in the value that people today place on the availability of the resource for their use and the use of future generations. If today's society has a strong concern for future generations, it may place as much value on the benefit in the future as today, implying a zero discount rate.

The following example helps show the profound effect the choice of discount rate has on the outcome of an analysis: Suppose a decision must be made on whether to

> Economists aggregate streams of costs and benefits over time through discounting. Discounting reflects the opportunity cost of not having access to money or any other benefit immediately

Table 4.1.
DISCOUNTED NET PRESENT VALUE OF BEACH RESTORATION PROGRAM.

Year	2000	2001	2002	2003	Present Value of Benefits	Net Present Value
Benefits of program	$0	$40,000	$40,000	$40,000	—	—
Program cost	$100,000	$0	$0	$0	—	—
0% discount rate	—	—	—	—	$120,000	$20,000
3% discount rate	—	—	—	—	$113,144	$13,144
5% discount rate	—	—	—	—	$108,930	$8,230
7% discount rate	—	—	—	—	$104,973	$4,973
10% discount rate	—	—	—	—	$99,474	-$526

restore an eroded beach in Sheboygan County, Wisconsin. Assume a one-time restoration cost of $100,000 (Table 4.1). The project will be completed in late 2000. The benefits associated with the program are projected to last for three years. They come in the form of increased benefits to local swimmers and other users of the beach: $40,000 each in 2001, 2002, and 2003. Discounting will be crucial in determining whether the beach restoration program is an efficient use of society's resources.

The benefits sum to $120,000. Without discounting (or at a zero discount rate), the net present value of the program is $20,000, the program may be considered economically efficient, and the investment should be viewed favorably. With a 5 percent discount rate, the net present value is $8,230. However, with a 10 percent discount rate, the program results in a net loss of $526, suggesting an inefficient use of resources. Which discount rate is "correct?"

Large discount rates put more weight on the value of benefits (or money) in the present relative to the future. They give less weight to environmental benefits or damages that accrue only in the long term. Real rates of between 0 and 8 percent appear regularly in the economics literature. Some economists have even argued for negative discount rates to reflect the implicit interest of future generations in resource management decisions.

Despite the extensive literature, a consensus does not yet exist on an appropriate procedure for discounting costs and benefits of public programs and regulations. This lack of consensus is evident in the fact that different government agencies employ different discount rates when evaluating public expenditures. For example, in 1990 the Office of Management and Budget used a discount rate of 10 percent. The Congressional Budget Office uses a rate of 2 percent. The U.S. Environmental Protection Agency (EPA) uses several discount rates for evaluating environmental programs. Some agencies also require sensitivity analysis, showing how a program's net benefits are affected when determined using a range of discount rates.

Although one can debate which is the most appropriate discount rate for environmental benefits, it is clear that the characteristics of natural resources (e.g., slow-growing, renewable, and typically held in the public trust) necessarily imply that they should be treated differently than other private capital assets. Standard discounting would result in greater resource exploitation or use of nature capital now, at the expense of the future.

Irreplaceable Amenities and Irreversible Outcomes

The fewer substitutes available for a good or service, the greater the loss if it is degraded. For example, a hunter or bird-watcher near Saginaw Bay experiences a greater loss with the development of a marsh site if no close-by substitutes are available. The overall value of the remaining wetland areas may be diminished by the loss of the developed wetland as well; elimination of one site could cause congestion at other sites and could reduce the overall abundance of wildlife in the area. Conversely, doubling the wetland acreage may not double the value of the site. When working out cost-benefit comparisons, the availability of substitutes and their effect on value must be considered in order to estimate net benefits or losses.

Some negative environmental effects are irreversible. Global warming, introductions of exotic species, and species extinctions are examples. The value of actions to reduce the risk of irreversible environmental impacts is higher than of actions to prevent otherwise equivalent but reversible ones. This differential value is reflected in U.S. law. The Endangered Species Act places greater restrictions on development activity on land where species extinctions are possible than on land where it is not.

Accounting for Natural Resource Capital

Our measures of national productivity still do a poor job of accounting for the environment's role in the economy. The United Nations System of National Accounts includes the value of environmental assets in national capital stock estimates, but these assets do not yet have a place in national income and product accounts. This scheme fails to reveal the effect on a nation's income of depletion of exhaustible resources through mining, timber harvest, or the pollution of aquifers and surface waters. The resulting error may bias economic policy aimed at increasing gross domestic product in favor of activities that exploit natural resources. To rectify this error, the United Nations Statistical Commission is revising the System of National Accounts to include guidelines for incorporating natural resource assets in national accounts.

Natural resource capital also may be relevant to valuation exercises. For example, actions to prevent destruction of an aquifer recharge area improve present day supplies of groundwater, but also maintain an exhaustible resource (the aquifer) over time. In the same way, remediation of contaminated sediment could reduce public health problems associated with consuming contaminated fish in the near term, but could also restore a source of wealth in the form of an on-going venue for marinas, fishing, and other recreational activities. Resource economists capture these values by measuring the value of the flows of goods and services that the clean-up intervention might alter and converting that value to a lump-sum present-day value, as discussed earlier in this chapter. Some economists argue that a larger geographic view is requisite to incorporating natural resource capital into valuation exercises. For example, the depletion or restoration of wetlands can affect recreational uses locally, but may improve wildlife abundance on a basin-wide level. Alternatively, an increase in local economic activities associated with a recently restored harbor could lead to a decrease in economic activity at a nearby harbor which has been serving as a substitute. These issues are not limited to benefits analysis; the cost side of the equation also should incorporate degradation of natural resource capital that an intervention (or lack of intervention) may create.

Risk and Uncertainty

Risk and uncertainty are two terms that can be used interchangeably to describe a situation in which one of several outcomes occurs with some degree of randomness. In practice, resource economists contend with a great deal of uncertainty. One source of uncertainty is in predicting the precise consequences of proposed environmental policies and actions. For example, will tighter regulation on air emissions from municipal incinerators in the Great Lakes region result in less discharge of pollutants to the environment? Or will the incinerators be shut down in favor of an alternative that also pollutes the environment?

A second source of uncertainty resides with biological and even meteorological unknowns. For example, will the remediation of contaminated sediments in Green

Bay in Wisconsin lead to reduced levels of pollutants in fish and reduced illness among anglers, and if so, to what extent? The answers to questions like these have strong bearing on the value to society of the regulation or cleanup effort.

A third source of uncertainty arises from the increasing use of models, both biological and economic, to predict outcomes. Modeling is inherently a source of error, as is the measurement error of data used to calibrate the models. We tend to measure complex technical and ecological relationships with simplified mathematical functions. Sometimes this is because the basic science studies themselves fail to provide the range of information needed by economists to estimate the full economic consequences of changes. At other times, economists simplify scientific models in order to make their models more tractable. Errors can arise in economic estimates from simplifying abstractions and aggregations.

There are no hard and fast rules for the correct way to incorporate risk and uncertainty into resource valuation studies. It is clear, however, that decision-makers should be given as much information as possible about the probability of potential outcomes of environmental actions and how these probabilities affect the valuation exercise. Three methods are often used to address risk and uncertainty explicitly: (1) direct enumeration (i.e., listing all possible outcomes); (2) probability calculus, in which statistics such as the means and variance of a probability distribution are calculated; and (3) stochastic simulation, also known as Monte Carlo simulation or model sampling.

One ready method of accounting for risk is to adjust discount rates upward for projects or decisions with more risk. This has the added effect of lessening the chance of adopting a given intervention, which may be a sensible safeguard against potential but unknown future environmental damage. An alternative is to establish risk rankings of projects or decisions, along with other measures of anticipated benefits. Decision-makers may select actions with lower net benefits, if they are more certain of the outcome. This is an example of risk aversion, which enters into the decision process. Environmental risk aversion should be especially high in cases displaying uncertainties, irreversibilities, or a lack of substitutes. For example, a proposal to create a new connecting channel to divert water from one watershed basin to another could lead to irreversible changes in the receiving basin due to organism transfers. This outcome is

Our measures of national productivity fails to reveal the effect on a nation's income of depletion of exhaustible resources through mining, timber harvest, or the pollution of aquifers and surface waters.

uncertain in type and magnitude. In such cases, a decision to delay an irreversible investment (or to avoid irreversible damage) is most often the best choice.

Sorting Through Benefits from Multiple Projects

In many cases, a single environmental problem is the subject of two or more proposed interventions. The interventions may be under consideration by different agencies, or possibly at different jurisdictional levels. Unless one intervention precludes the others, evaluation of the interventions separately could give a misleading picture of potential outcomes.

For example, suppose a state environmental agency is investigating the benefits associated with a potential cleanup of mercury-laden sediments from a commercial harbor. At the same time, EPA is considering more stringent restrictions on municipal incinerators, which would also reduce mercury loadings into the lakes. Studies show that the combination of projects could lead to a lifting of the fish consumption advisory for mercury for a particular lake, although either action alone would not. In this case, the value of each project would be greatly increased by the implementation of the other. Alternatively, and less likely, studies could indicate that either of the interventions could, by itself, put an end to the fish consumption advisory for mercury for a particular lake. In this case, a part of the economic value of each project would be contingent on the absence of the other.

As a result of these effects, interrelated policies and projects must be evaluated carefully. Correct estimations of the benefits of environmental interventions, and formation of the best policy decisions, often require coordination and communication among several agencies.

Accounting for Secondary Impacts

Economic analyses have a tendency to focus on the most prominent effects of environmental interventions. In many instances, however, measuring the benefits (and costs) due to the secondary effects of interventions can be quite important. For example, the primary effect of cleaning up Ashtabula Harbor in Lake Erie could be an increase in recreational opportunities in the harbor and the lake — a benefit of great value to the potential users. This increased use could in turn have the secondary impact of creating jobs in marinas and nearby hotels and restaurants, which is of even greater economic value to residents than the new recreational uses.

When incorporating secondary impacts, one must exercise caution in accurately defining the geographic scope of the analysis and the extent to which changes in economic activity versus economic value are being measured. If the cleanup of Ashtabula Harbor leads to an increase in demand for marina services that exploit previously unused resources, such as labor, then the increased employment should be considered added economic value resulting from the cleanup. If the increased employment needs are met by a shift in previously employed resources (e.g., marinas close at another site), then the increased employment, while representing increased economic activity in Ashtabula, does not represent a true increase in economic value resulting from the cleanup. This distinction does not diminish the importance and persuasiveness of the reallocation information to local decision-makers and possible funders of the cleanup in Ashtabula. It should simply be made clear that the net gain is a local one.

SOCIAL JUSTICE AND ETHICAL CHALLENGES

Social justice intersects directly with environmental economics. Justice matters arise in the distribution of environmental benefits across society and in the distribution of benefits across generations. Both concerns pose challenges for economists who historically have focused on economic efficiency and have had a relative lack of interest in distributional, or equity, considerations. This bias is changing as economists focus more attention on distributional concerns, both between generations and across society in today's generation. Ethics are also relevant to economics. Especially in the resource economics arena, environmental interventions can alter the risk of morbidity and mortality, necessitating valuation of human health and life itself.

Distribution of Benefits Across Society

It is well known that the distribution of environmental costs and benefits resulting from an environmental intervention, such as the siting of a waste disposal facility, are often geographically uneven, with most of the costs concentrated on neighbors and most of the benefits on more distant users of the facility. Economists have historically neutralized these geographic variables by, as a first step, defining the population

Social justice intersects directly with environmental economics. Justice matters arise in the distribution of environmental benefits across society and in the distribution of benefits across generations.

affected by an intervention, both local and distant, and sampling from that population in a representative way. The end result is an average measure of willingness to pay for the intervention. If the sample is truly representative, this average should be a good measure of value for the population.

An example might be an estimate of people's willingness to pay for a reduction in the release of smog-creating pollution in Chicago. An estimate of the average willingness to pay for the entire population of the greater Chicago area could be used to help develop policies for reducing smog. The feelings of those who are greatly affected by smog and of those who are little affected would all be included in the average.

Unfortunately, according to a report by the U.S. General Accounting Office (1995), environmental costs often are borne disproportionately by low-income segments of society. Frequently facilities that harm the environment are established in low-income areas where political clout is weakest. In other instances, low-income populations, attracted by low real estate prices, move near these facilities after they are sited. In addition, interventions aimed at improving the quality of our environmental resources can have differing effects on different segments of the population due to patterns of use. For example, if a contaminated harbor is not remediated, the effect is more important to people who want to (or must) eat the fish they catch in the harbor than for those who do not.

Problems arise when the differential impacts sustained by subpopulations directly correspond with gross differences in income. In these cases, environmental costs averaged over the entire population may not reflect the effect that the intervention would have on wealth (i.e., the opportunity costs) within the individual subpopulations. If the communities are studied separately, economists can clarify the differences in impacts reflected in each community's willingness to pay for environmental quality. However, interpreting these findings will also be tricky. Based on these findings, economists might falsely conclude that the low-income, near-neighbors are less willing to pay for environmental quality simply because they would have to sacrifice more meaningful goods and services (such as food or health care) to do so than would the rich community. In these cases, economists must attempt to differentiate willingness to pay from ability to pay.

The key question economists should ask is whether the effect of a given environmental problem is felt most strongly by a low-income subpopulation. If so, the average willingness to pay obtained by an economic study could be biased downward, precisely because the group most severely affected by the problem has low incomes and therefore relatively low willingness to pay.

In 1994, President Clinton called on all federal agencies to "make achieving environmental justice part of its mission by identifying and addressing, as appropriate, disproportionately high and adverse human health or environmental effects of its programs, policies, and activities on minority populations and low-income populations in the United States...." (Executive Order 12898). Can the economic valuation tools presented in this guidebook be used to comply with that executive order? Some economists believe the tools themselves should be re-evaluated to eliminate the interpretation problems that their neutrality may create. This goal is certainly worthy of intensive exploration. However, even if it became a priority for resource economists, it would take some time to develop reliable alternative approaches. In the meantime, it is important for economists to become well versed in the possible interpretation problems associated with social justice, so that they can present to decision-makers additional considerations that are not treated well by the resource economics analysis.

Distribution of Benefits Across Generations

Another social justice concern relates to the rights of our children and grandchildren to have their voices heard in today's environmental decisions. How do we derive a lump-sum present-day value for cost-benefit comparison purposes when the flow of goods or services from an environmental intervention spans generations? For example, should we sacrifice today to conserve habitat along Lake Superior even though in our generation an abundance of habitat may still exist? In many decisions related to environmental interventions, one generation stands to gain and another to lose. Historically, economics has focused on people alive today and their preferences. The choice of a discount rate bears directly on this issue. Commonly used discount rates place a very small weight on the preferences of future generations, and therefore discriminate heavily against them.

Some economists have proposed that decisions affecting the future should be made with decision-makers placed behind a "veil of ignorance" about which generation the decision-makers belong to. This impartiality criterion suggests equal use of irreplaceable resources across generations, implying a zero discount rate. But with a zero discount rate, if enough generations are involved, use of nonrenewable resources (such as oil) approaches zero for any given generation. Likewise, irreversible development (such as building a dam in a unique natural area) is essentially precluded. Perhaps more important, a zero discount rate may foreclose future options by undervaluing investments that produce wealth and new technology that would be of great value to future generations.

Clearly some compromise is needed between a zero discount rate, which would preclude many resource uses and perhaps prevent valuable technological advances, and a typical market rate that reflects only the atomistic time preferences of the current generation. This compromise has been called a *social rate of discount*; its argument is that the government in this role should consider the wishes (i.e., the values) of both current and future generations. Because the welfare of future generations depends on current consumption patterns, the government should assure protection of future welfare by interventions that force sufficient resource conservation. In essence, the government would proclaim what it deemed to be an appropriate discount rate.

Another argument takes a more democratic approach, recognizing that the government is run by and for the current generation; thus, any saving for the future must rely on the values of the current generation. The basis of this argument is that most citizens hold a set of values that include a concern for the larger group (including the future) as well as concern for self. If people value the welfare of the future, then what is needed is a way for that value to be expressed and measured — a way that avoids the singular context of the marketplace.

Alternatively, society could come to a political consensus regarding the validity of future generations' needs in present-day policy discussions, making future economic values automatically relevant. *Sustainable development* is a term often used to capture the idea that current generations should use environmental assets in a way that preserves the ability of future generations to enjoy these assets. There is a wide array of perspectives in the debate over sustainable development, and its very definition takes many forms. According to the World Commission on Environment and Development (1987), sustainable development is "development that meets the needs of the present without compromising the ability of future generations to meet their own needs."

Economists and others have formalized this idea in many ways. A key determinant of sustainability is whether or to what degree human-made capital (e.g., roads, buildings, and machinery) can substitute for natural capital (i.e., the atmosphere, mineral reserves, ecosystem services). If substitutability is high, then the danger to future generations of severe consequences from exploiting natural resources today is low. Technological advances, always difficult to forecast, have a great deal to say both about substitutability and about the sustainability of economic development.

Placing a Value on Human Life and Health

Because the resources available for use in preventing loss of life and health are scarce, society makes choices about where to invest them. Although they cannot solve the dilemmas posed by such choices, economists can contribute information for these choices by calculating the change in the probability of death or illness resulting from an environmental intervention and by placing a value on that change. In this way, economists do not value life so much as they do the reduction in the probability that life span or health may change for some segment of a population.

It is customary to express this value in terms of the number of statistical lives lost or compromised due to an environmental insult. The number of statistical lives lost is the sum of all the persons exposed to a given insult (e.g., a pollutant) multiplied by the change in probability of death for each individual. The value of a statistical life is the sum of the affected people's willingness to pay for these risk changes divided by the number of statistical lives saved.

The Implied Value of Life

Suppose that a particular environmental policy could reduce the average concentration of a toxic substance to which one million people are exposed. What if this reduction in exposure could be expected to reduce the risk of death from 1 out of 100,000 persons to 1 out of 150,000? This implies that the number of expected deaths would fall from 10 to 6.67 in the exposed population as a result of this policy. If each of the one million persons exposed is willing to pay $5 for this risk reduction (for a total of $5 million), then the implied value of a life is approximately $1.5 million ($5 million divided by 3.33).

If the change in risk is the same for everyone in a population, then the value of a statistical life is the average value all members of the population are willing to pay, or the rate at which the average individual is willing to trade risk for wealth. A drawback to this approach is that it does not reflect the age of people who are at risk and therefore the number of expected years of life that are lost. In Chapter 10, we take a more in-depth look at the value of health improvements.

CONCLUSION

Placing a monetary value on the effects of changes in environmental quality, from improvements in water quality to the introduction of exotic species, is a complex undertaking. The concepts presented in this chapter make up some of the biggest challenges in environmental economics. Though the methods that economists use to value environmental changes have limitations, economic analysis can be a critical factor in the evaluation of environmental policy. Policymakers should be aware of the strengths and limitations of economic models to inform decisions regarding changes in the environment. This is a useful thought to keep in mind as we turn in the following chapter to a discussion of some of those specific models and approaches.

References

World Commission on Environment and Development. 1987. *Our Common Future*. Oxford, UK: Oxford University Press.

United States General Accounting Office. 1995. *Hazardous and Nonhazardous Waste, Demographics of People Living Near Waste Facilities*. Washington, DC: General Accounting Office.

part II

Methods

Chapter 5

Models for Great Lakes Environmental Decision-Making[6]

n this chapter, we review formal analytical frameworks for incorporating economic information into environmental decision-making. The technique most familiar to many of us is cost-benefit analysis (CBA). Other formal frameworks include cost-effectiveness analysis (CEA), natural resource damage assessment, and economic impact analysis. These frameworks are restricted to the analysis of *economic* implications — a subset of the total information field that any environmental policy decision may involve. Yet, as we point out in Chapter 4, other issues such as social justice and ethics are often inextricably woven together with economic issues in real world environmental decisions. The extent to which economists should take responsibility for these additional considerations in the presentation of economic information is an open question addressed in Chapter 4.

While many of us have heard of each of these applications, few understand the varied objectives of the approaches. Yet information about the specific purpose of each technique is essential to meaningful discourse over the use of information generated by these models in environmental decision-making.

CBA is a specific technique designed to account as thoroughly and comparably as possible for the many economic costs and benefits that will accompany a given policy change or project. Although it is an old idea in economics generally and in environmental economics, CBA has recently become quite controversial. CEA compares the economic implications of two or more approaches to achieve a given societal objective. Natural resource damage assessment can be thought of as the mirror image of the typical benefits assessment. It is aimed at measuring the value of damages caused by an injury to the environment (i.e., foregone benefits). Economic impact analysis is a tool for evaluating the economic effects of a policy intervention, but it does not necessarily convert the measured effects into a single dollar measure.

---

[6] *Jay Coggins, Associate Professor of Applied Economics, University of Minnesota*

COST-BENEFIT ANALYSIS: WILL THE INTERVENTION PAY OFF?

Put simply, CBA is the estimation and comparison of the costs and economic benefits attributable to a given policy intervention. It answers the question of whether the intervention will pay off from an economic standpoint. In the most simple application, a private firm might conduct a CBA to decide whether to undertake an expansion project — say, building a new processing plant. Costs comprise capital, initial construction, and operating expenses over the next several years; benefits are the returns to the plant over the same time period. Economists would discount the flows of costs and benefits back to the present to make them comparable in time. The project should be undertaken if discounted benefits exceed discounted costs.

In environmental economics, CBA compares the present value of all current and future social benefits with the present value of current and future costs in using resources. It is most often encountered in the context of public project decisions, reflecting the concern that a level of economic efficiency be maintained in the use of public dollars. CBA was first used in conjunction with the U.S. Flood Control Act of 1936, which specified that federal participation in projects to control flooding on major rivers of the country would be justifiable "if the benefits to whomever they accrue are in excess of the estimated costs." Today's applications include physical projects, such as public waste treatment plants, beach restoration projects, sediment removal, and the restoration or purchase of wetlands. They also include regulatory programs whose goal it is to enforce environmental laws and regulations, such as water-quality standards, choice of water treatment technology, waste disposal practices, land use restrictions, and the like.

Predictably, the CBA task is far less simple in environmental evaluation than in a conventional business setting. First, the viewpoint of an entire society, not just a single company, is of concern. Indeed, "society" may refer to a local population, a state, an entire country, or even an international community and all the subpopulations it comprises. Second, the policies or programs under consideration may have outputs that are not valued by ordinary markets, such as improvements in environmental quality or degradation of natural resource capital.

CBA in environmental evaluation also involves judgment calls. One must choose the discount rate used to bring future costs and benefits back to the present, and there is no settled method for doing so. As we noted in Chapter 4, it is difficult to account properly for the interests of future generations. Distribution of costs and benefits in the current generation is also difficult to address. Finally, CBA is not adept at dealing with uncertainty and irreversibility.

Despite these limitations, CBA provides valuable insights into economic tradeoffs associated with a proposed environmental intervention and is probably here to stay. CBA is now being used for the economic evaluation of public programs in natural resource management such as flood control, irrigation, hydropower, harbor improvements, and alternate energy supply projects. It is an integral part of the environmental impact analysis process to evaluate the impacts of public and private developments on environmental resources.

Rules and procedures govern the use of CBA for public decision-making. For example, an interagency group consisting of representatives from the Office of Management and Budget and the Council of Economic Advisors was convened to describe best practices for preparing the economic analysis of a significant regulatory action called for by Executive Order 12866. Table 5.1 lists some of the primary recommendations produced by the group as they concern environmental regulations.

Table 5.1.
GUIDELINES FOR COST-BENEFIT ANALYSIS THAT INCORPORATES ENVIRONMENTAL VALUATION

In 1993, President Clinton signed Executive Order 12866, "Regulatory Planning and Review," which called for an increased level of economic scrutiny of proposed federal regulations.

Principles for Valuing Benefits That Are Indirectly Traded in Markets
(e.g., reductions in health and safety risks, the use values of environmental amenities, and scenic vistas)

1. To estimate the monetary value of such an indirectly traded good, the willingness-to-pay valuation methodology is considered the conceptually superior approach.

2. Alternative methods may be used when there are practical obstacles to the accurate application of direct willingness-to-pay methodologies.

3. A variety of methods has been developed for estimating indirectly traded benefits. Generally these methods apply statistical techniques to distill from observable market transactions the portion of willingness to pay that can be attributed to the benefit in question. Examples include estimates of the value of environmental amenities derived from travel-cost studies, hedonic price models that measure differences or changes in the value of land, and statistical studies of occupational risk premiums in wage rates.

4. For all these methods, care is needed in designing protocols for reliably estimating benefits or in adapting the results of previous studies to new applications.

5. Reliance on contingent valuation methods depends on hypothetical scenarios, and the complexities of the goods being valued by this technique raise issues about its accuracy in estimating willingness to pay compared to methods based on (indirect) revealed preferences.

continued on next page

Table 5.1 (continued from previous page)

6. Accordingly, value estimates derived from contingent valuation studies require greater analytical care than studies based on observable behavior. For example, the contingent valuation instrument must portray a realistic choice situation for respondents — where the hypothetical choice situation corresponds closely with the policy context to which the estimates will be applied.

Principles and Methods for Valuing Goods That Are Not Traded, Directly or Indirectly, in Markets
(e.g., goods such as preserving environmental or cultural amenities apart from their use and direct enjoyment by people)

1. For many of these goods, particularly goods providing nonuse values, contingent valuation methods may provide the only analytical approaches currently available for estimating values.

2. The absence of observable and replicable behavior with respect to the good in question, combined with the complex and often unfamiliar nature of the goods being valued, argues for great care in the design and execution of surveys, rigorous analysis of the results, and a full characterization of the estimates to meet best practices in the use of this method.

In general, CBA involves four steps:

1. *Specify the social values of concern.* There are actually many publics and many social values. The first step in CBA is to decide on the values and perspectives of concern to the decision-makers. This step offers the prime opportunity to incorporate social justice and ethical concerns into a CBA. If one is conducting a CBA for a national agency, the public normally would be the population of the entire country. But if an employee of a city or regional planning agency conducts a CBA of a local environmental program, a more appropriate focus would be on the costs and benefits accruing to people living locally in those areas. The first step also includes a complete specification of the main elements of the project or program: location, timing, groups involved, connections with other programs, and the like. This first step is sometimes called scoping, in which the scope of the problem — its size and the population affected by the intervention — are specified, and the environmental target or standard is selected.

2. *Identify and measure the physical and biological changes that should be measured.* All that public money for environmental monitoring could really pay off if quality data could be fed into CBAs in this step. For some projects, determining the changes of concern, including both input and output flows, can be reasonably easy. For example, in planning a wastewater treatment facility, the engineering staff will be able to provide a full physical specification of the plant, together with the inputs required to build it and keep it running. For other types of programs, such determinations can be much harder. For example, a restriction on development in a particular region can be expected to reduce runoff locally. But what could be the actual environmental consequences? Could the restrictions deflect development into surrounding "green fields?" In this step, we become acutely aware of the time it can take to complete large environmental projects and the even greater time involved as their impacts play out. Uncertainty manage-

COST-EFFECTIVENESS ANALYSIS: WHAT'S THE BIGGEST BANG FOR THE BUCK?

CEA comes into play in environmental decision-making in two ways. The first, which is most common, is a case in which society has decided to make a given environmental improvement. The role of CEA in this case is to identify the least-cost method of achieving the environmental goal. The second, which could more accurately be termed benefit-effectiveness analysis, is a case in which society has decided to spend a given amount of money to address a particular objective. The role of CEA in this case is to identify the specific project that will achieve the greatest social benefit while remaining within the fixed budget.

The first of these approaches, in turn, comes into play in two different circumstances. First, society may decide it wishes to accomplish an action regardless of cost. It may do so on other than economic bases; here, social justice or ethics may prevail over money concerns. An example is the 1990 Clean Air Act, which set forth an agenda for action for environmental improvement to protect public health and the environment and actually prohibited the consideration of costs. Another example could be a deci-

---

Table 5.1 (continued from previous page)

ment becomes a major factor in the process because the job of specifying inputs and outputs involves predictions of future events, sometimes many years after an intervention begins.

3. *Estimate the costs and benefits of changes resulting from the program.* Assigning economic values to input and output flows is done to measure social costs and benefits. Typically, costs and benefits are measured in monetary terms. This does not mean relying on market value because in many cases, particularly on the benefit side, the effects are not registered directly in markets. Neither does it imply that only monetary values count. It means we need a single metric to translate all of the effects of an intervention to make them comparable among themselves and with other public activities. When we cannot find a way to measure how much people value these effects, it is important to supplement monetary results of a CBA with estimates of intangible effects.

4. *Compare costs and benefits. In this final step, total estimated costs are compared with total estimated benefits.* However, if benefits are not to be realized until some time in the future, first they must be converted to the present-day value, factoring in the selected discount rate, as discussed in Chapter 4. This judgment call deserves special examination and discussion and is closely linked to Step 1, in which social values of concern are identified. The present value of the stream of benefits minus the present value of costs gives the present value of net benefits.

sion to undertake an environmental cleanup even though the beneficiaries will reside primarily in future generations.

Second, the economics of a cost-benefit comparison could be so straightforward that a sector doesn't waste time or money on calculating cost-benefit ratios. An example could be a decision within the maritime industry to develop technologies to prevent the introduction and spread of aquatic nuisance species into the Great Lakes and other U.S. waters by ships. The cost impacts of new species introductions are known to be so great that environmental decision-makers already know that prevention will prove a sound course of action.

GLI BENEFITS ASSESSMENT — AN AFTERTHOUGHT

an important benefit-cost analysis undertaken in the Great Lakes region in support of an environmental rulemaking was that carried out by the EPA on the Great Lakes Water Quality Initiative (the GLI). The EPA and the Great Lakes states launched the GLI in 1989 to coordinate and improve water quality programs in the Great Lakes basin. Federal legislation, the Great Lakes Critical Programs Act of 1990, health, aquatic life, and wildlife. Federal legislation, the Great Lakes Critical Programs Act of 1990, codified the GLI and created deadlines. The Critical Programs Act also required the specification of water quality criteria to protect human health, aquatic life, and wildlife.

Pursuant to Executive Order 12866, the EPA conducted an economic analysis comparing costs and benefits of the GLI. In March 1995, the EPA released the study as a requisite part of the regulatory impact analysis. The analysis provides insight into the difficulties created by the low priority that benefits assessments have received historically. It also reflects the very limited literature base on economic benefits of environmental improvements in the Great Lakes region

The GLI concerns 69 pollutants, with special emphasis on a set of "bioaccumulative chemicals of concern," i.e. toxic substances that accumulate in the food chain. The BCA consisted of a detailed estimate of the costs, together with a more cursory estimate of the benefits, of achieving the environmental objectives.

The cost analysis began with the GLI criterion levels for the 69 pollutants, each set to ensure that the threats to human health, aquatic life, and wildlife did not exceed a specified level. Researchers studied in detail the anticipated costs of complying with the new criteria for a representative sample of small and large sources. They derived two sets of cost estimates. The low-cost estimates described economic consequences given the most optimistic

(continued on next page)

In both of these instances, there may be several different approaches to achieving the known societal objective, some more economically efficient than others. CEA can help society and sectors within it to select the most efficient approach. To undertake this operation, economists estimate and rank the costs of various projects or approaches designed to accomplish the same outcome. For example, a CEA of a sediment remediation project could start with a reduction goal for contaminant concentrations in the harbor. Economists would examine several alternative designs for the remediation that meet the design objective. They would compare the cost of each approach and indicate the least costly. Identifying the costs of concern represents perhaps the only judgment call in this operation. For example, in the case of approaches to sediment reme-

---

(continued from previous page)

assumptions about the types of measures that industry would utilized to meet the objectives. The high-cost estimates reflected more pessimistic assumptions. The estimates of annual compliance costs, basin-wide, were $61.4 million in the low-cost scenario and $376.2 million in the high-cost scenario.

The benefits analysis was not nearly as comprehensive as this. Rather, it was based on three case studies, for the Fox River and Green Bay, the Saginaw River and Saginaw Bay, and the Black River. The benefits estimates were obtained using benefits transfer from other studies, in addition to some information from commercial markets and from value-of-life estimates. The costs of GLI compliance for each of the study areas were derived from the basin-wide cost analysis.

Two of the case studies, the Fox River/Green Bay and the Saginaw River/Saginaw Bay, revealed annualized benefits larger than annualized costs. But total costs over a 20-year horizon were expected to exceed total benefits over the same period. For the Black River, costs exceeded benefits by every comparison that was considered. The benefits work was criticized based on the limited scope of the benefits studies, the fact that they were benefits transfer efforts rather than primary research, and the fact that the source sites were not in the Great Lakes region.

Perhaps the most important lesson to the learned from the GLI benefit-cost analysis is that estimating benefits has been an afterthought, almost to the extent that it becomes meaningless. The EPA spent several years on the cost analysis, yet it apparently performed its benefits analysis in a few short months near the end of the project. By the time the work began, a comprehensive benefits study was infeasible. A preferred approach would be to devote a comparable level of resources to both the cost and the benefits analysis.

diation, the cost to the environment of resuspending sediments in a removal operation, or the risk of resuspension due to storms in a containment scenario, may or may not be incorporated into a cost comparison. However, in both cases, the benefits have already been accepted as important.

The second approach, in which a fixed amount of money is to be spent, is familiar to decision-makers in the Great Lakes region. Frequently, federal appropriations legislation contains earmarks that members of the Great Lakes delegations secure for environmental projects in the region. In these cases, CEA can help identify ways to gain maximum environmental benefits at a set cost. Where non-market and non-monetary benefits are in play, society will have to select the option with the most desirable types and distribution of benefits.

There may be several different approaches to achieving the known societal objective, some more economically efficient than others. CEA can help society and sectors within it to select the most efficient approach.

NATURAL RESOURCE DAMAGE ASSESSMENT: WHAT DID WE LOSE?

The objective of natural resource damage assessment is to estimate the value of the damages to an injured resource so that these amounts can be recovered from parties held liable by the courts. Presently, three federal statutes — the Clean Water Act; the Comprehensive Environmental Response, Compensation and Liability Act; and the Oil Pollution Act — impose liability assessments for injury to natural assets that result from oil spills, hazardous wastes, and other substances. Under these acts, regulations have been developed by the Department of the Interior and the National Oceanic and Atmospheric Administration for comprehensive natural resource damage assessments. The process includes three steps: (1) injury determination, (2) quantification of service effects, and (3) damage determination.

Environmental valuation plays a role in the third step. Natural resource damages are the sum of (1) restoration costs (i.e., the direct and indirect costs of rehabilitation, replacement, and/or acquisition of equivalent resources), (2) compensable value (i.e., the value of foregone natural resources services prior to restoration), and (3) damage assessment costs. The benefit of avoiding the environmental damage in the first place is the sum of all three components.

Environmental valuation tools play a particular role in estimating compensable value. Compensable value is the loss of natural resource services between the time of the release (for example, an oil spill) and the time when these services are fully restored to their baseline condition. Compensable value excludes any losses resulting from secondary economic impacts caused by the release, such as losses incurred by businesses patronized by users of the injured resources (e.g., bait and tackle shops). All of the issues discussed in Chapter 4 and the judgment calls they require come into play in compensable damage determinations. Yet the outcome of the valuations can be determinative of the amount of money that must change hands. Here, the "gray area" discussed in Chapter 1 has led to litigation. The guidelines for proper use of valuation methods outlined in Chapter 2 were developed to limit disputes around these estimates.

The objective of natural resource damage assessment is to estimate the value of the damages to an injured resource so that these amounts can be recovered from parties held liable by the courts.

ECONOMIC IMPACT ANALYSIS: DOES ECONOMIC ACTIVITY INCREASE?

Economic impact analysis is a methodology for determining how some change in regulation or policy, a new technological breakthrough or other intervention alters economic activity reflected in revenues, expenditures, and employment. These analyses are limited to goods and services traded in markets. A pure impact analysis is neutral with respect to the increased activity, even though changes in economic activity may or may not coincide with changes in economic value. A violent storm that destroys a town can have a positive economic impact as companies work overtime to rebuild the area. In the same way, proponents often justify a proposed development, such as a landfill, based on projected, though perhaps short-term, increases in local sales volume or employment. Sales and employment may also go up in response to an actual increase in local natural resource wealth, such as that resulting from a cleanup of a harbor that permanently unleashes a heretofore untapped tourism potential. Thus, sales and employment figures do not necessarily reflect changes in value, i.e., what things are worth to people, and they do not account for what is being given up, i.e. the alternatives that people have to forego.

Impact analyses can focus at any geographic level. For example, a town council might be interested in the impact of a wetland protection law on the tax base in their community. In the same way, the Council of Great Lakes Governors might be interested in the economic impacts of tougher ballast water treatment requirements on ships on the Great Lakes regional economy. Congress might seek an economic impact analysis on a new national water quality requirement. Meanwhile, international agencies might be interested in how efforts to control carbon dioxide emissions might affect the relative growth rates of rich and poor countries.

VALUE CLARIFICATION: DID WE MISS SOMETHING?

Each environmental problem and each environmental policy is unique. Whether evaluating the relative merits of alternative projects or deciding how much to spend, it can be useful to have a number of formal economic evaluation approaches on hand. Cost-benefit analysis, cost-effectiveness analysis, and economic impact analysis all have their roles. At times however, it is equally useful to use economic tools simply to uncover the tacit values that society holds. Chapter 1 refers to this function as that of "shining a light" on hidden values. Benefits assessments using the tools laid out in this guidebook can help array the trade-offs, and help estimate the relative value society may place on competing interests. As noted in an earlier section, perfect information is a simplifying assumption of economics. At times, economic benefits assessments also actually help inform us of the many services a resource provides and allow us to take stock of what those services may be worth to us. Thus, while all too often we "don't know what we've got 'til it's gone," benefits assessments can change the refrain. "We don't know what we've got 'til we are asked to reflect on it" is less poetic, but bodes a happier ending for society and the environment.

CONCLUSION

Most people have heard of the fundamental economic decision-making models: cost-benefit analysis, natural resource damage assessment, cost-effectiveness analysis and economic impact analysis. Benefits assessments could play a role in all but the conventional economic impact analysis model. We hope it is clear from this chapter that these methods have distinctly different purposes and products. They also are not the only way that economics can play a role in environmental decision-making. First and foremost, environmental benefits assessments can help reveal the otherwise hidden, but very real, value that society places on its natural resources.

Up to this point, our discussion has been rather general. Certain important pieces of the puzzle have been missing. For example, how exactly do economists measure the benefits of a sediment remediation program? The primary role for economists in environmental policymaking is usually to answer this type of question. In the next chapter, several different tools for valuing benefits are presented.

Chapter 6

Tools of the Trade: Placing a Value on Great Lakes Environmental Benefits

U p to this point, we have provided information on the general use of economics in environmental decisions, including statutory requirements, special issues, and information frameworks. Now it is time to explore the techniques available to economists to estimate the values of goods and services associated with the environment. These techniques fall into two fundamental categories: (1) techniques to estimate the value of environmental amenities traded in markets and (2) techniques for benefits not traded in markets.

A market comprises a group of suppliers who provide the good or service, a group of consumers who buy the good or service, and a price at which the good or service changes hands. The markets for automobiles and blue jeans and personal computers and long-distance telephone service, for example, include these components. In general, we are familiar with markets and are accustomed to participating in them. As a result, the techniques for placing a value on environmental amenities traded in markets are quite conventional and are not unique to environmental economics, although their application to environmental amenities has required some adaptations. The second set of techniques were developed specifically to help society understand changes in the value of nonmarket benefits, including those associated with the environment.

In this chapter, we describe the primary techniques in use today, including their applications, data needs, key strengths, and limitations. Chapter 7 contains case studies showing the application of these techniques to real-world problems.

VALUING ENVIRONMENTAL GOODS AND SERVICES TRADED IN MARKETS[7]

Goods and services traded in markets may be prominent components of, and even adequate to explain, the major benefits of many environmental interventions. For example, the primary benefits of a nonpoint source pollution prevention effort could be reduced maintenance requirements for a municipal water supply or reduced dredging needs for waterborne shipping. Because the market determines the cost of water plant maintenance and dredging, the cost savings caused by the nonpoint source pollution control effort can be estimated easily using market prices. These instances are fortunate ones for those seeking economic information because the methods for measuring the value of goods and services traded in the marketplace are relatively standard and well accepted.

Changes in Producer and Consumer Surpluses

For goods traded in markets, economists estimate changes in producer and consumer surpluses to determine the change in economic value associated with environmental interventions. *Producer surplus* is any benefit (including profits) suppliers receive when they sell the goods and services they produce at market prices. Clearly, they benefit more as production costs decrease relative to the market price. *Consumer surplus* is any benefit that consumers may receive when purchasing goods and services at market prices. Consumers benefit most when market prices are lower than what they are willing to pay. Both aspects of the market are dynamic and could be affected by an environmental intervention. Economists seek to quantify the effect of a change in environmental conditions on consumer and producer surplus as one measure of the overall value (positive or negative) of the intervention.

For example, the cost of shipping to harbors on the Great Lakes is in part affected by the amount of dredging that the harbors require. The more dredging, the higher the cost of shipping. Soil runoff into river systems increases the need for dredging — and the cost to keep harbors open. The dredging costs in turn drive up the cost of shipping, reducing the producer surplus available to Great Lakes industry. As the cost increases are passed on to consumers, consumer surplus also declines. Analysis of these changes gives important insight into some of the direct costs of siltation in the Great Lakes basin.

---

[7] Brent Songhen, Assistant Professor, Department of Agricultural, Environmental, and Development Economics, The Ohio State University

Of particular concern when conducting this sort of analysis is the need to accurately account for all the factors that affect the supply of shipping over time, because dredging costs will not be the only factor to change. Other changes could magnify or counteract the changes resulting from dredging requirements. For instance, technical advances in shipping, such as development of ships that draw less water, might reduce this cost impact of soil runoff. Meanwhile, regulation requiring additional containment measures for harbor sediment could increase the direct cost to society of that runoff. There are statistical means for parsing out the effects of the dredging costs. The data required for this analysis include time series data on input and output prices, shipping capacity, and possibly the prices offered by alternative transportation industries.

Estimates of consumer surplus must also be carefully controlled. Shifts in demand, if any, must be accounted for fully using time series data on market prices for the product and quantity consumed, along with measures of other factors that affect demand.

Defensive Expenditures

Defensive expenditures can also measure changes in the values of environmental benefits traded in markets. Defense expenditures can be measured either with consumer and producer surplus, as described in the previous section, or they can be measured with direct market expenditures used to avoid or mitigate for an environmental impact. They are a response to shifts in producer and consumer surplus caused by an environmental impact. Defensive expenditures occur when markets or individuals affected by the reduced environmental quality attempt to maintain existing production levels or consumer satisfaction by spending additional resources to offset environmental changes, particularly damages. For example, water treatment facilities downstream may add technology to remove zebra mussels from their intake pipes. This cost represents a defensive expenditure related to a failure to prevent aquatic nuisance species introductions. Similarly, if water quality is still below safe minimum standards, water alerts may be issued, and households may substitute bottled water or they may boil water. In either case, the defensive expenditures can be estimated with market techniques, similar to those described in the preceding section. The case study on the Maumee River basin (see Chapter 7) presents an example in which defensive expenditures were used.

VALUING NONMARKET ENVIRONMENTAL GOODS AND SERVICES

Many if not most environmental "goods" have no market in the usual sense. For example, one does not buy a day's worth of enjoyment of the scenic beauty along the north shore of Lake Superior. One could buy a trip, a guide, access to a site, and gasoline or supplies along the way, but the aesthetic enjoyment itself is free. The same is true of a beach or fishing opportunities on Lake Michigan. Although there are consumers of these aspects of the Great Lakes environment, there is no supplier in the usual sense, and there is no price that can be observed in the usual way. Markets for resources such as clean air, clean water, or abundant wildlife are also difficult to imagine.

The fact that many environmental goods and services are not traded in markets makes alternative approaches to measuring their value necessary. Some approaches, such as the travel-cost method and hedonic valuation, deduce nonmarket value indirectly from the value of associated market goods and services. Contingent valuation involves asking people directly how much a specific environmental good is worth to them. Responses to carefully crafted questions of this kind can be helpful in assessing benefits not easily associated with market goods and services. Existing estimates from similar interventions can also be transferred to new applications through benefits transfer and meta-analysis methods. All of these methods are described briefly below.

Travel-Cost Method[8]

Application

The travel-cost method is generally used to estimate economic values associated with the use of recreation sites. This technique assumes that visitors to a particular site incur economic costs, in the form of outlays of time and travel expenses, to visit the site. In effect, these economic expenditures, or travel costs, reflect the "price" for the goods and services provided by the site. As noted in Chapter 5, "price" and what a consumer is willing to pay, or the "value" of the site to the consumer, are two different things. However, by observing the number of recreation trips individuals make at different levels of travel cost, economists are able to estimate the demand for recreational trips, and how environmental interventions may alter a consumer's willingness to pay for them, i.e., the value.

The travel-cost method has a number of applications — it can be used, for example, to measure the effects that changes in access costs to a recreational area, elimination of a

---

[8] *Frank Lupi, Assistant Professor, Department of Agricultural Economics and Department of Fisheries and Wildlife, Michigan State University*

site, or changes in environmental quality have on a consumer's willingness to pay. A policy intervention could result in any of these changes. To use the travel-cost method to value an intervention, recreation behavior must be linked to the effects the intervention has on recreation sites. For example, if the intervention changes environmental quality, then the relationship between the environmental quality at recreation sites and the number of trips to these sites must be established. Changes in environmental quality at a site can be valued only if they result in changes in trips to a site (i.e., the change in quality changes the demand for the site). The *recreational use value* of the change in environmental quality is the change in net benefits (i.e., consumer surplus) that accompanies the change in the trip demand.

To use the travel-cost method to value an intervention, recreation behavior must be linked to the effects the intervention has on recreation sites.

There are two main types of travel-cost models: single-site and multiple-site models. The two approaches differ in how explicitly they account for the ability of individuals to take trips to alternative recreation sites. These alternative recreation sites are often referred to as *substitutes*.

To see the importance of alternative recreation sites, suppose quality changes at site A. If similar recreation opportunities are widely available at alternative sites, then trips to site A will be more responsive to changes in the quality at site A than if site A was quite unique. The availability and comparability of substitutes determines the relative scarcity of any given recreation site. With many high-quality alternatives, decrements in quality at any one site will result in larger reductions in trips to that site, and improvements in quality will result in larger increases in trips. Consequently the availability of alternative recreation sites plays a dual role: mitigating some of the losses from decreases in site quality, and enhancing the gains from improvements in site quality. Thus, as with market goods, omitting the prices and qualities of relevant substitutes will bias the resource valuations.

The single-site travel-cost model simply measures trips to a single site. Single-site travel-cost models underlie the bulk of the travel-cost methods in the literature until the early 1990s. More recent literature, however, relies almost exclusively on multiple-site models.

Several variants of the multiple-site travel-cost model have appeared in the literature. The basic goal behind these variants is to estimate a system of trip demand equations for several sites rather than for a single site. The majority of multiple-site models use a method referred to as the *random utility model* (RUM). The RUM is a theoretical and statistical model used widely by economists to model the choice of a single alternative from a larger set of alternatives. In travel-cost applications, the RUM is used to estimate the choice of which recreation site to visit. When coupled with a method for predicting quantity of trips, the RUM provides a tractable way to model the number of trips to each site when a large number of potentially relevant substitutes is available.

Data Needs

Typically data are collected through surveys of individual travelers. The survey data usually include the characteristics of individuals, the number and locations of their trips, and information for deriving travel costs. On-site surveys can provide heavy sampling of users, but these surveys oversample frequent users and need to be augmented with general population data to learn what proportion of the population uses the resource. Although they are often more costly than on-site surveys, general population surveys also provide data that help the economist estimate decisions about whether to visit the site. Finally, if the travel-cost method is to be used for valuing environmental quality, data are needed to establish the linkage between the behavior of visitors and the level of environmental quality.

Single-site surveys require all the basic data needed to use the travel-cost method: the characteristics of individuals, the number of visits they made to the site, and information for deriving their travel costs. In most cases, some proxy variables for the prices and qualities of substitute sites are needed. If the method is to be used to value changes in environmental quality, then site-quality data are needed that vary over time or across individuals.

Data needs are greatest in the multiple-site models. In addition to the characteristics of individuals, data are needed to delineate the set of sites that is to be included in the model. Behavioral data are needed for the total recreation trips for all sites that will be included in the model and for the specific locations for some of these trips. In addition, the travel costs and quality characteristics are needed for each of the substitute sites.

Strengths of the Travel-Cost Method

The travel-cost method is relatively uncontroversial because it mimics empirical techniques used elsewhere in economics. Some economists tend to prefer techniques of this sort because they are based on actual behavior rather than verbal responses to hypothetical scenarios. In the travel-cost method, individuals must spend money and time, and their economic values are deduced from their behavior. The resulting demand concept is fairly intuitive: The travel-cost method explains how trips are related to personal characteristics, travel costs, and site-quality variables. In addition to valuation, the estimated demand model can be used to predict changes in behavior (i.e., trips) in response to changes in model variables that may be useful for other policy purposes. In some circumstances, a travel-cost model can be applied without enormous expense.

Single-site models can often be easy to implement. They are most useful when potential policies will affect only a single site that has few substitutes. Data can be collected on-site and combined with other data sources to estimate the demand function and correct for the on-site sampling. General population surveys can be more targeted because behavioral data need to be collected for only one site.

Multiple-site models deal explicitly with potentially important site substitution (i.e., switching from one site to another when site quality changes). These models can generally be used to value the addition of new sites as well as the elimination of some sites. Because these models are well suited to examining changes in the quality characteristics of the substitutes, they can be used for environmental valuation and for the valuation of policies that affect numerous sites. When only a small number of substitutes is available, some versions of the RUM are easy to estimate. Most economists consider multiple-site models to be the state-of-the-art.

Limitations of the Travel-Cost Method
The greatest disadvantage of the travel-cost method is that it cannot be employed unless some observable behavior can be used to reveal values. Thus the method is inappropriate for measuring nonuse values. In the case of nonuse values, there is no observable interaction between the individual and the resource in question. Again, if the travel-cost method is to be used to value changes in environmental quality, then travel to the site(s) in question must be linked to alternative levels of environmental quality.

It is important to recognize that any relationship between the site characteristic and recreational use must be established statistically. As a result, a host of data issues are involved in identifying this linkage. Some of these data issues are listed below:

- The data must exist to describe (i.e., quantify) the aspect of environmental quality to be valued;

- The data must be available for all sites to be modeled;

- The data should exhibit sufficient variation across sites;

- The data cannot be highly correlated with other variables that influence site choice; and

- The range of variation in the data should be sufficient to cover the range of policies to be examined.

Most of these concerns apply to any statistical modeling effort. However, they are particularly important in the travel-cost method because the linkage between site-quality characteristics and recreation trips is used to infer the value of changes in environmental quality. Ultimately, any travel-cost method valuation of environmental quality is only as good as the statistical link between site-quality characteristics and the number of trips to the site.

In contrast to most market goods, the market outlays and time costs that comprise travel costs vary across individuals and are not observed directly in a market transaction. Instead, these time and money costs are inferred by the economist. Therefore, the values derived from travel-cost models are sensitive to the specification of travel costs. In addition, the data about individuals and their trips that are needed to implement the travel-cost method must be gathered through surveys. Although collecting data through surveys is not a disadvantage per se, it is important to bear in mind that any survey data can suffer from poor design and implementation. The following issues must be considered when using travel-cost modeling:

- Accurate information on costs (both travel and time costs are not observed directly in a market transaction, and these costs are often critical in recreational consumption);

- Characterization of the quality dimensions of the site and statistical linkage of demand to site quality;

- Consideration of substitute sites and their characteristics; and

- Gathering of accurate and representative survey data on how much individuals use sites (i.e., which sites are used and how many visits are made).

Several disadvantages have led to a decrease in the popularity of single-site travel-cost models. First, if numerous substitutes are available, then the prices and qualities of these sites should enter the demand function. Second, single-site models give little information regarding the value of additional sites. Third, single-site models cannot be used to evaluate policies that affect multiple recreation sites. Thus, if the scope of the intervention is larger than a single site, this method is not appropriate.

Finally, and most important, single-site models are difficult to use for measuring the value of changes in environmental quality because such valuation requires knowledge of how the recreation trips (i.e., demand) will change when quality changes. Gathering such knowledge usually requires variation in the measure of environmental quality to identify statistically how different levels of environmental quality affect trip demand. With a single site, most users will face the same level of environmental quality. Sometimes the requisite variation exists if the study extends over longer time periods during which quality is changing (e.g., trip behavior has been measured before and after the intervention). In other cases, the variation might be available if individuals have different perceptions of quality or different skill levels (e.g., fishing success). In some cases, hypothetical surveys can be developed to generate data on visitation levels under various environmental quality conditions.

Multiple-site models are more demanding of data than are single-site models. The researcher needs to identify the set of sites that will enter the model, and this decision usually involves a fair amount of the researcher's judgment. The models become increasingly difficult to estimate as the number of sites grows. The RUM by itself deals only with site choice; it does not address the quantity of trips to these sites. If trips are anticipated to change in response to policies, then a method of modeling the trip quantity dimension must be adopted. In addition, the typical RUMs assume choices are independent over time. Modeling interrelatedness among the choices made by each individual is challenging in the multiple-site models.

> Although collecting data through surveys is not a disadvantage per se, it is important to bear in mind that any survey data can suffer from poor design and implementation.

Because environmental quality can vary across sites, multiple-site models provide a means of valuing changes in environmental quality. However, the valuation results cannot be divorced from the empirical adequacy of the site-quality data. As with any statistical analysis, the estimate of the effects of environmental quality may be affected by data difficulties. A key difficulty is a potential lack of variation in the quality variable across sites. Moreover, because recreation site choices are based on perceived quality, there is no guarantee that site choices are related to the scientific measures of site quality. Finally, as with any statistical analysis, the estimated results are most reliable when they are applied within the range of variation in the data used to estimate the model.

Hedonic Valuation of Environmental Improvements[9]

Application

Virtually any commodity or service purchased by consumers is really a bundle of attributes. A car has attributes of size, number of doors, color, power, durability, and electronic conveniences. A house has attributes of location, lot size, scenery, number of rooms, floor space, mechanical systems, age, school district, and property tax level. Although a single price is paid for a good or service, this price reflects the cumulative value of the various characteristics. Hedonic valuation uses statistical methods to deduce how much of the overall price is due to each attribute.

Hedonic valuation has been useful in estimating the economic value of certain types of environmental quality. A major area of application is environmental amenities associated with housing — amenities such as the quality of the ambient air; proximity to parks, water bodies, or contamination sites; noise levels; and the presence of scenic vistas. Hedonic valuation can reveal how the market prices of residential properties are affected by changes in the level of environmental amenities. This is done by statistically comparing the prices of residential properties that differ, among other things, in the amount of one or more of these amenities. The results indicate how residences that are otherwise identical differ in price because of differences in the levels of the environmental amenities.

Another major use of the technique is in the valuation of occupational risks. Many occupational risks stem from exposure to toxic chemicals, carcinogens, or other workplace environmental hazards. Hedonic valuation of wage rates for similar occupations in workplaces with different exposure levels can help reveal how much compensation workers require in order to accept more environmental risk.

Hedonic valuation proceeds in two stages. The first stage analyzes the relationship between attributes (independent variables) and the observed market prices (dependent variables). The analyst collects data for these variables on as many parcels of property or wage rates as is practical. The data are examined statistically to produce estimated coefficients for an equation called the *hedonic price function*. The coefficients of the price function express a unit dollar value (marginal price) associated with a unit of measurement of each attribute. For example, say that a particular study produces a price function relating house prices, measured in dollars, to proximity to a hazardous waste site, measured in miles, and produces a coefficient of 3,025. The coefficient

[9] *John Braden, Professor, Department of Agricultural and Consumer Economics, University of Illinois at Urbana-Champaign and Sudip Chattopadhay, Assistant Professor, Department of Economics, San Francisco University*

implies that the value of the average house in the group being analyzed would increase by approximately $3,025 if the average distance to the waste site could be increased by one mile.

The values revealed by the hedonic price function reflect not only the willingness of consumers to pay or be compensated for environmental attributes, but also the costs borne by producers to supply the attribute. This confounding of demand and supply is not a problem if the goal of the analysis is to evaluate a very small proposed change in the level of the environmental attribute. Then, the unit dollar value revealed by the hedonic price function is an appropriate estimate. However, in many cases the analyst will be interested in the benefits of a large change — of 25 percent or more — from the baseline level. In these instances, consumers' unit values can change. For example, the value of an additional mile of distance from a hazardous waste site is likely to be much higher for houses within one mile of the site than for houses four or more miles away. The unit value associated with houses four miles from the site cannot simply be multiplied by four to arrive at a unit value for houses only a mile away. Most likely, the unit value increases for homes closer to the site. An accurate evaluation of a large environmental quality change should allow for these changes in unit values.

The first stage of hedonic valuation analyzes the relationship between attributes (independent variables) and the observed market prices (dependent variables).

Fortunately, methods have been developed to determine how unit values change with changes in the level of environmental quality. These methods are applied in the second stage of the hedonic valuation method. The second stage takes the unit prices estimated in the first stage (one for each data point in the sample) and estimates their relationship to consumer variables, such as income, educational level, family demographics, and so forth as well as to the level of the environmental amenity. Statistical analysis of this relationship produces another equation. The coefficients of this equation express the importance of each demand-side variable on the average unit value. Because one of those demand-side variables is the current level of environmental quality, the equation can be used to evaluate the willingness to pay for large changes in the environmental amenity. Thus the two-stage hedonic valuation method produces values for both a one-unit change and a multi-unit change from the sample average value of the environmental amenity. Both steps are essential if (1) the analyst wants to consider an environmental quality change from baseline levels of more than a few percentage points, and (2) the hedonic price function turns out to be something other than a simple linear equation, in which case multiplying the average unit value times the proposed change in the environmental attribute could seriously misrepresent true economic values.

Data Needs
Data needs depend on the type of hedonic study being carried out. Table 6.1 summarizes the types of data needed for each type of hedonic study and lists possible data sources.

Strengths of Hedonic Valuation
A leading strength of the hedonic valuation method is its use of actual market transactions. The values derived are not merely hypothetical or expressions of intent; they reflect real commitments of consumer resources to achieve specific environmental quality improvements through the choice of residences or jobs.

Table 6.1.
DATA SOURCES FOR HEDONIC VALUATION STUDIES.

Type of Study	Type of Data	Sources
Property value studies	Data on homes and purchasers	Federal Housing Administration Department of Housing and Community Development Local real estate associations County recorder of deeds Property tax agencies
	Survey data on all types of houses, including the owner's estimated valuation	American Housing Survey
	Socioeconomic data by census tract	U.S. Bureau of the Census
	Monitoring data on air and water quality	State or regional environmental agencies
	Fiscal data on local governments	State revenue agencies
	Fiscal and demographic data on local school systems	State education agencies
Wage studies	Data on employment and wages	U.S. Bureau of Labor Statistics
	Occupation risk data	National Institute of Occupational Health and Safety

Hedonic valuation is also useful because the transactions typically analyzed represent a large share of most consumers' welfare. A house purchase is the single largest transaction that most consumers ever make, and the largest portion of one's time is typically spent at home. Thus the value attached to the residential environment should represent a large share of the overall value attached to environmental quality. Similarly, a job is the major source of income and the second-largest time commitment for most people. Environmental risks associated with employment accordingly represent a major share of the overall social value of certain types of environmental problems.

Another strength of hedonic valuation is the availability of a variety of statistical techniques to apply to hedonic data. Some of these techniques essentially collapse the two-stage process into a single step. The availability of several different ways to examine the data makes it possible to cross-validate the valuation results.

Limitations of Hedonic Valuation

The hedonic valuation method seems straightforward: Gather all the data one can on market transactions of a good or service likely to be influenced by environmental quality, then statistically estimate two relationships, one based on the other. In practice, however, the technique can be quite challenging. Data availability often limits what can be included in a hedonic study and, more generally, the types of environmental quality that can be analyzed. Price, attribute, and socioeconomic data are needed for a large number of individual transactions, and such detailed data are routinely available for only a few goods and services. Housing and labor market transactions are notable cases where a good deal of data are available, but even in these markets the data may not truly represent the full population. For example, the most readily available housing data are for transactions that involve federal subsidies or guarantees, and these tend to be lower-priced residences. Another data problem is that key variables are likely to be available only with very coarse measurement — by census tract, city, school district, or air quality monitoring district in the case of housing — reducing the ability to distinguish precisely between individual transactions and increasing the number of transactions that must be analyzed to gain meaningful insight.

In interpreting the results of hedonic valuation, some debate exists as to whether objective measures of environmental quality such as the ambient concentrations of certain chemicals or distance to a contamination site accurately capture human perceptions of environmental conditions. Human sensory systems may perceive environmental quality changes in ways very different from the objective measures, and in such cases, the value relationships established through hedonic methods would be misleading.

Many economists are skeptical that the second stage of the hedonic valuation method can separate consumer preferences from the cost factors influencing supply — the so-called *identification problem*. The ability to make this distinction is essential if the results are to provide meaningful information about consumer welfare effects. Otherwise, it is not clear whether price changes are due to environmental quality effects on producers or on consumers. Economists have shown that this problem is not important for hedonic valuation studies that (1) use household-level data on prices and property characteristics, not data aggregated at the census tract or community level, and (2) introduce additional, relevant data at the second stage, both socioeconomic- and market-level, beyond the data included in the first stage.

The specific point estimates produced by hedonic valuation could be unreliable for environmental quality levels quite different from the status quo. This is because hedonic valuation, like any type of statistical analysis, is most trustworthy within the range of the data on which its estimates are based.

Another limitation of hedonic valuation is that it provides only partial estimates of the value of environmental quality changes — estimates clearly connected to the actual consumption of a particular good. For example, improvements in urban air quality could affect the quality of life not only at home but also in the office, at the park, and in the car. Value changes might be expected at all of these locations, but hedonic valuation of housing prices would pick up only the share experienced at home. Although residential or job values may capture large shares of the value attached to environmental improvement, they probably do not capture all of that value.

A final limitation of hedonic valuation is that it is confined to environmental attributes that are closely associated with market transactions. It would be unrealistic to expect these methods to be helpful with attributes about which consumers have less ability or incentive to make choices, such as stratospheric ozone depletion or reductions in biological diversity.

Recent advances in econometric techniques have resolved many of the concerns surrounding the hedonic valuation method, and alternative approaches have been developed to provide cross-checks on the results and to circumvent the identification problem. As a consequence, hedonic valuation is a viable tool for use in valuing certain types of environmental quality outcomes.

Contingent Valuation Method[10]

Application

Contingent valuation (CV) uses survey methods to estimate values of environmental amenities. In personal or telephone interviews or in mail surveys, respondents are asked to make hypothetical choices that will reveal their willingness to pay to achieve environmental improvements or avoid environmental degradation. The more meaningful and well defined are the choices placed before participants, the more their responses will reveal about the choices they would make if the situation were real. Monetary values estimated using CV are used in cost-benefit analyses and other efforts to inform public decision-making and in estimating damages for litigation involving environmental resources.

Though relatively new, CV has been applied in literally hundreds of cases, both in North America and abroad (Carson et al. 1994). One well-known recent example valued the environmental effects of the Exxon Valdez oil spill (Carson et al. 1992). Another application focused on the effects of upstream dam operations on the environmental and cultural resources along the Colorado River in Grand Canyon National Park (Welsh et al. 1995; Bishop and Welsh, 1999). So far, applications to Great Lakes resources have been limited mostly to fisheries (Milliman et al. 1992; Lyke 1993). However, the potential for applications is broad, including possible remediation of contaminant sediments, wetland and fish habitat restoration, marina development, and redevelopment of harbors and other coastal areas.

Unfortunately, CV studies have acquired a reputation for being expensive. The truth is that CV studies vary greatly in cost, from a few thousand dollars to millions of dollars. Much depends on the circumstances and the degree of accuracy needed in the specific application. In applications in which respondents are familiar with the resources in question and in which researchers have conducted a great many similar studies, costs may be quite modest. An example might be a straightforward application to recreational fishing. Costs are also low when accuracy is not required. For example, suppose a government agency is contemplating a new policy or regulation that will enhance local environmental quality. If the only issue is whether the benefits exceed the costs or vice versa, a small pilot study may be all that is needed. Suppose a pilot study shows that a full study would in all likelihood turn up benefits in the hundreds of thousands of dollars. This may be all that is needed if the new policy or regulations will cost many millions of dollars or only a few thousand dollars.

[10] *Richard C. Bishop, Professor and Chair, Department of Agricultural and Applied Economics, University of Wisconsin-Madison*

At the other extreme are studies in which accurate values are needed and the resource issues being debated involve complex ecological and other relationships about which many respondents are poorly informed. In such cases, designing a survey that can communicate large amounts of complex information can be a long, demanding process. Expensive personal interviews may be necessary. Sample sizes must be large enough to support precise estimates. Extra care may be needed in analyzing the data once the survey is complete. Each of these requirements can run up the costs. Still, in the history of CV, studies costing millions of dollars or even several hundred thousand dollars have been the exception rather than the rule.

Dissecting a typical CV survey would reveal three parts: the scenario, the valuation question, and other survey questions. Considering each part in turn may help the reader visualize how the method is applied.

Scenario. One major purpose of the scenario is to explain to study participants how their circumstances might change if some proposed action is taken to modify environmental amenities. By "proposed actions," we mean steps being considered primarily by government, possibly involving proposed new regulations, policy changes, or public projects. Examples from the Great Lakes might include changes in fish stocking, regulations to limit unintentional introduction of aquatic nuisance organisms, and cleanup of contaminated sediments. After the proposed action has been described, the typical scenario would detail how environmental resources would be affected. In addition, the proposed action might affect incomes, market prices, and other economic variables. Study participants must be aware of all potentially relevant effects of proposed actions before they can be expected to successfully consider how valuable those effects are to them. Verbal descriptions of the changes, possibly aided by photographs, maps, diagrams, and other visual aids, are central to any CV scenario.

Respondents also usually like to know something about the circumstances under which they are being asked to reveal their values. Thus the other major role of the scenario is to convey information to respondents about the context of valuation. For example, a valuation exercise may be framed as a referendum similar to a ballot referendum people might encounter during an election. Or, as another example, suppose that the action will affect amenities at a recreation site. In that case, the context of valuation might ask respondents to imagine a situation in which they must choose whether to visit the site with improved amenities if their costs for such a visit were higher.

An important issue regarding the context of valuation is the mechanism through which payments would be collected. The payment mechanism in the case of a referendum might be taxes, whereas in the case of recreation, it might be increases in recreational expenses. Those who apply CV seek payment mechanisms that will seem realistic to respondents yet be neutral in their effects on responses to the upcoming valuation question. Property taxes, for example, are so controversial that they are rarely used because responses are likely to reflect more about respondents' opposition to property taxes than about their willingness to pay for environmental amenities.

Choosing a payment mechanism often involves compromises. For example, state or federal income taxes are sometimes used. Although income taxes may be less contentious than property taxes, they are not likely to be perfectly neutral, because many people object to tax increases regardless of the form. On the plus side, income taxes to support governmental actions often seem plausible to respondents, and they seem to take the possibility of such taxes seriously.

Valuation question. Once the scenario is complete, the valuation question itself is posed. If the context of valuation involves a referendum, then the CV question would ask how respondents would vote if given the opportunity to do so. In the recreational example, the CV question might ask respondents about their intentions to visit the site under conditions posed in the scenario. Various question formats can be used. Assuming that the question is posed as a referendum, in one commonly used format, respondents would be asked to vote yes or no at a specified cost, much as they do in a real referendum. The cost, which might be in the form of an increase in income taxes or in taxes and prices more generally defined, is varied from respondent to respondent in order to understand willingness to pay across a wide range of possible values. Another format would ask respondents simply to write in a blank in the survey the maximum increase in their taxes or other costs they would accept and still vote positively on the proposed change. So-called payment cards are sometimes used, where a range of amounts appears in the survey and respondents are asked to mark the maximum amount they would pay.

An alternative measure of economic value — *willingness to accept* compensation or simply willingness to accept — might also be estimated using CV. If the proposed action under consideration would degrade environmental resources, for example, a

> Unfortunately, CV studies have acquired a reputation for being expensive. The truth is that CV studies vary greatly in cost.

CV study might investigate how much members of the public would have to be compensated before they would find the loss of environmental amenities acceptable. Although in concept it might make perfect sense to try to measure willingness to accept in such cases, responses to willingness to accept questions have generally not been very reliable. Hence, CV researchers usually stick to willingness-to-pay questions.

Other survey questions. CV surveys invariably include questions other than the valuation question. Such questions may provide additional information to decision-makers by providing data on respondents' characteristics and their preferences and opinions about the proposed action. They may also provide data to be used in evaluating the validity of the CV estimates in ways described below.

Data Needs

Designing a successful CV survey involves several steps. To begin with, the proposed action and its potential environmental effects need to be fully understood by the investigator. This normally involves collaboration between the economists conducting the study and decision-makers and environmental scientists. As the scenario begins to take shape, initial contacts with the sorts of people who will eventually complete the survey are often made. This may take place in focus groups. In such groups, a moderator engages a group of 8 to 10 people in discussions aimed at developing a high-quality survey instrument. The purpose of such groups is to improve communications between researchers and study subjects. Early focus groups may explore what sorts of language future respondents might use to describe the proposed action and its environmental and other effects. Other goals include identification of the attributes of the environment that are important to potential respondents and how they react to draft material for the scenario. To develop a high-quality survey, an iterative process of revising the survey materials and holding focus groups may be required. Once the survey is in semifinal form, individual interviews with people from the future population of respondents may help to further refine it. Surveys are then often pretested on small samples. Pilot surveys of larger, more representative samples may be used to finalize the instrument.

Administration of the final version of the CV survey involves choosing a representative sample from the relevant public. Both theoretical and practical considerations come into play in defining the population from which to draw the sample. In theory, all members of society who are potentially affected by the proposed action should be considered part of the population. For example, if a study were focusing on a major Great Lakes issue of concern to both Americans and Canadians, the relevant potential population might be all the citizens of the two countries. In practice, narrower definitions may be a necessary expedient. For example, the scenario may need to include complex information about environmental resources. Such information is usually more easily grasped by those familiar with the resources in question. This may necessitate restricting the population to people living near potentially affected resources even if effects extend to people living farther away. We return to issues related to information that respondents receive when we consider the limitations of CV, below.

Once the population has been defined and a representative sample chosen, survey administration procedures are implemented that will, it is hoped, obtain a response rate sufficient to support extrapolation of the sample results to the population. Responses are computerized and the analysis conducted to provide value estimates for the population and to provide whatever other statistics from the survey decision-makers might use. Ideally the study report summarizes the procedures followed and all decision-relevant results.

Strengths of Contingent Valuation
As should be clear by this point, CV is not the only method of investigating nonmarket environmental values. However, its proponents argue that it has two potential advantages over other methods. They believe that it is the most comprehensive in terms of the range of potential values that can be included, and that it is the most flexible of the valuation techniques.

The proponents of CV believe that it is more comprehensive than other approaches in that it is capable of measuring not only use values, but also values associated with environmental amenities. Examples of use values include values obtained from enjoying a fish dinner from uncontaminated Great Lakes waters or breathing clean air in one's neighborhood. Nonuse values are values that do not depend on personal use of environmental amenities (e.g., recreational fishing) or products derived from nature (e.g., commercially caught fish). Instead, nonuse values are rooted in the desire to leave environmental bequests to one's heirs or future generations more generally, the desire simply to know that pristine environments continue to exist, or other such motives.

> The proponents of CV believe that it is more comprehensive than other approaches in that it is capable of measuring not only use values, but also values associated with environmental amenities.

All other major valuation approaches fall short in this regard because they depend on observing actual behavior, particularly behavior in market settings. For example, the travel-cost method examines choices about how much to spend in markets for gasoline, food, hotels, and other travel goods and services in order to engage in outdoor recreation. In hedonic valuation, researchers try to tease out the values of air and water quality from data on housing prices, housing characteristics, and environmental quality across housing markets in one or more urban areas. In economics jargon, all commonly applied valuation methods except CV are termed *revealed preference methods*. This term calls attention to the fact that economists believe people reveal their economic preferences for goods and services through the choices they actually make in markets. All of the other methods of valuation discussed in this guidebook, including the travel-cost method, the hedonic price method, and market valuation, are revealed preference methods. (Benefits transfer and meta-analysis simply summarize and extrapolate from studies using revealed preference or CV methods).

The problem with nonuse values is that they are expressed only imperfectly, if at all, in actual behavior. People may join environmental groups or volunteer in times of emergency, such as during oil spills, but beyond such gestures there may be few opportunities for them to express nonuse values through overt behavior. For this reason, most environmental economists are pessimistic about prospects for measuring nonuse values with revealed preference techniques. CV is the only method of estimating total values, including nonuse values, that has gained substantial acceptance among economists. Of course, CV measures of total value are useful only to the extent that they are judged to be scientifically valid. We revisit the issue of validity in the next section. At this point, we can only say that if a CV total valuation study were judged to be valid, it would allow decision-makers to consider the broader values that the public may hold for environmental amenities rather than basing their choices on use values alone.

CV is more flexible than other methods in at least two dimensions. First, CV is less demanding in terms of data and statistical procedures than other methods. Revealed preference methods depend on statistical techniques to unravel economic values implicit in choices that people actually make. The econometric difficulties in applying revealed preference methods are always formidable, and sometimes the data are simply insufficient to estimate valid economic values. Because it does not depend on data from actual choices, CV is potentially flexible enough to provide value estimates when econometric methods and data fall short. Second, CV places fewer constraints on the analyst in terms of values to be measured. The potential measurement of nonuse values using CV has already been stressed. It is also worth pointing out, however, that nonuse values need not be included if research goals call for estimating a narrower range of values. For example, restoration of lake trout to the Great Lakes may involve both use values (e.g., sport and commercial fishing) and nonuse values (e.g., people may value restored ecosystems as bequests to future generations). If decision-makers were interested only in the values of lake trout restoration to anglers, it might be feasible to focus a CV study only (or at least mostly) on sport-fishing values.

Limitations of Contingent Valuation
The chief limitation of CV stems from the fact that it is still rather new and remains controversial. Economists have a long history of using revealed preference data and methods to estimate economic values. Those who have developed the CV method are proposing that data from surveys be accepted as valid economic evidence as well. Some economists have greeted this proposal with considerable skepticism (Hausman 1993; Diamond and Hausman 1994). The concerns that have been expressed mean that validity is not merely an academic issue. Decision-makers who base choices on CV results should expect to be challenged based on arguments against the validity of the method or of the individual studies on which they are drawing.

CV studies vary so greatly in quality that the results of any given study probably should not be taken at face value. The merits of each study need to be considered on a case-by-case basis. Criteria for evaluating the validity of individual studies have been developed (Mitchell and Carson 1989; U.S. Department of Commerce 1993; Bishop et al. 1995). Some criteria focus on whether the survey procedures applied were conducive to accurate measurement, whereas others would test for consistency of the results with economic theory. For example, theory tells us that environmental economic values will often be sensitive to income and environmental attitudes. Thus CV studies often gather data on income and attitudes as a part of the survey and test for such relationships statistically. Where values are correlated with income and attitudes in the expected way, this lends support to the validity of the results.

Because CV is so new, the full limitations of the method are not fully delineated. Research aimed at understanding those limitations continues. Although definitive results on the exact boundaries are still to be determined, most researchers would agree that even the best studies face limits in terms of how much information can be conveyed to study participants in scenarios. This is particularly true when nonuse values of resources unfamiliar to the participants must be assessed. Personal interviews can push this limitation somewhat but are very expensive. As research continues, other limitations may become clearer.

In the meantime, enough research has accumulated to begin to form some judgments about the validity of CV as a method. The question here is whether results from individual studies that meet high standards as defined by leading researchers in the field should be considered valid evidence about economic values. Although some economists might continue to argue that the proverbial glass is at least half empty, many others would argue that it is at least half full. That was certainly the conclusion of the NOAA Panel on Contingent Valuation (U.S. Department of Commerce 1993). The NOAA panel was charged by the National Oceanic and Atmospheric Administration (NOAA, an agency of the U.S. Department of Commerce) with assessing whether CV should be considered sufficiently reliable to be used to assess damages to public resources from oil spills. The NOAA panel was composed of several prominent economists and a survey researcher, and was cochaired by Nobel-laureates in economics Kenneth Arrow and Robert Solow. The NOAA panel concluded (p. 4610),

CV studies convey useful information. We think it is fair to describe such information as reliable by the standards that seem to be implicit in similar contexts, like market analysis for new and innovative products and the assessment of other damages normally allowed in court proceedings… Thus, the Panel concludes that CV studies can produce estimates reliable enough to be the starting point of a judicial process of damage assessment, including lost passive use [nonuse] values.

> **Enough research has accumulated to begin to form some judgements about the validity of CV as a method.**

Most economists would agree that any method that is sufficiently reliable to be used in court is sufficiently reliable to be used in public decision-making more generally, including decision-making about the future of Great Lakes resources.

Benefits Transfer[11]

Application
Benefits transfer is the application of the results of one or more studies developed for addressing particular environmental or natural resource valuation questions to another intervention. In one context, this is normal procedure. A thorough review of past work is a necessary first step in addressing a new research question or policy

---

[11] *Leroy J. Hushak, Professor Emeritus, Department of Agricultural, Environmental, and Developmental Economics and The Ohio Sea Grant Program, The Ohio State University*

problem. In this sense, researchers and policymakers have always applied research results to other issues or settings as a first step in assessing an issue. In this section, however, we focus on cases in which the use of past results may be the only information used to estimate the value of the intervention.

Benefits transfer can be a reasonable and inexpensive method for determining economic values. If, for example, it is important to establish a value for recreational fishing in one's location, and time or resources are not sufficient for an explicit study of that location, then one might consider making a benefits transfer estimate using values from studies of other locations in the Great Lakes or elsewhere. However, benefits transfer does not add to the total knowledge about environmental or natural resource values; it only borrows knowledge about values at selected study sites to infer something about value at an intervention site.

Benefits transfer applications can be divided into two approaches: (1) Benefits transfers based on the best or average estimated results of a study, adjusted if possible for known differences between the study and intervention sites; and (2) benefits transfers that combine the statistically estimated model from the original study and estimated values of the model variables at the intervention site.

In the first and simpler approach, estimated willingness to pay (e.g., average consumer surplus from a market, travel-cost, or hedonic model), or mean willingness to pay from a CV study, is used as the benefits transfer estimate. These average values could be adjusted for site differences if information about how to adjust the estimates is available. For example, walleye or yellow perch fishing in Lake Erie during 1987 had an estimated consumer surplus of about $7 per day. If one wanted an estimate of the economic value of walleye or yellow perch fishing in Saginaw Bay, a benefits transfer estimate would be the estimated Lake Erie consumer surplus per day of $7 times the estimated number of fishing days for walleye or yellow perch in Saginaw Bay.

In the second and more detailed approach, the statistically estimated model for the study site is combined with intervention site data to obtain estimates specific to the intervention site. In the Saginaw Bay case, for example, estimated mean travel costs, income, and other variables for anglers in Saginaw Bay would be used in the statistical Lake Erie travel-cost model to generate an intervention site estimate of consumer surplus. Suppose this came out to be $6 per day. The benefits transfer estimate of walleye or yellow perch fishing in Saginaw Bay would then be $6 per day times the number of fishing days. Similarly, estimated values of intervention site variables would be used in an estimated statistical willingness-to-pay choice function to generate estimates of willingness to pay at the intervention site.

A more sophisticated application of the second approach is to use a *meta function* to generate a benefits transfer estimate of economic value. A meta function is a composite statistical function relating estimated economic values from a set of studies to a set of characteristics about those studies. For example, a meta function of the willingness to pay or consumer surplus estimates of sport angling is a statistical relationship between the standardized value estimates (per trip or per day) for the studies and such characteristics as mean price, mean income, species (individual or type such as warm water versus cold water), type of water body, year of study, estimation method, plus other factors expected to affect the value estimates. The goal of a meta study is to estimate the systematic variation among value estimates for variations in site characteristics. If available, the use of a meta function as the basis for benefits transfer can result in an estimate superior to one from a site-specific study, in particular if resources are limited.

Benefits transfer is considered to be valid under well-defined conditions. The more similar the conditions between the intervention site and the study site(s), the more reliable is the transfer estimate.

Several questions must be answered in evaluating a benefits transfer opportunity; these questions concern the assumptions underlying previous studies, the methodologies used in the studies, the economic methods used in evaluation, and the resource evaluated. For example, are the purposes of the source study similar to the intervention site? What groups are considered in generating the initial estimate (e.g., duck hunters or sport anglers versus all citizens in an area)? Does the source study address a specific or unique problem that may have influenced the magnitude of the estimates obtained? For example, was the study conducted during a period of heightened concern or crisis for the resource in question? Have general attitudes, perceptions, or levels of knowledge changed in the period since the existing study was performed in a way that would influence the value of the benefits estimate? Are these values likely to be consistent over time? If the value being considered is for a generic resource category (e.g., common songbirds), are the species considered in the original study relevant to the case at hand? Were any adjustments to the data made in the existing study? For example, were outliers deleted? Were any adjustments made for perceived biases? Does the existing study consider the same or a similar geographic area? Are the demographic and socioeconomic characteristics of the two areas similar?

A specific set of questions must be posed with respect to the resource subject to study. How does the resource at the intervention site compare to that considered in the source study site? For example, is the species of concern more common in the intervention study area than in the initial study area? What was the nature of substitute resources or sites in the initial study area, and how does this compare to the intervention study area? For example, are alternative recreational opportunities more or less available in the intervention study area? Was the original analysis conducted to value all organisms of a given species, a subpopulation, individual members of the species, or some other grouping?

Sometimes the source study presents a composite of existing values based on an earlier literature review. That is, the source study may already be a benefits transfer estimate. If so, the following questions must be asked: What methods were used to derive these composite values, and what was the nature of the underlying studies? Were baseline conditions (e.g., ambient water quality) in the existing study similar to baseline conditions at the intervention site? Were variables omitted from the original study that are believed to be relevant to the intervention site? To what extent does such omission prohibit the transfer? If current best-research practices were not used to generate the value estimate(s), can the estimate(s) be adjusted to reflect changes in the state-of-the-art? Given the rapid development of economic valuation methodologies, studies that are several years old will not be using state-of-the-art models.

Benefits transfer is considered to be valid under well-defined conditions. The more similar the conditions between the intervention site and the study site(s), the more reliable is the transfer estimate.

Finally, a close review of the quality of the source study is also in order. Was the study used to generate the value estimate published in a peer-reviewed journal, or did it receive other forms of peer review? How was the original study viewed in the professional community? How was the study viewed by its investigators? In many cases the defensibility of the transferred economic benefits estimate will depend on the quality of the underlying research. However, no globally accepted, standard criteria are available to judge the quality of existing studies. The professional and academic community can provide guidance with regard to the current minimum conditions for quality assurance of benefits transfer.

Once a final set of values has been chosen from the literature, consideration should be given to their general magnitudes. If the existing value estimates differ significantly, or if values generated using alternative models differ significantly from one another, consideration should be given to whether they differ in a predictable and consistent manner. In some cases, it may be possible to combine these estimates formally through a meta-analysis (described later in this chapter). In all cases, more defensible benefits estimates will result from comparative analysis.

In the final analysis, the decision of whether benefits transfer is the most appropriate approach requires (1) comparatively assessing the quality of the benefits transfer estimate, (2) assessing the level of study required to generate a site-specific estimate that is of the minimum quality required, and (3) deciding whether the benefits of the site-specific estimate exceed the costs of getting that estimate.

Data Needs

At it simplest level, there are no primary data needs for a benefits transfer estimate. One applies to the intervention site the best results from a literature review of appropriate previous studies. The quality of the benefits transfer estimate will be improved as more information is known about the intervention site. For example, in a benefits transfer of fisheries values, the estimate will be improved as one incorporates information about species harvested, type of water, catch rates, demographic characteristics of anglers, and other factors affecting how a fishery is valued by anglers.

Strengths of Benefits Transfer

Although not formally a method or technique of estimation, the discussion and conditions for evaluating the applicability of benefits transfer do provide somewhat formal procedures for making benefits transfer estimates. The strengths of the benefits transfer process are three: First, a benefits transfer estimate can be quick and of low cost. Existing studies form the basis for the estimate, and no original work is conducted. Second, the focus is on the generic value of the intervention, to the exclusion of its unique elements. That is, only those traits of the resource that are in common with other similar resources are evaluated. Unique characteristics of the resource will be excluded (this can also be a disadvantage, see next section). Third, if a meta function is available, the intervention can be valued by inserting the intervention site values of the explanatory variables into the meta function and calculating the intervention site result (see meta-analysis, below).

Limitations of Benefits Transfer

The weaknesses of using benefits transfer are in many respects the opposites of its strengths. First, the unique elements of the intervention are not valued. If the resource being valued has a unique characteristic judged to be important that is not found in other similar resources that have been studied, serious consideration should be given to a special study of the resource. Second, the quality of the benefits transfer estimate is no better than the quality of the value estimates in the literature. If a type of resource or an issue has been studied in depth in several different projects, then one can expect benefits transfer to yield a reasonably good estimate. In contrast, if the existing studies are weak, any benefits transfer estimate will be weak as well.

Meta-Analysis

Application

Meta-analysis is another method that can be used to estimate the value of a particular environmental project or intervention without acquiring new data and conducting a complete, original study. It can be thought of as a fancy form of benefits transfer, one that might be useful in certain situations for which there is no comparable study that can serve as the basis for a direct benefits transfer. Meta-analysis is a method for synthesizing many comparable estimates of the benefits to a given environmental change, using information from all of them to come up with an estimate of benefits that draws from a broader collection of underlying information.

Consider, for example, the dozens of studies conducted over the years that used hedonic methods to estimate the effect of particulate matter on property values. [This is precisely the set of studies that were themselves the object of study in Smith and Huang (1995).] Each of these hedonic studies arrived at an estimate of the marginal effect of particulate matter on property values. But the studies used data from different places, at different times, and under different environmental conditions. The estimates arrived at are, understandably, different. Now imagine that one wishes to estimate the effect of particulate matter on property values in Gary, Indiana, but that no previous study has been done for a locale that is comparable to Gary. Benefits transfer is not an option in this case. But meta-analysis may be.

The meta-analysis method treats as individual data points the hedonic estimates of willingness to pay for reduced particulate matter from the many existing studies. Each such estimate is one observation in the new meta-data set, which is then examined using statistical techniques. The statistical model is designed to relate the willingness-to-pay estimates from individual studies to the various properties (or explanatory variables) of the individual models. These properties will typically include information such as income levels and other demographic variables, the level of particulate matter from each study, a measure of property desirability (e.g., vacancy rates in the local market), the time period in which the original studies were conducted, and finally some features of the individual studies' own statistical models.

The result is an estimated, statistical relationship between willingness to pay and the explanatory variables. This statistical estimate is capable of telling us, in a way that a single study cannot, which factors seem to affect the relationship between environmental quality and property values. In some studies, an additional step is taken that allows one to derive new estimates of the effect that a reduction in pollution levels would have on property values. Thus a true benefits measure is obtained, one that could be used to make decisions about a policy intervention under consideration.

Meta-analysis can also be used to synthesize many CV studies (Smith and Osborne 1996) or many travel-cost studies. As long as the source studies use the same basic approach, a meta-analysis is possible.

Data Needs
The data needs for a meta-analysis are, in one sense, modest. One does not need to acquire new data or perform a new survey. In another sense, though, they are extensive. One must scour the literature for all of the relevant studies so as to maximize the breadth of the information base of the meta-analysis. The difficulty of performing this step well should not be underestimated.

Strengths of Meta-Analysis
As with benefits transfer, the fact that no new data must be acquired is an important strength of the method. Unlike benefits transfer based on a single source study, the information on which a meta-analysis is based is quite broad. Because the estimate relies on many underlying estimates, it can be argued that a meta-analysis provides more reliable estimates than any other method applied to a single data set. Any errors in the underlying estimates should wash out in the meta-analysis, because some will be too high and some will be too low.

Limitations of Meta-Analysis
As with benefits transfer, the main limitation of meta-analysis is that no original data are used. This means that the relevance of the results for any given location could be questioned. If no data are available for Gary, Indiana, then how can one be sure that the estimates apply to Gary? Even when examining a site for which one or several

studies have been conducted, researchers must consider that the use of information from other places in deriving the benefits estimate could be said to limit the applicability of such information to any one specific place.

References

Bishop, Richard C., and Michael P. Welsh. Contingent Valuation: Incorporating Nonmarket Values. In *Better Environmental Decisions: Strategies for Governments, Businesses, and Communities.* Ken Sexton, Alfred A. Marcus, K. William Easter, and Timothy D. Burkhardt, eds. Washington, D.C.: Island Press, 1999, pp. 177-194.

Bishop, Richard C., Patricia A. Champ, and Daniel J. Mullarkey. 1995. Contingent valuation. In *Handbook of Environmental Economics.* Edited by Daniel W. Bromley. Oxford, UK: Blackwell Publishers, pp. 629-654.

Carson, Richard T., et al. 1992. *A Contingent Valuation Study of Lost Passive Use Values Resulting from the Exxon Valdez Oil Spill.* A Report to the Attorney General of the State of Alaska. La Jolla, CA.: Natural Resource Damage Assessment, Inc.

Carson, Richard T., et al. 1994. *A Bibliography of Contingent Valuation Studies and Papers.* La Jolla, CA: Natural Resource Damage Assessment, Inc.

Lyke, Audrey J. 1993. *Discrete Choice Models to Value Changes in Environmental Quality: A Great Lakes Case Study.* Unpublished doctoral dissertation, Department of Agricultural and Applied Economics, University of Wisconsin, at Madison.

Milliman, Scott, et al. 1992. The bioeconomics of resource rehabilitation: a commercial-sport analysis for a Great Lakes fishery. *Land Economics* 68(2):191-210.

Mitchell, Robert C., and Richard T. Carson. 1989. *Using Surveys to Value Public Goods: The Contingent Valuation Method.* Washington, DC: Resources for the Future.

Smith, V. K., and J. Huang. 1995. Can markets value air quality? A meta-analysis of hedonic property value models. *Journal of Political Economy* 103:209-227.

Smith, V. K., and L. Osborne. 1996. Do contingent valuation estimates pass a 'scope' test? A meta-analysis. *Journal of Environmental Economics and Management* 31:278-301.

U.S. Department of Commerce, National Oceanic and Atmospheric Administration. 1993. Natural Resource Damage Assessments Under the Oil Pollution Act of 1990. *Federal Register* 58:4601-4614.

Welsh, M. P., R. C. Bishop, M. L. Phillips, and R. M. Baumgartner. 1995. GCES *Non-Use Value Study Final Report.* Madison, WI: Hagler Bailly Consulting.

Recommended Reading

Benefits Transfer

Carson, R. T., et al. 1996. Contingent valuation and revealed preference methodologies: comparing the estimates for quasi-public goods. *Land Economics* 72(1):80-99.

Investigation and Valuation of Fish Kills, American Fisheries Society Special Publication 24, 1992.

Sorg, C., and J. Loomis. 1984. *Empirical Estimates of Amenity Forest Values: A Comparative Review.* General Technical Report RM-107. Washington, DC: U.S. Department of Agriculture.

LMSOFT. 1995. Valuing the Economic Benefit of Wetlands: Case Studies in Ontario, prepared for Environment Canada, Ontario Region, August.

Smith, V. K. 1992. On separating defensible benefit transfers from "smoke and mirrors." *Water Resources Research* 28(3):685-694.

Contingent Valuation

Bishop, Richard C., and Michael P. Welsh. "Contingent Valuation: Incorporating Nonmarket Values." *Better Environmental Decisions: Strategies for Governments, Businesses, and Communities.* Ken Sexton, Alfred A. Marcus, K. William Easter, and Timothy D. Burkhardt, eds. Washington, D.C.: Island Press, 1999, pp. 177-194.

Bishop, Richard C., Patricia A. Champ, and Daniel J. Mullarkey. 1995. Contingent valuation. In *Handbook of Environmental Economics.* Edited by Daniel W. Bromley. Oxford, UK: Blackwell Publishers, pp. 629-654.

Carson, Richard T., et al. 1992. *A Contingent Valuation Study of Lost Passive Use Values Resulting from the Exxon Valdez Oil Spill.* A Report to the Attorney General of the State of Alaska. La Jolla, CA.: Natural Resource Damage Assessment, Inc.

Carson, Richard T., et al. 1994. *A Bibliography of Contingent Valuation Studies and Papers.* La Jolla, CA: Natural Resource Damage Assessment, Inc.

Diamond, P. A., and J. A. Hausman. 1994. Contingent valuation: is some number better than no number? *Journal of Economic Perspectives* 8:45-64.

Hanemann, W. Michael. 1994. Valuing the environment through contingent valuation. *Journal of Economic Perspectives* 8(4):19-43.

Hausman, Jerry A. 1993. *Contingent Valuation: An Assessment.* Amsterdam: North-Holland.

Krieger, Douglas J. 1994. *The Economic Value of Environmental Risk Information: Theory and Application to the Michigan Sport Fishery.* Unpublished doctoral dissertation, Department of Agricultural Economics, Michigan State University.

Lyke, Audrey J. 1993. *Discrete Choice Models to Value Changes in Environmental Quality: A Great Lakes Case Study.* Unpublished doctoral dissertation, Department of Agricultural and Applied Economics, University of Wisconsin, at Madison.

Milliman, Scott, et al. 1992. The bioeconomics of resource rehabilitation: a commercial-sport analysis for a Great Lakes fishery. *Land Economics* 68(2):191-210.

Mitchell, Robert C., and Richard T. Carson. 1989. *Using Surveys to Value Public Goods: The Contingent Valuation Method.* Washington, DC: Resources for the Future.

Portney, Paul R. 1994. The contingent valuation debate: why economists should care. *Journal of Economic Perspectives* 8(4):3-17.

U.S. Department of Commerce, National Oceanic and Atmospheric Administration. 1993. Natural Resource Damage Assessments Under the Oil Pollution Act of 1990. *Federal Register* 58:4601-4614.

Welsh, M. P., R. C. Bishop, M. L. Phillips, and R. M. Baumgartner. 1995. *GCES Non-Use Value Study Final Report.* Madison, WI: Hagler Bailly Consulting.

Hedonic Valuation

Epple, D. 1987. Hedonic prices and implicit markets: estimating demand and supply functions for differentiated products. *Journal of Political Economy* 87:59-80.

Gegax, D. S., S. Gerking, and W. D. Schulze. 1991. Perceived risk and the marginal value of safety. *Review of Economics and Statistics* 73:589-596.

Michaels, R. G., and V. K. Smith. 1990. Market segmentation and valuing amenities with hedonic models: the case of hazardous waste sites. *Journal of Urban Economics* 28:223-242.

Palmquist, R. B. 1992. Valuing localized externalities. *Journal of Urban Economics* 31:59-68.

Smith, V. K., and J. Huang. 1995. Can markets value air quality? A meta-analysis of hedonic property value models. Journal of Political Economy 103:209-227.

Meta-Analysis

Smith, V. K., and Y. Kaoru. 1995. Can markets value air quality? A meta-analysis of hedonic property value models. *Journal of Political Economy* 103(1):209-227.

Smith, V. K., and L. Osborne. 1996. Do contingent valuation estimates pass a 'scope' test? A meta-analysis. *Journal of Environmental Economics and Management* 31:278-301.

Travel-Cost Method, General Overviews

Freeman III, A. Myrick. 1993. Recreation uses of natural resource systems. In *The Measurement of Environmental and Resource Values: Theory and Methods*, Washington, DC: Resources for the Future.

Bockstael, Nancy E., Kenneth E. McConnell, and Ivar E. Strand, Jr. 1991. Recreation. In *Measuring the Demand for Environmental Quality*. Edited by Braden, John B., and Charles D. Kolstad. New York: North-Holland Publishing, pp. 227-355.

Kling, Catherine and Joseph Herriges, eds. 1999. *Valuing Recreation and the Environment: Revealed Preference Methods in Theory and Practice*, Edward Elgar Publishing.

Travel-Cost Method, Multiple-Site Models and Random Utility Models

Bockstael, Nancy E., W. Michael Hanemann, and Catherine L. Kling. 1987. Estimating the value of water quality improvements in a recreational demand framework. *Water Resources Research* 23(5):951-960.

Hausmann, Jerry A., Gregory K. Leonard, and Daniel McFadden. 1995. A utility-consistent, combined discrete choice and count data model: assessing recreational use losses due to natural resource damage. *Journal of Public Economics* 56:1-30.

Morey, Edward R., et al. 1995. Searching for a model of multiple recreation demand that admits interior and boundary solutions. *American Journal of Agricultural Economics* 77(1):129-140.

Travel-Cost Method, Single-Site Models

Knetsch, Jack L. 1963. Outdoor recreation demands and benefits. *Land Economics* 39(4):387-396.

McConnell, Kenneth E. 1985. The economics of outdoor recreation. In *Handbook of Natural Resource and Energy Economics*, Vol 2. Edited by Kneese, Allen V. and James L. Sweeny. Amsterdam: North-Holland Publishing.

Chapter 7

Case Studies

n this chapter, we move from theory into practice by applying the valuation methods described in Chapter 6 to actual environmental problems in a series of case studies. The case studies illustrate how the methods are used in practice and the various practical problems that may be encountered along the way. The cases, four of which take place in the Great Lakes, cover a cross-section of environmental concerns. In each case, the end result is an estimate, in dollars, of benefits that would attend a change in environmental quality.

The first case study demonstrates ways in which changes in the value of environmental goods and services traded in markets can be assessed to understand economic implications of an environmental intervention. This case study concerns the effect that reduced soil erosion could have on dredging costs in Toledo harbor. This study found that reduced soil erosion in the Maumee River basin could cut dredging costs by up to $13 million.

The remaining four case studies show ways to assess nonmarket environmental benefits. The travel-cost approach is applied to recreational fishing in the Great Lakes. This large-scale model represents the high end of the technique, in terms of sophistication and cost. It also demonstrates that you get what you pay for. The model greatly aids understanding of policies to improve the fishery and the effect of those policies on recreational fishing and the economic welfare of anglers. The hedonic valuation method is used to value changes in air quality in Chicago. This study found that the value to Chicago-area homeowners of a 5 percent reduction in either particulate matter or sulfur dioxide would be in the hundreds of millions of dollars. The contingent valuation approach, applied in a study of sediment remediation in the Pacific Ocean off the coast of Los Angeles, found that residents would be willing to pay about half a billion dollars for a remediation program that would protect the local marine resources from polychlorinated biphenols (PCBs) in the sediment off shore. The Los Angeles case is similar in many ways to contamination problems found in the Great Lakes, most notably Green Bay in Lake Michigan. Finally, the benefits transfer approach is applied to a restoration project in the Saginaw Bay wetlands. Based on a source study for Lake Erie wetlands, the Saginaw Bay study showed that Michigan residents value Saginaw wetlands at over $150 million.

Through their detail, these case studies reveal the complexities of resource valuation exercises. If they are to be useful, economic studies must conform to the rigors of other scientific studies, such as controlling variables, while addressing the many problematic analytical and social issues we outlined in Chapter 4. These case studies will help readers (1) appreciate what may be involved in undertaking an economic study and (2) evaluate the quality of studies already performed. Although sound economic valuation studies are not simple, they are clearly quite feasible.

CASE STUDY OF A MARKET-BASED ANALYSIS: SOIL EROSION IN THE MAUMEE RIVER BASIN[12]

Background

This case study describes how to estimate the benefits of reduced dredging costs arising from lower soil erosion upstream. It is an example of the defensive expenditure approach described in Chapter 6. In the Maumee River basin in northwestern Ohio, soil erosion from upstream land uses damages Toledo harbor, into which the river drains. Although both market goods (i.e., dredging) and environmental goods (i.e., water quality) are affected by sediment deposition from the Maumee River, this case study focuses on market impacts, in particular dredging and confining sediment.

Dredging is considered a market impact because the U.S. Army Corps of Engineers must expend resources by hiring private contractors to dredge the harbor. Other economic impacts of soil erosion are ignored here in order to focus our attention on the techniques necessary to value dredging impacts. Market impacts include increased water treatment costs and increased drainage ditch cleaning costs. Nonmarket impacts include impaired fish spawning habitat or altered aquatic ecosystems. In addition, the move to confine all dredged materials may require building of additional confinement space. Depending on where the facility is built, other nonmarket values may be affected, such as loss of wetlands or recreation space. Given the low levels of remaining coastal wetlands along Lake Erie shores, the impacts of sedimentation on these resources in the Maumee Bay may be substantial.

[12] Brent Songhen, Assistant Professor, Department of Agricultural, Environmental, and Development Economics, The Ohio State University and Jon Rausch; Extension Associate; Department of Food, Agricultural, and Biological Engineering; The Ohio State University.

These other market and nonmarket impacts of soil erosion are important, but the economic value of avoided dredging and confining costs alone may be sufficient to justify the costs of reducing soil erosion. The objective of this analysis is to measure the decrease in dredging and confining expenditures associated with a 15 percent reduction in sediments entering the harbor. Although we do not do so in this case study, in a cost-benefit analysis, the savings, or benefits, afforded by upstream runoff control to achieve that objective would ultimately be compared to the costs of reducing soil erosion by that amount (see Nakao and Sohngen, 2000 for a cost-benefit analysis).

Understanding the Site

Toledo harbor serves as a shipping port for many regional commodities, including grain from midwestern farms and coal from Ohio mines. The Maumee River basin drains 4.2 million acres in northwestern Ohio, southern Michigan, and northeastern Indiana. Approximately 75 percent of the land is used for farming, 5 percent for forests, and the remaining land for urban and other uses. In the Maumee River basin, total soil erosion is estimated to be 10.3 million tons per year. Approximately 7.4 million tons arise from land where crops are produced.

Only a portion of the 10.3 million tons of soil erosion actually enters streams. Some soil moves only from the top of the field to the middle or edge of it. Of all the soil that moves during rainstorms, only a portion will leave the field. Even when soil enters the waterway, only part of it ends up in Toledo harbor. Some will be deposited in fields downstream (inducing net benefits for the farmers who own those fields), at the bottom or sides of the river, or in drainage ditches. Table 7.1 shows that (1) only a portion of all soil erosion leaves the field, (2) some sediments are

Table 7.1.
SOURCES AND SINKS FOR SOIL EROSION FROM THE MAUMEE RIVER BASIN

Sources	Tons/Year	Percent
Agriculture	7,418,900	72
Streambank	100,000	1
Geologic (riverbed)	20,000	0
Gully and urban	2,761,100	27
Total	10,300,000	

Sinks	Tons/Year	Percent
Fields or river bank	8,515,128	83
Drainage ditches	484,872	5
Ship channel	468,000	5
Lake	832,000	8
Total	10,300,000	

Source: USDA Soil Conservation Service (1993), except for drainage ditch estimates, which are from Forster and Abrahim (1985).

deposited in drainage ditches, and (3) only a portion of the sediments entering the harbor are deposited in the shipping channel (the rest end up elsewhere in the lake). Of the 10.3 million tons of soil (or 2.39 tons per acre) that erode each year, about 1.3 million tons of sediment make it to the Toledo harbor (USDA Soil Conservation Service 1993). The delivery ratio, or the proportion of total soil erosion in the Maumee River basin that ends up in Toledo harbor, is 12.7 percent (1.3/10.3), for the Maumee River basin.

The Toledo harbor is a federal navigation channel, and the Army Corps of Engineers spends an average of $2.2 million each year to dredge 468,000 tons of sediments from the shipping channel (both in the harbor and the approach to it in Lake Erie). The possibility that these sediments are contaminated by toxic chemicals leaching from local landfills causes the Army Corps of Engineers to confine about half of the dredge spoils in a disposal facility. Although material dredged from farther out in Lake Erie currently is dumped in the open lake, the U.S. Environmental Protection Agency has issued an order that all sediments eventually must be confined.

The quantity of sediment dredged in any year is directly related to soil erosion in the upland basin. If soil erosion is reduced, the Army Corps of Engineers does not need to dredge as much to keep the harbor open, resulting in a reduction in costs associated with dredging. The Army Corp of Engineers and the Natural Resource Conservation Service are examining the impact of reducing soil erosion from agricultural land in the basin on the costs of dredging sediments. They have undertaken a project that attempts to establish conservation tillage across 75 percent of the corn and soybean fields in the basin. Conservation tillage is a farming practice that reduces soil erosion by leaving more of the soil, up to 30 percent, covered with crop residues (i.e., corn or soybean stalks) during the winter and spring months. The USDA Soil Conservation Service (1993) predicts that additional residue cover can reduce the quantity of sediment dredged downstream by up to 15 percent. This case study estimates the savings that a 15 percent reduction in harbor sediments could create.

Estimating the Cost of Dredging and Transporting the Spoils

Because dredging and storing costs are based on the volume of sediment removed, we must first translate the tonnage of sediment removed into cubic yards. This is accomplished by using estimates of the average density of soils in the basin. These estimates suggest that each ton of sediment equals 1.82 cubic yards, so that 468,000 tons of sediment equal 850,000 cubic yards.

Dredging costs have three components: (1) costs of dredging material from the lake bottom and putting it in a boat, (2) costs of transporting the material to a confined disposal facility, and (3) costs of confining the material. The first two costs, dredging and transportation, are annual costs related directly to the total quantity of sediments dredged. Confining costs, however, are capital costs. As capital costs, they depend on additional variables, such as interest rates, and they must be treated differently.

The annual costs of dredging and transporting material to a disposal point have both variable and fixed components. Variable costs depend directly on the quantity of material dredged and transported each year. They include expenditures such as fuel or labor used to operate dredging machinery. Variable costs increase as more material is dredged and transported to the disposal point. Fixed costs, in contrast, are the capital costs associated with owning and maintaining dredging equipment. They do not vary with the quantity of sediments dredged each year. No matter how much sediment is dredged, contractors must pay for the machinery to do the dredging. Total costs are the sum of variable and fixed costs.

Dredging activity in the Toledo harbor area actually occurs in two different areas — the river/harbor area and the lake. Dredging costs will differ in the two regions because it generally takes more effort and time, and even different equipment, to extract sediments in the river/harbor area. Furthermore, these two areas are different distances from the disposal area, so that different transportation costs will apply to each region. Separate dredging and transportation cost functions can be estimated from historical Army Corps of Engineers dredging contracts (1978 to 1995) to determine specific cost functions for the two regions:

(1) River/harbor: Total Cost = $331,879 + ($2.10 x $Q_{R/H}$)

(2) Lake: Total Cost = $215,815 + ($1.78 x Q_L)

The first component of each equation is the fixed cost of a contract to remove sediment. The second part is the variable cost. Variable costs are the cost per cubic yard multiplied by the cubic yards, $Q_{R/H}$ or Q_L. Because of differences in the type of machinery that may be used for dredging, and differences in the channels that must be dredged, the fixed and variable costs differ depending on where the sediments are dredged.

When the annual quantity of sediments dredged is 850,000 total cubic yards,[13] these equations suggest that annual dredging and transportation costs in the Toledo harbor amount to $2,188,534 per year. Under the sediment reduction plan, sediments are

[13] *399,500 cubic yards in the river/harbor area and 450,500 cubic yards in the lake.*

reduced 15 percent in the harbor, and dredging costs decline to $1,942,408. Although it is possible that dredging may decline more in one particular region (i.e., river/harbor or lake), this case study assumes a proportional reduction in each region. This points out an area of uncertainty based on the underlying science. Reductions may not occur proportionally in each region, but this could be determined only with more thorough sediment transportation modeling. Economic analysis with such uncertainty should contain relevant discussions pertaining to such difficulties.

Estimating the Cost of Confining Dredge Spoils

A confined disposal facility is a landfill that removes contaminated sediments from the environment. Because of the presence of heavy metals in the Toledo harbor and Lake Erie, sediments dredged in the harbor must be confined in such a facility. Currently the confined disposal facility is located on the eastern shore of the entrance to the harbor. At historical rates of storage (approximately 400,000 cubic yards per year), the existing facility would last another 20 years. However, this case study assumes that all sediments dredged after 1997 are stored in the facility, and the effective life of the facility is instead nine years. When the existing facility fills, it is assumed that a new 20-year facility will be built to replace it.

This case study examines two costs associated with building a confined disposal facility. The first is the cost of renting land. Clearly these costs depend on the location of the facility. For example, purchasing part of the lake floor to extend the current facility would be without cost to the Army Corps of Engineers. However, purchasing additional harbor-front property would cost up to $25,000 per acre near the existing facility, based on real estate values in December 1997. In this case, we assume that a new facility will be built farther out into the lake, next to the existing one, using no new lake frontage. At the moment, there are few market uses of the additional lake in this area, although there may be substantial nonmarket uses such as habitat for fish, recreation area, and aesthetic beauty. Loss of these uses is important, but we ignore them here in order to focus the analysis of market damages. Techniques for measuring nonmarket uses are described elsewhere in this guidebook, and such estimates could be used within the context of this study.

The second cost is the capital cost of building the facility. Construction costs for the existing extension of the Toledo facility were $1 per cubic yard in 1994, and construction costs for a recently constructed facility in Cleveland, Ohio, were approximately $7 per cubic yard (personal communication with Weiner Cadet of the U.S. Army Corps of Engineers). Current estimates of construction and construction management

Table 7.2.
**COMPARISON OF CONFINED DISPOSAL FACILITY DATA
FOR TWO STRATEGIES**

	Plan I: No Sediment Reduction	Plan II: Sediment Reduction
1. Original facility life	9 years	11 years
2. New facility opens	2006	2008
3. New facility capacity	12.75 million cubic yards	10.86 million cubic yards
4. Total cost of new facility	$95.6 million	$81.5 million
5. Present value of total cost	$61.6 million	$47.7 million
6. Annual cost	$4.1 million	$3.1 million

Note: Because the calculations presented above involve several additional decimal places, you may obtain slightly different results if you calculate these values on your own.

costs for a new facility in Toledo are nearly $10 per cubic yard. These costs are notably higher for two reasons. First, the last site was cheaper because it was not difficult to establish. Second, waste handling costs may be higher due to new environmental regulations. For this analysis, a cost of $7.50 per cubic yard is used to accommodate recent expenditures and potential future increases. For 20 years of capacity at existing dredging rates, this amounts to $95.6 million.[14]

Table 7.2 presents information for two scenarios: (1) no sediment reduction (plan I) and (2) 15-percent sediment reduction (plan II). Row 1 indicates that the original facility will last for 9 more years in under plan I and 11 years under plan II (i.e., plan II pushes back construction by 2 years). Row 2 presents the date of construction for the new facility. In addition to extending the life of the existing facility, construction costs for the new facility are reduced because the new facility is smaller (rows 3 and 4).

Row 5 introduces the concept of discounting. Discounting is important when the costs and benefits of environmental programs occur at different times. Here, for example, the Army Corps of Engineers must expend resources now to reduce soil erosion, but these activities do not provide benefits until later when they defer the costs of

[14] This value is calculated as follows: 850,000 cubic yards per year (20 years ($7.50 per cubic yard (0.75. This last multiplier (0.75) incorporates the assumption that volume of sediments will subside 25 percent over the life of the facility as water evaporates or is drained from the sediments.

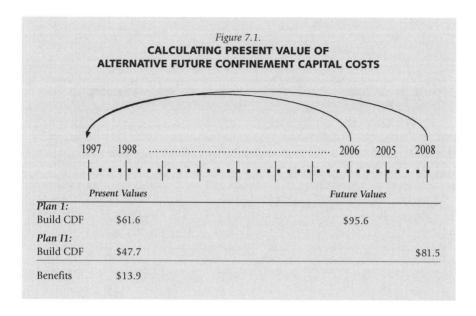

Figure 7.1.

CALCULATING PRESENT VALUE OF ALTERNATIVE FUTURE CONFINEMENT CAPITAL COSTS

	Present Values	Future Values
Plan 1:		
Build CDF	$61.6	$95.6
Plan I1:		
Build CDF	$47.7	$81.5
Benefits	$13.9	

installing a new facility. Without a sediment reduction plan, the new facility must be built in the year 2006, but with sediment reduction it can be built in 2008.

Although a large share of benefits under the sediment reduction plan arises because the Army Corps of Engineers can build a smaller facility, additional benefits accrue because the Army Corps of Engineers can put off the building costs for two more years. Putting off large capital expenditures is some benefit because it allows the Army Corps of Engineers to pursue alternative activities in the meantime.

Figure 7.1 shows the present value of building costs under the two alternatives. Under plan I, future costs are $95.6 million and they occur in 2006; under plan II they are $81.5 million and they occur in year 2008. These values are discounted to 1997 to determine the present value of future costs, $61.6 and $47.7 million under the two plans, respectively. Present values are calculated with the following formula:

(3)   Present value of cost in year $(1997 + n)$ = Future value x $(1 + r)^{-n}$,

where r is the interest rate (in this case, 5 percent), and n is the number of years into the future when construction occurs. For example, under plan I, the present value is calculated as follows:

(4)   Present value of cost in 2008 = $95.6 x $(1.05)^{-9}$ = $61.6

The overall benefits of building a smaller facility and pushing that two years into the future is $13.9 million ($61.6 – $47.7).

The values in row 5 of Table 7.2 are the present value of construction costs for different size facilities. These costs, however, are not comparable to our estimates of dredging and transportation costs because those are annual costs, and these are the costs of a facility that can be used for multiple years. Discounting techniques can be used again to determine a set of equal annual payments that just equal the present values shown in row 5. These annual equal payments are shown in row 6. For a description of how to obtain the values in row 6, please see the appendix to this chapter.

Comparing Costs with Prevention Alternatives

With costs for each underlying component expressed annually, we are prepared to compare the costs of two alternatives (no sediment reduction versus sediment reduction). The benefit of the sediment reduction plan in terms of avoided downstream costs is the difference between the total annual costs of the two proposals. The total costs for each plan are shown in Table 7.3. Plan II (i.e., the 15-percent sediment reduction plan) benefits the Army Corps of Engineers $1.3 million per year.

Table 7.3.
ANNUAL COSTS OF DREDGING, TRANSPORTING, AND CONFINING SEDIMENTS IN THE MAUMEE RIVER BASIN, IN MILLIONS OF DOLLARS (1995)

	Plan I: No Sediment Reduction	Plan II: Sediment Reduction
Dredging and transportation costs	$2.2	$1.9
Confined disposal facility		
Land rent	$0.0	$0.0
Building	$4.1	$3.1
Total costs	$6.3	$5.0

The benefits of each additional cubic yard of dredging avoided can be calculated as the reduction in total costs divided by the reduction in quantity dredged. This is $1.3 million divided by 127,500 cubic yards, or $10.19 per cubic yard.[15] These benefits can also be translated into the benefits of a reduction in soil erosion on land upstream. To do this, one must account for three factors: (1) the delivery ratio (12.7 percent), (2) the ratio of cubic yards to tons of sediments (1.82 cubic yards per ton), and (3) the ratio of sediments dredged to the total quantity of sediments that enters the Toledo harbor (65 percent). By accounting for these factors, one calculates that soil erosion in the basin would have to be reduced by approximately 1.5 million tons in order to avoid 127,500 cubic yards of dredging. The benefits per ton of soil erosion in the basin could therefore be calculated as $1.3 million divided by 1.5 million tons, which equals $0.87 per ton of soil erosion.

Conclusion

The estimates provided in this case study capture only one impact of soil erosion. There may be impacts in many other areas, including recreational boating, sport and commercial fishing, housing, aquatic life, and ecosystem integrity, to name a few. Although improvement in these areas would be expected to increase the economic benefits of reducing erosion, it may not be important to estimate any or all of them. If the benefits calculated in this case study exceed the costs of reducing sediments, it may be enough to justify efforts at lowering soil erosion.

There are several uncertainties surrounding these estimates. First, weather is uncertain from year to year, and actual costs may differ dramatically from these average conditions. Second, some assumptions above are based on hydrological modeling that is itself uncertain. Finally, the economic estimates themselves contain uncertainty. Although this case study does not attempt to provide estimates of the possible error, readers should be aware that these errors can exist in studies they conduct or evaluate.

References

Cadet, Weiner. U.S. Army Corps of Engineers, 1776 Niagara Street, Buffalo, NY 14207.

Forster D. Lynn, and Girmai Abrahim. 1985. Sediment deposits in drainage ditches: A cropland externality. *Journal of Soil and Water Conservation* 40: 141-143.

Personal Communication. 1993. USDA, Natural resources Soil Conservation Service.

---

[15] *The additional benefit of each additional cubic yard of dredging avoided is constant for the first 15 percent of dredging avoided.*

CASE STUDY OF A TRAVEL-COST ANALYSIS: THE MICHIGAN ANGLING DEMAND MODEL[16]

Background

This case study estimates the demand for recreational angling in Michigan using the travel-cost model. By "demand for angling," we mean both where and how often anglers go fishing. Michigan has abundant water resources that provide a diverse array of freshwater recreational fishing opportunities. The application discussed here attempts to account for this richness. The result is a large-scale, state-of-the-art model that lies at the upper end of the spectrum in terms of complexity, cost, and effort involved in travel-cost method studies. The model was developed at Michigan State University by the authors and their colleagues. The work was supported by the Michigan Department of Environmental Quality and Michigan Department of Natural Resources (MDNR), and the findings are summarized in Lupi, et. al. (1997). We refer to the estimated model as the Michigan angling demand model, or the Michigan model.

Great Lakes fish population levels interact with a host of Great Lakes environmental quality issues including fish stocking, fish habitat restoration and preservation, and control and prevention of aquatic nuisance species. To illustrate how one might estimate some of the economic value associated with changes in fish populations, we use the Michigan model to value changes in trout and salmon catch rates at Great Lakes fishing sites in Michigan. Because Great Lakes trout and salmon are mobile species, valuing changes in these fisheries requires a model with a broad geographic scope.

As we mentioned in Chapter 6, the travel-cost method establishes a relationship between recreational use and the costs and characteristics of recreation sites. Given this demand relationship, the travel-cost method cannot tell us anything about values that are not associated with recreational use. Fortunately, environmental quality often is a value associated with recreational use, and in these cases the travel-cost method can link changes in environmental quality to the demand for recreation trips and the value of these trips. This is accomplished by including measures of environmental quality as variables that describe site characteristics in the travel-cost model.

In this study, trout and salmon catch rates were key site characteristics in the model revealing any linkage between catch rates and angler behavior. Valuing environmental quality through the fish variables requires appropriate evidence from the physical sciences linking some change in environmental quality to changes in fish, and these

[16] *Frank Lupi, Assistant Professor, Department of Agricultural Economics and Department of Fisheries and Wildlife, Michigan State University, and John P. Hoehn, Professor, Department of Agricultural Economics, Michigan State University.*

changes in fish must be translated into changes in catch rates (Figure 7.2). Clearly, establishing such a valuation pathway involves several types of knowledge and data.

This case study does not investigate the entire valuation pathway. Rather, the Michigan model is directed at the later portions of the pathway, as indicated in Figure 7.2. As we stated in the Chapter 6, any travel-cost method valuation of environmental quality is only as good as the statistical link between site-quality characteristics and the travel-cost method demand for trips to the site. Nonetheless, we use the example to highlight some of the environmental data needed in order to establish pathways for valuing environmental quality with the travel-cost method.

In addition to establishing the portion of the pathway that the case study addresses, it is also important to define all possible valuation pathways to clarify what values are being measured in any particular environmental valuation. This study focuses on *catch rates*, a measure of the number of fish that anglers can expect to catch. Although catch rates often have a direct relationship to angler satisfaction and, therefore, to the use value of the fishery, catch rates speak only to quantity, not quality. Angler satisfaction also depends on the size of fish, their fitness, their fight, their suitability for human consumption, and so on. As a result, a change in catch rates captures only a portion of the use values accruing to anglers. Figure 7.2 depicts a valuation pathway for a change in environmental quality that affects catch rates, yet there is nothing that prevents a change in environmental quality from causing a complex array of changes in a fishery other than population density and catch rates. For example, sediment remediation might increase fish populations as well as the size of fish. Alternatively, an aquatic nuisance species could supplant native forage fish and lead to smaller fish, although populations are just as numerous. Both of these scenarios might affect angler behavior. However, in Michigan, because data on the size of fish do not exist for all the sites in the Michigan model, fish size cannot be linked to angler behavior.

What Makes the Model Tick

Fishing destinations differ in their travel costs and characteristics, and anglers must make a tradeoff between travel costs and site characteristics. Anglers' choices reveal

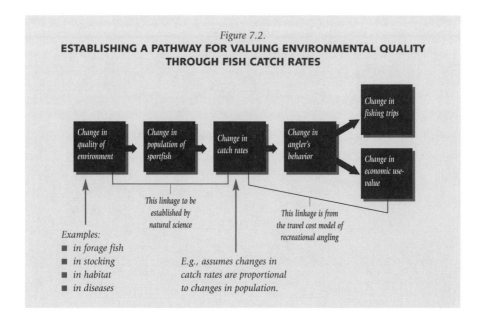

Figure 7.2.

ESTABLISHING A PATHWAY FOR VALUING ENVIRONMENTAL QUALITY THROUGH FISH CATCH RATES

Change in quality of environment → Change in population of sportfish → Change in catch rates → Change in angler's behavior → Change in fishing trips / Change in economic use-value

This linkage to be established by natural science

This linkage is from the travel cost model of recreational angling

Examples:
■ in forage fish
■ in stocking
■ in habitat
■ in diseases

E.g., assumes changes in catch rates are proportional to changes in population.

their relative preferences for site characteristics and travel costs (i.e., anglers' willingness to trade costs, or money, for site characteristics). This is what makes the travel-cost model tick.

The travel-cost method used by the Michigan team is referred to as a random utility model (RUM). The RUM approach assumes that anglers pick the site they consider to be best and applies advanced statistical techniques to data on individual trips to explain angler choices. The model relates these choices to the costs and characteristics (e.g., environmental quality) of alternative fishing sites.

Categorizing Angler Opportunities

To increase the precision of the study with respect to angler choices, researchers carefully categorized the broad array of fishing opportunities available to Michigan anglers. The study differentiated opportunities by trip duration (single versus multiple day trips), water body (Great Lakes, inland lakes, rivers/streams), and species targeted for fishing (so-called warm species, such as bass, perch, and walleye, versus so-called cold species, such as salmon and trout). Figure 7.3 presents a diagram of the different types of fishing activities and sites included in the Michigan model. The model structure builds on previous research in Michigan (Kikuchi; Jones and Sung 1993).

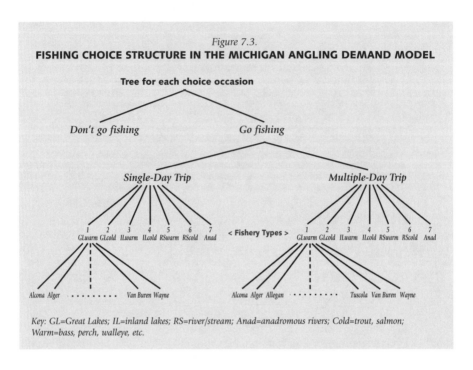

Figure 7.3.

FISHING CHOICE STRUCTURE IN THE MICHIGAN ANGLING DEMAND MODEL

Tree for each choice occasion

Don't go fishing — *Go fishing*

Single-Day Trip — *Multiple-Day Trip*

| 1 | 2 | 3 | 4 | 5 | 6 | 7 |
| GLwarm | GLcold | ILwarm | ILcold | RSwarm | RScold | Anad |

< Fishery Types >

| 1 | 2 | 3 | 4 | 5 | 6 | 7 |
| GLwarm | GLcold | ILwarm | ILcold | RSwarm | RScold | Anad |

Alcona Alger · · · · · · · · · Van Buren Wayne

Alcona Alger Allegan · · · · · · · · · Tuscola Van Buren Wayne

Key: GL=Great Lakes; IL=inland lakes; RS=river/stream; Anad=anadromous rivers; Cold=trout, salmon; Warm=bass, perch, walleye, etc.

The Great Lakes destination sites were defined by the stretch of Great Lake shoreline within the county (the bottom level of Figure 7.3) and categorized within fishery types. There are 41 Great Lakes counties in each of two Great Lakes fishery types, Great Lakes warm and Great Lakes cold. Within the Great Lake cold branch of the Michigan model, sites were further described by the catch rates for each of the following species: coho salmon, chinook salmon, lake trout, and rainbow trout. These catch rates are specific to each county and vary on a monthly basis over the open water season (April to October). They are based on an analysis of angler party interview records from the Michigan creel survey data.

For river and stream fishing, destinations are distinguished according to the three types of species that can be targeted on a fishing trip: warm species, nonanadromous cold species, and anadromous species. Anadromous run refers to Great Lakes trout and salmon on migratory runs up or downstream. Destinations within the river and stream fishery types are defined as the counties in Michigan that contain river fishing opportunities for that species type. Inland lake warm and cold fishing sites are also defined at the county level.

Discovering Angler Choices

Angler choices can be discovered through direct surveys. Clearly, the quality of the travel-cost method survey is critically important to the accuracy of the study, as evidenced in the wide divergence between various state and federal estimates of the amount of fishing in Michigan and on the Great Lakes (Bence and Smith, 1999). There are pitfalls particular to data gathering on recreational trips. Survey research conducted by the Fisheries Division of MDNR and other agencies has established that surveys asking anglers to recall the number of trips they have taken over some period of time tend to contain upward biases that increase with the length of the recall period. Because the economic use values derived from the travel-cost method are directly related to use (i.e., the number of trips taken by anglers), potential recall biases are a concern. In light of these results, one goal of the study reported here was to collect data on the number of annual fishing trips made by individual anglers that were as accurate and representative as possible.

The data for this study describing where and how often anglers go fishing in Michigan were collected in an extensive telephone panel survey that followed over 2,000 anglers during the course of the 1994-1995 fishing year. The panel members were recruited from the general population of Michigan residents to ensure that the results would be representative. Computer-assisted telephone interviewing was used to streamline all interviews and improve response accuracy. Techniques to ensure response accuracy included a large pilot survey, fishing logs as memory aides, placing bounds on the dates anglers were asked to recall to avoid double counting of trips across panel interviews, and provision of multiple opportunities to revise trip counts. To balance the need to collect timely and accurate data against the burden of the interviews, frequent anglers were called more often than infrequent anglers — panel interview frequencies ranged from eight interviews for the most avid anglers to three interviews for the least avid anglers.

Calculating Site Choice Occasions

As we noted above, the basic RUM model describes site choice. In a repeated RUM such as the Michigan model, the season is divided into a series of *site choice occasions*. In each occasion, anglers decide whether to take a trip and, if so, where to fish. In the Michigan model, the choice occasion depicted in Figure 7.3 is repeated twice-weekly over the course of the season. Consequently, the repeated RUM can explain site choices and the number of trips (i.e., where and how often anglers fish). In all, the Michigan model contains over 850 distinct fishing opportunities in each choice occasion (the number of nodes at the bottom of Figure 7.4), and this set of opportunities is available for over 60 occasions for each sampled angler in the model. Moreover, the model contains about 80 parameters that were estimated statistically.

Although our focus is on fishing for trout and salmon, it is essential to include all the potential alternative (i.e., substitute) types of fishing available in Michigan. Generally, the more high-quality substitutes that are available, the less valuable a specific fishing site will be. The Michigan model is appropriate to the Great Lakes valuation task because it is a statewide model and it includes the full range of fishing opportunities available in Michigan. Few models combine such a range of activities and cover such a broad geographic area. By tabulating the predicted patterns of trips, we use the catch rate scenarios to illustrate the extent to which Michigan anglers are likely to switch in to (or out of) Great Lakes trout and salmon fishing as catch rates change. The trip predictions underscore the role of the potential substitute sites and activities.

Table 7.4 displays the estimated user days by Michigan fishery types (as defined in Figure 7.3). The Great Lakes trout and salmon fisheries account for 13 percent of the user days (the sum of the user days for Great Lakes cold and anadromous run fishery types). The table shows that most of the fishing trips taken in Michigan by resident anglers are taken to inland water bodies such as lakes and rivers, and that warm species are targeted on most of the trips.

One does not need an economic model to generate use information as presented in Table 7.4. Use estimates can be obtained by extrapolating appropriately from the survey data. However, an economic model is needed to predict changes in trip demand, to translate the use information into values, and to link use to environmental quality. We turn to these issues in the next section.

Table 7.4.
USER DAYS BY FISHERY TYPE

| Fishery Type | Total User Days[1] | |
	Number *(thousands)*	Percent
Great Lakes warm	2,776	23
Great Lakes cold	922	8
Inland warm	5,513	46
Inland cold	198	2
RS warm	1,452	12
RS cold	588	5
Anadromous run	663	5
Totals	*12,111*	*100[2]*

[1] *Estimated sport fishing user days in Michigan by resident anglers from April to October 1994, for each fishery type defined in Figure 7.4.*
[2] *Percentages add to more than 100 due to rounding.*

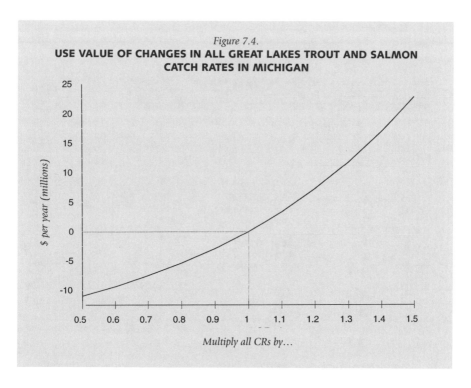

Figure 7.4.

USE VALUE OF CHANGES IN ALL GREAT LAKES TROUT AND SALMON CATCH RATES IN MICHIGAN

Multiply all CRs by...

Linking Angler Choices to Catch Rate and Value

The Great Lakes trout and salmon valuations presented here consist of multiplying catch rates by factors ranging from 0.5 to 1.5 (50 percent decreases to 50 increases). The species affected are chinook salmon, coho salmon, lake trout, and rainbow trout in the Great Lakes cold fishery type, and chinook salmon, coho salmon, and rainbow trout in the anadromous run fishery type. For each valuation scenario, angler well-being under the baseline array of catch rates is compared to angler well-being under the altered catch rates. For decreases in catch rates, anglers experience losses; for increases in catch rates, anglers experience gains. A description of the methods and associated caveats are described in Lupi et. al.(1997).

Figure 7.4 presents a graph of the valuation results, and Table 7.5 presents the results used to plot the figure. The estimated values represent the aggregate annual use values accruing to Michigan residents in 1994 dollars as a result of the hypothesized change in catch rates. The estimated economic values for the changes in catch rates range from a benefit of about $23 million for a 50 percent increase to a loss of about $11

Table 7.5.
GREAT LAKES TROUT AND SALMON VALUATIONS

Multiply Great Lakes Trout and Salmon Catch Rates by	Value (million $)	Great Lakes Trout and Salmon User Days (thousands)	Change in User Days (thousands)
0.5	−10.95	1,189	−395
0.6	−9.36	1,250	−334
0.7	−7.52	1,320	−265
0.8	−5.38	1,398	−187
0.9	−2.89	1,486	−99
1.0	0.00	1,585	0
1.1	3.35	1,690	111
1.2	7.23	1,819	235
1.3	11.71	1,956	371
1.4	16.86	2,106	521
1.5	22.75	2,268	683

million for the 50 percent decrease. Table 7.5 also presents the changes in the estimated user days associated with the Great Lakes trout and salmon fishery types (i.e., the Great Lakes cold and anadromous run fishery types). The 50 percent decrease in catch rates results in a 25 percent decrease in estimated user days, and the 50 percent increase in catch rates results in an estimated 43 percent increase in user days.

From Figure 7.4 and the results in Table 7.5, one can see that the estimated gains from increasing catch rates exceed the estimated losses for an equivalent decrease in catch rates. These results are due to the role of site and activity substitution embodied in the model. *Site and activity substitution* refers to the possibility that anglers would switch fishing sites or activities in response to a change in the characteristics of some sites. In the case at hand, when the catch rates for the Great Lakes trout and salmon fisheries decrease (increase), anglers substitute out of (in to) this fishery. Thus, for decreases in catch rates, anglers who are taking trips to fish for Great Lakes trout and salmon experience losses, but the magnitude of these losses is limited by their ability to switch to their next best alternative. Their next best alternative could be fishing for a different species, fishing at a different site, or fishing less. Because the values being measured are use values, once an angler switches sites, he or she does not experience any further losses if catch rates at the site he or she is no longer visiting continue to decrease.

Conversely, when the catch rates at a site increase, anglers who are currently using the site experience benefits. In addition, some anglers are induced to switch to the site where catch rates increase, and these additional users also benefit from the increase in catch rates. Thus site substitution in travel-cost models plays a dual role, mitigating losses and accentuating gains relative to models that ignore such substitution possibilities. These factors help explain the shape of the benefits frontier depicted in Figure 7.4. The difference between the values for increases and decreases in fishing quality demonstrates the importance of accounting for potential substitutes in travel-cost models.

Conclusion

Although the valuation scenarios reported here illustrate how the travel-cost method can be used to value changes in environmental quality, the scenarios represent a fairly simple use of the model. More generally, models such as the Michigan model can be used to value any spatial and temporal pattern of catch rates relative to any other pattern of catch rates. For example, if one wanted to evaluate fish stocking programs at different Great Lakes, one might want to compare the benefits associated with stocking a certain number of fish in Lake Huron to the benefits associated with stocking those fish in Lake Michigan. If the effect of stocking the fish can be translated into changes in the catch rates at each lake, the model can then be used to produce benefit estimates that are specific to the individual lakes.

As another example, one might be interested in the value of a change in river habitat at a major Great Lake tributary that is expected to affect spawning success. Over time, the habitat change might translate into larger fish stocks for the lake and, hence, larger catch rates for the whole lake. However, over some initial periods of time, the changes in fish stocks might be more localized. Such a scenario can be evaluated in the Michigan model, provided that the temporal pattern of catch rate changes can be specified for each site in the model. Obviously, changes in catch rates that would occur at some subset of the Great Lakes sites would be less valuable than a comparable change at all Great Lakes sites (the latter is depicted in Figure 7.4).

A real benefit of the travel-cost method is that it yields a standing demand model that can be used repeatedly to predict changes in fishing trips associated with changes in characteristics of the fishing sites.

References

Bence, James R., and Kelly D. Smith. 1999. An overview of recreational fisheries of the Great Lakes. In *Great Lakes Fisheries Policy and Management: A Binational Perspective*. Edited by W. W. Taylor and P. Fererri. East Lansing: Michigan State University Press.

Jones, Carol Adair, and Yusen D. Sung. 1993. *Valuation of Environmental Quality at Michigan Recreational Sites: Methodological Issues and Policy Applications*. Final Report, EPA Contract No. CR-816247-01-2.

Kikuchi, Hideo. 1996. *Segmenting Michigan's Sport Fishing Market: Evaluation of Two Approaches*. Ph.D. dissertation, Michigan State University.

Lupi, Frank, John P. Hoehn, Heng Chen and Theodore Tomasi. 1997. The Michigan Recreational Angling Demand Model. *Agricultural Economics Staff Paper* 97-58, East Lansing, MI: Department of Agricultural Economics, Michigan State University.

CASE STUDY OF A HEDONICS ANALYSIS: THE BENEFITS OF AIR QUALITY IMPROVEMENT IN THE GREAT LAKES REGION[17]

Background

With major industrial and urban centers, the Great Lakes are stressed by a variety of airborne pollutants, including particulates, volatile hydrocarbons, and oxides of sulfur and nitrogen. Airborne contaminants are known to have terrestrial and human impacts, including acidification of forests, lakes, and soils; reduced productivity of agricultural crops; and various respiratory and cardiovascular complications for humans. In addition, large fractions of some of the most pervasive water pollutants in the Great Lakes arrive through deposition of airborne contaminants.

Two major air pollutants in the Great Lakes region are particulate matter and sulfur dioxide. One of the most troublesome forms of particulate matter is the small particles that can penetrate deep into the human respiratory tract. This form is known as PM-10, for particulate matters of diameter smaller than 10 micrometers (μm). PM-10 includes dust, dirt, soot, and smoke, and arises from factories, power plants, cars, construction, and land use. It can cause breathing problems, aggravate respiratory and cardiovascular diseases, damage lungs, and induce respiratory cancers; in short, higher levels of PM-10 can cause illness and shorten life expectancy. Sulfur dioxide is usually associated with acid precipitation, but it also contributes to haze, and damages buildings and historic monuments. It arises mainly from combustion in industries and power plants. Individuals experience sulfur dioxide through irritation and inflamma-

[17] *Sudip Chattopadhyay, Assistant Professor, Department of Economics, San Francisco University and John B. Braden, Professor, Department of Agricultural and Consumer Economics, University of Illinois at Urbana-Champaign*

tion of tissues that it contacts directly, generally causing bronchial constriction, which results in increased respiratory and heart rates.

This case study concentrates on the Chicago metropolitan area and shows how the hedonic valuation method can be used to estimate the economic benefits of reduced air pollution. Chicago is a nonattainment area according to National Ambient Air Quality Standards (NAAQS) for both PM-10 and sulfur dioxide. The Chicago metropolitan area includes Cook, DuPage, McHenry, and Will counties in Illinois as well as several counties in northwestern Indiana. Owing to the availability of data on air pollution and the proximity of these counties to the center of the Chicago metropolitan area, this case study focuses on Cook and DuPage counties.

The goal of this case study is to identify the economic value of reducing PM-10 and sulfur dioxide levels as perceived by Chicago area homeowners. In a sense, the study establishes the value of air pollution abatement to Great Lakes residents, an important consideration in determining how much air pollution should be allowed. During 1989 and 1990, the reference period for this study, Chicago had 16 monitoring stations for PM-10 and 11 for sulfur dioxide, located in different parts of the region. In 1987 the U.S. Environmental Protection Agency promulgated new, tougher air quality standards for PM-10 and sulfur dioxide. The new standards for PM-10 are (1) that the average annual concentration must be within 50 µg/m^3, and (2) that there should be no more than one daily mean concentration measurement greater than 150 µg/m^3 at any monitoring site in the entire area. In Chicago, during 1989 and 1990, the average annual concentration ranged from 28 µg/m^3 to 48 µg/m^3. These values were within the NAAQS limits for the annual average. However, the region did not meet the NAAQS standard based on the daily mean concentration because three of its monitoring stations recorded a daily mean concentration higher than 150 µg/m^3 in 1990.

The 1997 standard for sulfur dioxide is a maximum of 30 parts per billion (ppb) average annual concentration. Chicago met the standard for sulfur dioxide during the reference period; the annual average during the period ranged from 4 to 11 ppb. But there are years when Chicago has failed to meet the standard. For instance, in 1991, the sulfur dioxide level at nearby monitoring points rose well beyond the acceptable level, owing to the localized impact of a specific industrial source.

The fact that the standards for these pollutants were generally satisfied during the period of this case study does not necessarily mean that the ambient air quality in Chicago was benign. Consumers may be sensitive to pollution levels below those believed to have serious health impacts, the standard used for national air quality standards. For example, haziness due to sulfur dioxide may be negatively valued even

Public

perception of

the value of

environmental

improvements

may not mirror

regulatory

compliance.

if it does not impair health. Thus public perception of the value of environmental improvement may not mirror regulatory compliance. The public may have a strong desire to reduce some pollutants below the regulated level while also being relatively uninterested in other pollutants, such as those with invisible or latent consequences. What we learn from hedonic analysis is a value of the perceived effects, which may be different from scientifically based projections of real health or other effects.

What Makes Hedonics Tick

The way that people actually respond to air quality variation provides an indication of the benefits they attach to cleaner air. One of the major choices people make — where to live — reflects not only on their places of employment and incomes but also their perception of environmental quality. For example, a house situated with a nice view, less industrial noise, or less smoke and haze would probably be more attractive to most people than comparable houses in unscenic, noisy, or smoky settings. The greater attractiveness should translate into a higher market price for the more desirable properties. The price differential expresses consumers' willingness to pay for the benefits to be realized over time from a home with better environmental quality. By carefully separating out the effects of air quality on home prices, we can gain insight into the value the public places on improvements.

Hedonic valuation can provide several types of specific information depending on the depth of the study. This case study took place in two stages, demonstrating two levels of effort. The first stage provides information on marginal improvement to the air quality. The results are sufficient if we are concerned only with small changes in the environmental quality variable. We could simply multiply the (small) size of the expected change by the unit price and by the number of households that would experience the change in order to determine an aggregate benefit. However, if a large change in environmental quality is of interest, the marginal price is not enough. The value that people place on environmental improvements may decline as people obtain more and more of such improvements. This implies that the first unit of improvement is worth more than succeeding units. Depending on the environmental quality starting point, the unit price for marginal environmental improvement could overstate or understate the public's willingness to pay for large improvements. This is why we go to the second stage of hedonic valuation — deducing the demand dynamic for environmental quality as we move away from the status quo.

Profiling the Study Area

This case study estimates how much a typical Chicago household is willing to pay for a reduction in PM-10 and sulfur dioxide levels and, based on these estimates, draws conclusions about aggregate benefits of reduced air pollution in the Chicago area. The household willingness to pay is deduced from housing prices and consumer choices regarding where to live. Housing is clearly not the only thing people purchase, and it is important to acknowledge other purchases. However, data on the annual nonhousing expenditures of households are not readily available, whereas detailed information on housing is available.

To accurately correlate housing prices (the dependent variable) with air pollution levels (an independent variable), it is necessary to carefully characterize the attributes of the housing options and purchasers and to statistically control for all the other independent variables that affect consumer choice. Specifically, for the first stage of the hedonic valuation, we require data on home prices, other factors likely to influence home prices (e.g., neighborhood and city characteristics), and ambient air quality levels. For the second stage of the study, in which we attempt to characterize the demand for improvements in air quality, we need data on the socioeconomic characteristics of the buyers.

We compiled a sample consisting of 3,044 home sales located in 659 census tracts within 103 jurisdictions in the Chicago metropolitan area. Altogether, 18 independent variables are considered to influence house price in the first stage of this study. The details of all the variables, their sources, and the units in which they are measured are given in Table 7.6.

To assess housing prices, we followed an indirect approach, using information on monthly Federal Housing Administration (FHA) mortgage interest rates prevailing during the period under study. Because FHA mortgages are mostly 30-year loans with zero down payments, the monthly mortgage payment can be calculated using a routine loan payment formula. The monthly payment is then multiplied by 12 to arrive at the annual payment for each household, which is then subtracted from the purchaser's annual income to arrive at the final figure of annual nonhousing expenditure.

House sale prices and associated household demographic data for federally insured mortgages are often obtained from FHA records. The FHA sample represents households that are slightly less wealthy and larger in size than the population averages. For example, the FHA-insured sample has a median household income of $39,780, whereas the corresponding 1990 Census figure is $41,745; the median family size in

Table 7.6.
VARIABLES AND DATA SOURCES

Variable	Definition	Data Source
Purchaser Characteristics		
PURINC	Total annual income of purchaser ($)	Federal Housing Administration (FHA), U.S. Department of Housing and Urban Development
R	Purchaser's race: 1 = white; 0 = other	FHA
C	Number of dependent children in household	FHA
X	Household's annual nonhousing expenditure ($)	FHA
Property Characteristics		
SPRICE	Contract sale price of house ($)	FHA
NROOMS	Number of habitable rooms enclosed	FHA
LVAREA	Total living area of home (ft2)	FHA
HAGE	Age of dwelling (years)	FHA
LSIZE	Total area of lot (ft2)	FHA
AIRCON	Air conditioning: 0 = no; 1 = window unit; 3 = central	FHA
NBATH	Number of bathrooms	FHA
GRAGE	Parking: 0 = none; 1 = on-site parking; 2 = detached garage; 3 = carport; 4 = attached garage	FHA
Neighborhood and Political Characteristics		
PCTWHT	Percentage of white population in 1990 (%)	Bureau of the Census, U.S. Department of Commerce
MEDINC	Median income of census tract in 1990 ($)	Bureau of the Census, U.S. Department of Commerce
DFCL	Distance from the Chicago Loop (0.1 mile)	City maps
DFNI	Distance to the nearest interstate highway interchange (0.1 mile)	City maps

continued on next page

the sample is 2.80, whereas the same in the 1990 Census is 2.55. Moreover, the sample has a white population of about 43 percent, whereas the corresponding figure in the 1990 Census is 60 percent.

U.S. Bureau of the Census studies at the census tract level are a good source for information on other variables relevant to housing choice, such as neighborhood and city attributes. These variables include percentage of white population as a barometer of ethnic composition, and median income of the area as an indicator of socioeconomic status. Whether ethnic composition has a positive or negative effect on property values is not known in advance, but Chicago does have significant ethnic clustering, which may have some effect on housing choice. Higher incomes often exert an upward influence on property values.

Political variables that could affect house prices include aggregate property tax rates, per-capita municipal spending, and per-pupil spending by school districts. Other things being equal, higher taxes should depress housing prices, and higher public spending on public services and schools should increase them. These data were obtained from state revenue and education agencies and from the U.S. Census. This study included 103 distinct government jurisdictions in the two counties.

Table 7.6 (continued from previous page)

Variable	Definition	Data Source
PARTICLE	Average PM-10 concentration in 1989 and 1990 for nearest monitoring station ($\mu g/m^3$)	Illinois Environmental Protection Agency
SULFUR	Average annual sulfur dioxide concentration in 1989 and 1990 for nearest monitoring station (ppb)	Illinois Environmental Protection Agency
PTAXES	Property tax rate in municipality during year of purchase (%)	Illinois Department of Revenue
SSPEND	Operating expense per pupil in local school district ($)	Illinois State Board of Education
MSSPEND	Expenditure per person by the municipal government in 1987 ($)	Census of Government
COOK	Cook County = 0; DuPage County = 1	Maps
OHARE	Beyond 5 miles of O'Hare Airport = 0; within 5 miles = 1	Maps

Fortunately, census tracts also are a convenient geographic unit to which other potentially important location-related variables can be attached. One such variable is travel distance to commercial centers. We included two travel distances, one to the Chicago Loop, the primary business and employment center, and a second to the nearest interstate highway intersection. In general, proximity to a commercial center should have a positive effect on property values. The effect of highway proximity could be either negative, because of noise and congestion, or positive, by facilitating travel. We calculated both distances manually from maps. (In some cases, geographic information systems might be capable of automating this work.)

As with most large cities, commercial activities in Chicago are no longer concentrated exclusively in the central city. To represent the effect of outlying commercial centers on dwelling price, we introduced a dummy variable to capture the effect of proximity to the second major commercial center, around O'Hare Airport. Census tracts near the airport were assigned a value of one; those far away were assigned a value of zero. Like proximity to the downtown, we expect the O'Hare dummy variable to reveal a positive effect on property value. Also, to account for known differences in tax assessment practices from county to county, we assigned another dummy variable to each census tract, assuming a value of one if the dwelling unit is in Cook County and zero otherwise.

Another attribute that can be attached conveniently to census tracts is air quality. The information on PM-10 and sulfur dioxide pollution is collected by the Illinois Environmental Protection Agency for specific monitoring sites scattered throughout the Chicago metropolitan area. These readings can be associated with census tracts according to proximity and wind directions. In this analysis, each home is assigned the pollution readings of the monitoring station closest to the census tract in which the home is located. We expect higher pollution readings to produce lower housing prices.

Correlating Variables

Hedonic valuation requires the use of mathematical formulas to reveal the specific relationships between the dependent variable (housing prices) and the independent variables (including air quality). As you can imagine, one major issue in hedonic valuation is what type of equation to use. Rather than choose among them, we tried six different equations for estimating the hedonic price function in the first stage of this study and two different specifications for consumer demand in the second stage. All of the models provided good and largely consistent results, indicating that the results are not very sensitive to model choices. This is a desirable feature of any statistical analysis.

We report the best results (based on how well the equations fit the data) in Table 7.7. Altogether, the variables we studied explain just over half of the variability in housing prices. This level of explanatory power is quite acceptable for studies of this type. Factors we cannot measure or do not understand are responsible for the remaining variation. With the exception of local government expenditures, the direction of effect of each variable is consistent with our expectations.

In the first stage, we identified a unit price for each air quality variable. For each property, we obtained a unit value for PM-10 and another for sulfur dioxide. Taking all the unit values, we computed an average unit household value for PM-10 and another for sulfur dioxide. We report the results in the top row of Table 7.8. It is important to stress that these estimates are approximations, but informative ones. The various equations for the first-stage regression yielded a range of $268 to $363 for a 1 μg/m³ change in PM-10 and $88 to $104 for a 1 ppb change of sulfur dioxide.

In the second stage, we used the results of the first stage and added to them. For each environmental quality factor, we estimated the statistical relationship between the unit values developed in the first stage and household characteristics likely to influence unit values for environmental quality improvements. In our study, we selected the following characteristics of the purchaser: household income, race, number of dependent children, and nonhousing expenditures. Because unit prices and amenity levels are determined interactively, rather than one clearly determining the other, we used a statistical technique called three-stage least squares that is designed to handle such situations. The result of the estimation, using the sample average values of the purchaser characteristics, is the average demand curves for PM-10 and sulfur dioxide,

Table 7.7.
UNIT VALUES FOR HOUSING ATTRIBUTES

Variable	Mean Unit Value ($)
NROOMS	147[a]
LVAREA	16[a]
HAGE	−372[a]
LSIZE	1.785[a]
PCTWHT	230[a]
MEDINC	0.900[a]
DFCL	−1340[a]
DFNI	−275
PARTICLE	−268[b]
SULFUR	−100[a]
PTAXES	−3404[a]
SSPEND	0.963[d]
MSPEND	−12[b]

[a] *Significant at the 0.1% level of potential error (highest level of confidence in quality of estimate).*

[b] *Significant at the 1% level of potential error.*

[c] *Significant at the 5% level of potential error*

[d] *Significant at the 10% level of potential error (lower level of confidence in quality of estimate)*

Adj. R^2 = 0.54 (summary statistic expressing percentage of price variation

ESTIMATES OF HOUSEHOLD AND AGGREGATE BENEFITS OF POLLUTION REDUCTION

Value	PM-10 (1989-1990 $)	Sulfur Dioxide (1989-1990 $)
Unit household mean value	268	100
Household value for a 5% reduction	463	283
Citywide aggregate value of a 5% reduction	602,000,000	368,000,000

Note: Estimates are one-time payments for an expected stream of benefits over the duration of residency.

which relate unit prices for improvements to the level of environmental quality. The average value for a large change in the level of a contaminant is derived by summing together the unit values from the starting level of quality to the projected level.

In the middle row of Table 7.8, we report the estimated household value associated with a 5 percent change in the air pollution variables PM-10 and sulfur dioxide. The willingness to pay takes the form of a one-time payment covering the benefits expected for the duration of the homeowner's expected stay at the residence being purchased. Once again, these are approximations. By using a number of different specifications in the second as well as the first stages of the analysis, we obtained values ranging from $463 to $829 for a 5 percent reduction in PM-10 and from $283 to $369 for a 5 percent reduction in sulfur dioxide.

One way to check the validity of our results is to refer to other studies of similar environmental issues. Smith and Huang (1995) reviewed 37 hedonic studies conducted during the period 1967 to 1988 and found the average household marginal willingness to pay for PM-10 to range from $0 to $366 in 1982-1984 dollars. Adjusting for inflation, their results are the equivalent of $0 to $470 in 1989-1990 dollars. Thus our estimates for PM-10 agree well with previous studies. With respect to sulfur dioxide reduction, the only known study is by Atkinson and Crocker (1987), who found a negative value based on household data from Chicago for the period 1964-1968. Thus their results are seemingly at odds with ours. However, public awareness of sulfur dioxide pollution and associated problems was minimal in the 1960s, so it is not surprising that our findings are quite different.

In the bottom row of Table 7.8, we extrapolated the household mean unit values for the best-fit model to values for the 1.3 millions households in the Chicago metropolitan area, assuming our sample is representative of the general population. Once again, the reported values are approximations: The range of estimates using other specifications was $602 million to $1.078 billion for PM-10 and $368 million to $480 million for sulfur dioxide. Because the harmful effects of PM-10 are more direct and visible to humans, it is perhaps to be expected that households are more willing to pay for its reduction.

Placing the Results in Context

The aggregate benefit needs to be placed in context. First, our data pertain to single-family, detached, owner-occupied housing units, whereas the aggregation is based on all owner-occupied housing units. Households living in units other than the ones considered in the study may have, on average, higher or lower willingness to pay for reduction in air pollution. Second, the hedonic valuation method provides benefit estimates for an environmental amenity associated directly with housing consumption. Although housing choice captures a major fraction of the value of reducing air pollution, it is not the whole picture, and the benefit estimates we have derived probably understate the total value of reducing PM-10 and sulfur dioxide pollution. Third, it is not possible to disaggregate the benefit estimates to account for the individual effects on health, visibility, residential soiling, and other specific impacts.

In order to make the estimates more precise, a number of extensions could be attempted. For example, we might have tried to factor prevailing winds into the assignment of air monitoring stations to census tracts, rather than simply using linear distances. This might have produced more precise and significant value estimates for the environmental variables. We might have expanded the number of commercial centers used and the number of ethnic groups represented. We might have included other variables that could influence property values, improving the overall explanatory power of the model. We might have used average demographic characteristics for the Chicago metropolitan area, rather than averages for the sample, when determining average unit prices and willingness to pay.

Although some of these extensions would not require much time or expense, others would. Gathering data is particularly difficult and costly, unless it is already available in convenient census or transactions databases. For example, local governments gather a lot of data about housing transactions, but it can be difficult to correlate the local records to FHA and census records.

Although benefit studies could always be improved or replicated with different modeling assumptions, a study such as this one produces some valuable insights. Based on actual decisions in the marketplace, we can be reasonably confident that Chicago residents in the late 1980s valued a 5 percent decrease in PM-10 pollution at least on the order of $600 million to $1.1 billion per year. They valued a 5 percent reduction in sulfur dioxide at least on the order of $350 million to $500 million per year. Their actual values were probably greater, given that housing does not capture all value of environmental improvement. If these changes could be achieved at a cost below these dollar values (again, in late 1980 dollar values), they would probably be worth pursuing.

References

Atkinson, S. E., and T. Crocker. 1987. A Bayesian approach to assessing the robustness of hedonic property value studies. *Journal of Applied Econometrics* 2(1): 27-45.

Smith, V. K., and J. Huang. 1995. Can markets value air quality? A meta-analysis of hedonic property value models. *Journal of Political Economy* 103: 209-227.

CASE STUDY OF A CONTINGENT VALUATION ANALYSIS: THE BENEFITS OF SEDIMENT REMEDIATION[18]

Background

Sediments contaminated by industrial pollutants are common in the Great Lakes region. Unfortunately, remedial actions for contaminated sediments often carry hefty price tags. A commonly mentioned estimate for remediation of Green Bay and the Fox River, for example, is roughly $100 billion. As citizens and governmental bodies contemplate such expenditures, questions are bound to arise about potential economic benefits. Contingent valuation (CV) can help address such questions.

As we pointed out in Chapter 6, CV has some distinct advantages over other methods of approaching benefits questions. In particular, CV can include in benefit estimates a more

---

[18] *Richard C. Bishop, Professor and Chair, Department of Agricultural and Applied Economics, University of Wisconsin –Madison.*

comprehensive set of environmental values held by the general public, including both use and nonuse values, whereas other methods will limit values to those directly associated with resource uses such as recreational fishing. Limiting benefit estimates to use values carries a risk: Based on an overly narrow definition of benefits, the costs of remediation projects may be judged to exceed benefits when in fact a more complete accounting of benefits using CV would lead to the opposite conclusion.

Though a prime setting for CV, Great Lakes sediment remediation has not been the subject of any completed CV study. Here, we illustrate CV's potential contribution to the Great Lakes through a case study carried out in California.

Choosing a Question That Will Reflect Value

Beginning in the 1940s, a plant in Los Angeles manufactured DDT and discharged waste into the county sewer system. The DDT along with other sewage was discharged to outfalls in the Southern California Bight, an area in the Pacific Ocean off the Palos Verdes Peninsula. Polychlorinated biphenols (PCBs) also entered the marine environment through the sewage outfall. Even though discharges ended in the 1970s, DDT and PCBs continue to enter the food chain from sediments covering an area about five miles long and two miles wide. Bald eagles and peregrine falcons are very rare in a large area of southern California, and efforts to reestablish the birds there have been hampered be near-total lack of reproduction. Two species of fish — kelp bass and white croaker — have also experienced reproduction problems in areas near where the chemicals were released. Commercial fishing for white croaker has been banned in the area (kelp bass are not fished commercially). Recreational anglers have been warned about the dangers of eating both species. These environmental problems have been linked directly to the sediments of the Southern California Bight. Other effects are probably present but have been more difficult to document.

This case study summarizes research that estimated the value Californians would place on remediation actions that would prevent further uptake of DDT and PCBs into the food chain. The study was done in the context of a lawsuit being brought by the U.S. Department of Commerce and the state of California under Superfund.

The specific remediation proposal was to "cap" the contaminated sediments with a layer of clean material. It is important to note at the outset that this proposal was not a realistic one, nor was it intended to be. Covering perhaps 10 square miles and lying under 100 feet of water, the sediments would be difficult, expensive, and perhaps technically impossible to cap. Hence, they are expected to continue to affect birds and fish for at least 50 years. Instead the capping proposal was a tool the researchers used to

This case study summarizes researchthat estimated the value Californians would place on remediation actions that would prevent further uptake of DDT and PCBs into the food chain.

assess the amount Californians would be willing to pay for the abatement (i.e., for clean sediments). As long as researchers convinced respondents that the proposal was real and plausible, the reality of the proposal was of little importance. Only a very brief summary of the study is presented here. Full details are given in the study's report (Natural Resource Damage Assessment, Inc. 1994).

Presenting the Question

The CV survey for the Southern California Bight study began with a couple of questions focusing on how respondents felt about several alternative activities that the state of California spends money on, including building new prisons, providing public transportation, improving education, and the like. This general background data about how each respondent felt about various governmental programs introduced the topic of government spending and helped researchers control for blanket attitudes.

Next came the CV scenario overview (see Chapter 6 for a general discussion of CV scenarios). The CV scenario was quite long and detailed, and we present only a brief outline here. It began by telling respondents the following:

- Proposals are sometimes made to the state for new programs. The state does not want to undertake new programs unless taxpayers are willing to pay for them. One way for the state to find out about this is to give people like you information about a program so that you can make up your own mind about it.

- In interviews of this kind, some people think the program they are asked about is not needed; others think it is. We want to get the opinions of both kinds of people.

The scenario then introduced the elements of the contamination problem and the capping project, including:

- A description of the reproductive problems of the affected birds and fish and where they were located, including sketches of the organisms and maps.

- An explicit statement to the effect that there are many other species of birds and marine life in the area that are not currently affected.

- An explicit statement about the status of the affected species. (The fish were not endangered, whereas both birds were listed as endangered in California and several other states. However, populations of both birds were increasing elsewhere in California and in other states.)

■ A description of how the problems for these species are due to DDT and PCBs and how these chemicals got into the environment in the first place.

■ A discussion of how such compounds remain in the sediments and continue to get into the food chain many years after their release is discontinued.

■ Explanations of how commercial fishing controls and consumption advisories for recreationally caught fish protect human health.

■ A discussion of how new clean sediments from natural sources are slowly covering the contaminated sediments and will ultimately form a barrier between the contaminated sediments and the food chain, thus solving the problem in about 50 years without human intervention.

■ A description of a "speed-up program" that would cap the sediments and allow the birds and fish to recover in only 5 years rather than 50. (Several diagrams were presented here to make the speed-up program seem realistic.)

■ A statement to the effect that the capping project, if carried out, would be paid for by a one-time increase in next year's California income taxes.

Next in the survey came two valuation questions. They were posed as referenda and specified the amount by which the respondent's household income tax bill would increase. Each time, the respondents were asked whether they would vote for or against the proposal. Depending on whether they answered that they would vote yes or no to the first valuation question, they were asked about a higher or lower tax in the second question.

The sample was designed to be representative of English-speaking Californians, 18 years of age and older. The survey was administered in the first half of 1994. Trained interviewers from a leading survey firm completed 2,810 personal interviews, which constituted 72.6 percent of the eligible households in the original sample. Statistical procedures were used to analyze responses to the valuation questions. They were designed to estimate a lower bound on the average value per household.

The lower bound average value per household turned out to be $55.61. Multiplied by the total number of affected households, the per household level yields an aggregate value of the capping project's benefits of at least $575.4 million (estimated standard error = $27.5 million).

Summary and Implications

Results from the California study reported here underscore the need for a full accounting of benefits. Remediation of sediments in the Southern California Bight would lead to improved fishing and bird watching, but this is only the tip of the iceberg. Results from the CV study reported here indicate that much larger values lie just underneath the surface, values associated not with immediate direct uses of affected resources but with the public's broader concerns about the environment. To a greater or lesser degree, the same conclusion may be true for contaminated sediments elsewhere, including the Great Lakes region. The only way to know is to estimate the full range of values using CV. In this way, CV is capable of contributing much toward sound decision-making about where and when to apply remedial measures to contaminated sediments.

References

Natural Resource Damage Assessment, Inc. 1994. *Prospective Interim Lost Use Value Due to DDT and PCB Contamination in the Southern California Bight.* 2 Volumes. Washington, DC: U.S. Department of Commerce, National Oceanic and Atmospheric Administration.

CASE STUDY OF A BENEFITS TRANSFER ANALYSIS: WETLANDS RESTORATION IN SAGINAW BAY[19]

Background

Saginaw Bay coastal wetlands have declined by about 50 percent from roughly 37,440 acres in 1857 to 17,800 acres in 1963-1973 (Jaworski and Raphael 1978; The Nature Conservancy 1995). Conversations with Michigan Department of Natural Resources (MDNR) and the Michigan Department of Environmental Quality (MDEQ) personnel suggest that wetland area has not changed much since 1973.

MDNR and MDEQ have recognized the potential for restoring significant natural resource and recreation value to the coastal wetlands along the southern shore of Saginaw Bay. In order to inform future policy, the potential benefits of these uses from wetland restoration must be estimated. This case study shows how benefits transfer can be used to estimate the potential value of a wetlands restoration project in Saginaw Bay.

The MDEQ effort, called the Saginaw Bay Watershed Initiative, is part of a U.S. Environmental Protection Agency national watershed initiative. The Saginaw Bay water-

---

[19] *Leroy J. Hushak, Professor Emeritus, Department of Agricultural, Environmental, and Development Economics and The Ohio Sea Grant Program, The Ohio State University.*

shed was selected as the first area to be designated under the national initiative. The initiative was developed to bring together local, state, and federal resources, with citizens' input, to ensure that the programs and projects undertaken by the respective agencies are directed toward actions that will have the greatest impact within the watershed (MDEQ 1995).

Identifying Concerns

As we discussed in Chapter 6, the values of concern in the subject site must be outlined clearly in order to compare them with potential source study sites. The following programmatic concerns for the Saginaw Bay wetlands project were identified in focus group sessions: (1) Any restoration plan must be a partnership between local stakeholders and MDNR and MDEQ, (2) it must be a voluntary effort, (3) it must include visible involvement of the Michigan Department of Agriculture, (4) direct compensation or incentives must be considered, and (5) the preservation of existing wetlands must be assured before new ones are created (Saginaw Bay Watershed 1994, pp. 11-12). There were three focus groups comprised of business, agricultural, environmental, and local government leaders from within the Saginaw Bay watershed. The initiative will be more acceptable (i.e., valued more highly) if the concerns of these local leaders are addressed in the program. Also, a preliminary background analysis of economic and demographic characteristics of the Saginaw Bay area was compiled (The Nature Conservancy 1997, Appendix I).

Finally, a survey of Saginaw Bay residents was conducted by The Nature Conservancy (1997, Appendix II) to determine whether and under what conditions local residents would support the purchase of Saginaw Bay wetland areas by MDNR or other organizations. The Nature Conservancy survey included one referendum-type question that has bearing on this benefits transfer analysis. The survey's core question was, "In general, do you support or oppose buying farmland near Saginaw Bay and restoring it to wetlands?" About 51 percent of respondents said they opposed the action, 39 percent said they supported it, and 10 percent were indifferent (The Nature Conservancy 1997, Appendix II). Many of those who voted no on the question believed that wetlands restoration would hurt the economy by reducing agricultural output and employment, but did not see potential employment benefits from increased wetlands-related recreation. The referendum showed that a majority of residents opposed the purchase of farmland for wetlands restoration and showed the project team that to build support from these residents, it would be necessary to provide education about the potential economic benefits of wetlands restoration.

We focus
here on the
use of
benefits
transfer
analysis to
estimate the
value of
Saginaw Bay
wetlands
based on the
estimated
value of
Ohio's coastal
wetlands.

Identifying a Source Study

We were fortunate in finding a wetlands contingent valuation (CV) study of a proposed wetlands purchase and improvement of Ohio's Lake Erie coastal wetlands that is similar to the Saginaw Bay wetlands proposal (de Zoysa 1996, Randall and de Zoysa 1996). We focus here on the use of benefits transfer analysis to estimate the value of Saginaw Bay wetlands based on the estimated value of Ohio's coastal wetlands.

De Zoysa (1996) provides a comprehensive study estimating the values of reducing nitrate levels and sediment in the Maumee River basin and of coastal wetlands restoration in the coastal area of Lake Erie. Using a split-sample design, the sample was divided into six subsamples, and each subsample was asked a different version of the CV question.

Each respondent was asked to respond to a referendum question about one, two, or three of three programs. The three programs were (1) stabilization and reduction of nitrate levels in groundwater in the Maumee River basin, (2) reduction of sediments due to soil erosion in streams and lakes of the Maumee River basin, and (3) protection and enhancement of wetlands along the shore of the western basin of Lake Erie. The referendum question asked respondents if they would vote on the next election ballot in favor of or against a program meeting the following description:

The program would be funded by an additional tax collected from each household for *one year only*. This money would be placed in a special fund and used only to [protect groundwater quality, surface water quality, wetland habitat, depending on the options offered in the questionnaire]. Scientists expect the program would cost your household a *one-time extra payment of [$XX]*.

In this case study, we use only the values of coastal wetlands restoration from the source study and exclude values associated with nitrate levels and sediment reduction.

Comparing the Populations

As we discussed in Chapter 6, it is important to closely evaluate the match between the source study and the Saginaw wetlands subject study populations. The major shortcoming was that the source study sample did not include actual residents of the

Lake Erie coastal wetlands area. De Zoysa (1996) sampled three different populations: (1) rural residents of the Maumee River basin, (2) urban residents of the Maumee River basin, and (3) residents of the Columbus and Cleveland metropolitan areas. Residents of the Lake Erie coastal area where wetland restoration would take place were not sampled because the coastal wetland area is not in the Maumee River basin; it is only highly affected by it. In this case study, we assume that wetlands values of Maumee River basin residents are transferable to Saginaw Bay watershed residents. This assumption has not been tested and thus must be treated with caution. It may be that Maumee River basin resident values should be considered as part of the nonresident group; the nonresident values appear to be highly applicable to Saginaw Bay wetlands. Though problematic, the assumption that Maumee River basin resident values are transferable to Saginaw Bay watershed resident values allows us to illustrate the distinction between resident and nonresident values and how they are used in policy analysis.

The sample respondents for the De Zoysa study were asked to provide the total value they placed on the coastal wetlands. Therefore, the estimates generated for the Saginaw Bay wetlands proposal also are total wetlands values. Therefore, it was not necessary to find studies estimating the value of specific activities supported by wetlands such as fishing, hunting, bird watching, and hiking; conduct a benefits transfer analysis of these studies; and then add the components to obtain a total estimated value. However, such an exercise would still be useful to obtain confirming evidence of the values generated by the De Zoysa study.

Comparing Restoration Proposals

The goals of the Saginaw Bay restoration proposal appear in a recent application to the North American Waterfowl Management Plan for the Saginaw Bay area. They are to (1) protect 3,500 acres of wetlands by public acquisition, (2) restore 4,000 acres of wetlands on both public and private land, and (3) develop 1,000 acres of improved nesting cover in association with wetland habitat (SBCWRP 1995). Recall that Saginaw Bay coastal wetlands declined from about 37,440 acres in 1857 to 17,800 acres in 1963-1973 (Jaworski and Raphael 1978), or by about 50 percent (The Nature Conservancy 1995).

The goals of the Ohio restoration proposal were to protect and improve existing wetlands, restore 3,000 additional acres of wetlands, and provide about 20 percent more wildlife habitat for migrating birds and waterfowl. Lake Erie marshes once comprised

The smaller

size of the

Saginaw Bay

wetlands

ecosystem

could affect

the value that

residents

place on

restoration

positively,

negatively,

or both.

300,000 acres of wetlands from Sandusky to Toledo. Today only 10 percent (30,000 acres) of the original wetlands remain.

Consider the following comparisons: (1) Ohio has 30,000 acres of coastal wetlands, compared to 17,000 in Saginaw Bay; (2) the Ohio proposal would add 3,000 acres of new wetlands and restore and maintain existing wetlands, compared to the Saginaw Bay proposal to protect 3,500 acres by public acquisition and to restore 4,000 acres on public and private land; (3) the Ohio proposal would add 20 percent to wildlife habitat to enhance hunting, fishing and wildlife viewing, whereas the Saginaw Bay proposal would develop 1,000 acres of improved nesting cover.

The major difference appears to be that Saginaw Bay is a much smaller ecosystem with initial coastal wetland area of about 37,400 acres, compared to 300,000 acres in Ohio's western basin of Lake Erie. The current Saginaw Bay coastal wetland area is just over 50 percent of the Ohio area. The acres of proposed new wetlands and the wetland and habitat restoration reflect similar proportions. The smaller size of the Saginaw Bay wetlands ecosystem could affect the value that residents place on restoration positively, negatively, or both. With fewer acres in wetlands, each acre might be valued more highly. Also, each acre to be restored might also have a higher marginal value. Yet, with a smaller ecosystem, there may be less value on natural attributes generally. For discussion purposes, we assume that each household would place the same value on either proposal.

Estimating the Benefits Transfer Value

The total value of wetlands restoration is the value per unit (in this case per household) times the number of units that value wetlands restoration. A major issue is the population over which to aggregate values. In this case, drainage basin residents are distinguished from the broader population interested in wetlands restoration represented by the state of Michigan. We use the number of households of the drainage basin and of the state of Michigan and compare them to the Maumee River drainage basin (rural plus urban) and the state of Ohio, using the assumption that Maumee River drainage basin resident values are transferable to Saginaw Bay basin residents. In either case, Lake Erie or Saginaw Bay, the appropriate nonresident population might be larger or smaller than the number of households.

In addition, the Maumee River basin sample may not be representative of the resident populations of either the Ohio coastal wetlands area or the Saginaw Bay area. The Saginaw Bay area survey (Richard Day Research 1997) showed that 51 percent of the resident respondents opposed the acquisition of land for wetlands, thus placing a negative value on wetlands. The respondents voted this way because they viewed loss of agricultural land as leading to loss of employment and income; apparently they did not recognize the potential for generating new employment and income from an increase in tourism. At the same time, the CV model does not allow negative values in estimating willingness to pay, but truncates responses at the minimum of zero. Ohio respondents were asked to vote yes or no on referendum questions with positive costs only.

A third major issue is how to allocate the total benefits across the activities of the wetlands restoration programs. The De Zoysa study established per acre values of wetland restoration by dividing the total value by the 3,000 acres to be restored. This is problematic, however, because the restoration proposal is multifaceted, with maintenance and improvement of existing wetlands and habitat restoration as additional parts of the program. For illustrative purposes, we provide three alternatives:

1. Division by new acres restored or protected — 3,500 in Saginaw Bay and 3,000 in Ohio;
2. Division by new acres restored plus acres protected — 7,500 in both cases; and
3. Division by total wetland acres when the project is completed — 21,300 (17,800 + 3,500) in Saginaw Bay and 33,000 (30,000 + 3,000) in Ohio.

In Table 7.9, we present the CV estimates for the Ohio proposal using the two primary results from de Zoysa (1996) and calculate the total estimated wetlands benefits of Saginaw Bay for the water basin and for the state. Estimated wetlands benefits for Saginaw Bay range from $500 to $9,000 per acre for residents of the drainage basin and from $7,199 to $61,153 for residents of the state of Michigan. The estimated values for the Saginaw Bay drainage basin are more than double those for Lake Erie coastal wetlands because there are more than twice as many households within the Saginaw Bay drainage basin as in the Maumee River drainage basin. For the state, the per-acre Michigan estimates are in general smaller than the Ohio estimates because Michigan has fewer households, except in estimate 3, in which the total wetland area is the divisor.

Which per-acre estimate is best? We look first at the three alternative estimates and then at the drainage-basin- versus state-level estimates. In our judgment, estimate 1 is too large because the divisor includes only area of wetlands purchased, and the pro-

Table 7.9.
COMPARISON OF LAKE ERIE AND SAGINAW BAY
COASTAL WETLANDS VALUES

| | Saginaw Bay, Michigan | | Lake Erie, Ohio | |
	Median*	LBM**	Median*	LBM**
Drainage-basin level				
No. of households, 1990	496,000	496,000	236,000	236,000
Wetland value per household ($)	21.50	63.50	21.50	63.50
Total wetlands benefit (million $)***	10.66	31.50	5.07	14.99
Wetlands benefits per acre ($)				
Estimate 1+	3,050	9,000	1,690	5,000
Estimate 2++	1,420	4,200	675	2,000
Estimate 3+++	500	1,479	155	455
State-level				
No. of households, 1990	3,575,000	3,575,000	4,270,000	4,270,000
Wetland value per household ($)	42.89	59.87	42.89	59.87
Total wetlands benefit (million $)***	153.33	214.04	183.14	255.64
Wetlands benefits per acre ($)				
Estimate 1+	43,808	61,153	61,046	85,214
Estimate 2++	20,444	28,539	24,419	34,085
Estimate 3+++	7,199	10,049	5,550	7,747

*Median value of willingness to pay (i.e., the value of the middle respondent).

**LBM — Lower bound mean of willingness to pay, a mean calculated from subgroups of a sample where the smallest value any member of a subgroup places on the resource is used as the value for all members of that subgroup.

***Wetland value per household times no. of households.

+Division of total wetlands benefit by new acres restored or protected (3,500 in Saginaw Bay and 3,000 in Ohio).

++Division of total wetlands benefit by new acres restored plus acres protected (7,500 in both cases).

+++Division of total wetlands benefit by total wetland acres when the project is completed (21,300 in Saginaw Bay and 33,000 in Ohio).

gram proposes to improve some existing wetlands. Estimate 3 is too small because the proposal will not improve all existing wetlands, although it is hoped that it would ensure that they continue as wetlands (an important concern to the focus groups). The divisor for estimate 2 most closely represents the distribution of revenues for the wetlands acquisition and restoration proposal being valued, and is the best benefits transfer estimate from the de Zoysa study.

In the case of Ohio coastal wetlands, nonresidents place large values on the coastal wetlands. By inference using benefits transfer, this also applies to the Saginaw Bay wetlands. These high values of wetlands to nonresidents imply that nonresidents can appropriately be asked to pay for much if not all of the wetlands restoration program and that involvement of MDNR, MDEQ, the Michigan Department of Agriculture, and other state agencies in the acquisition and financing of wetlands acquisition and improvements is appropriate.

Conclusion

It is difficult to transfer estimates from one study to another. Although the study and intervention site proposals are highly similar in this case study, there are also significant differences in the two proposals. This is likely to be the norm, not an exception. De Zoysa (1996) is the only CV study of wetlands restoration of which we are aware; there are not numerous alternatives, although other studies have estimated the use values of wetland-related recreation activities.

In addition, the Saginaw Bay wetlands restoration effort has reached the stage at which a local land conservancy is developing an educational program and is carrying out the planning needed to proceed with wetlands restoration. Although a basin-wide CV survey on a program such as the one evaluated here provides a valuable first estimate of per-acre values, targeted studies estimating the economic value and economic impacts from conversion of specific smaller parcels to wetlands will be needed in the future. Benefits transfer can be used when one or more of the few available studies is applicable.

References

de Zoysa, A., and N. Damitha. 1996. *A Benefit Evaluation of Programs to Enhance Groundwater Quality, Surface Water Quality and Wetland Habitat in Northwest Ohio*. Ph.D. dissertation, The Ohio State University.

Jaworski, Eugene, and C. Nicholas Raphael. 1978. *Fish, Wildlife, and Recreational Values of Michigan's Coastal Wetlands*. Report prepared for Great Lakes Shorelands Section, Division of Land Resource Programs, Michigan Department of Natural Resources.

MDEQ (Michigan Department of Environmental Quality), formerly MDNR. 1995. *Saginaw Bay National Watershed Initiative*. Office of the Great Lakes.

The Nature Conservancy. 1995. *Michigan Natural Features Inventory of The Nature Conservancy. Saginaw Bay Coastal Wetland Restoration Feasibility Study.* Proposal submitted to MDNR Coastal Zone Management Program.

The Nature Conservancy. 1997. *Michigan Natural Features Inventory of The Nature Conservancy. Saginaw Bay: A Coastal Wetland Restoration Feasibility Study.* Final report to MDEQ, Coastal Zone Management Program and Office of the Great Lakes, and MDNR, Wildlife Division.

Randall, Alan, and Damitha de Zoysa. 1996. Groundwater, surface water, and wetlands valuation for benefits transfer: a progress report. In *Benefits and Costs Transfer in Natural Resource Planning.* Western Regional Research Publication W-133. Compiled by Joseph A. Herriges, Department of Economics, Iowa State University, Ames, Iowa.

Saginaw Bay Watershed. 1994. *A Strategy for Wetland Restoration.* Prepared by Saginaw Valley State University with assistance from Public Sector Consultants, Inc. and Resource Management Group, Inc.

SBCWRP (Saginaw Bay Coastal Wetland Restoration Plan). 1995. Draft.

part III:
Discussion

Chapter 8

Designing a Benefits Assessment: Sediment Remediation at Fox River[20]

W e have made clear by now that each resource valuation tool has specific strengths and limitations and that complexities of nature and society make the quality and usefulness of a study dependent on correct design decisions. Combine these facts with the reality that budgets for economic studies rarely afford economic analysis for its own sake, and we begin to understand the importance of front-end planning to successful economic benefits assessments. Important considerations include research design, geographic scope, and the valuation tool(s) used.

The design stage of the research effort can be substantial or quite cursory depending on the question being asked, the magnitude of the research under consideration, and the quantity of information already available. In this chapter, we provide insight into the scoping activities and planning decisions that economists undertake prior to conducting resource valuation exercises. We do so by walking the reader through a hypothetical scenario involving sediment remediation at the Fox River in Wisconsin. Although existing economic analyses of the Fox River cleanup are fragmentary and incomplete, enough is known about the problem to make it a useful illustration of how planning a full economic analysis would work.

The planning exercise we describe here has three stages, each involving several steps: (1) clarifying the scenario and question to be asked, (2) scoping the benefits as they compare to estimated costs, and (3) selecting the tool to answer the question (i.e., considering the geographic scope and research approach). This planning work then would be followed by implementation of the full benefits assessment study.

CLARIFYING THE SCENARIO AND THE QUESTION TO BE ASKED

Basic information about the study site and the exact policy question that requires an answer are critical to effective planning of a benefits assessment. We take as an exam-

---

[20] *Richard C. Bishop, Professor and Chair, Department of Agricultural and Applied Economics, University of Wisconsin-Madison*

ple pending proposals to deal with polychlorinated biphenols (PCBs) in the Fox River and Green Bay. The scenario entails facilities that recycled carbonless carbon paper and other industrial sources that discharged PCBs into the Fox River over many years. Some of the pollutants flowed downstream to Green Bay immediately. The rest became entrained in the sediments of the Fox River and continue to slowly wash downstream and into Green Bay to this day. PCBs also may enter Green Bay from the rest of Lake Michigan, although experts currently believe that the Fox River is the main source of PCBs now in Green Bay. Governments prohibited new discharges of PCBs many years ago, but high concentrations of PCBs remain in the environment from historic uses. PCBs cause many problems in the river and the bay, including contamination of fish consumed by humans and adverse effects on wildlife.

An important question is the extent of the proposed cleanup scenario subject to study and the possible environmental effects it could have. Sediment remediation projects involve efforts to remove, cap, or otherwise neutralize sediments containing toxic substances or other materials deleterious to environmental resources or humans. Proposals are currently under consideration to dredge Fox River sediments at several locations. Sediment deposits in Green Bay itself are too vast and dispersed to make dredging feasible there. For purposes of this example, we will proceed as if full cleanup of the Fox River PCBs is the sediment remediation project under consideration. Obviously, it would not be possible to recover all the PCBs in the Fox River sediments, but full cleanup would require that all significant deposits be dealt with. It is important to recognize that real-world remediation projects can involve any level of effort toward cleanup that decision-makers and the public want to consider. We could equally well have taken partial cleanup of Fox River PCBs as the project. Benefits and costs would be different (i.e., lower), but otherwise the analysis would take much the same form.

A second critical question is how the benefits estimate will be used in policy decisions. Economic analysis could be used to determine how economic benefits to society as a whole would compare to the expenditure of public or private funds on sediment remediation projects. Other questions might also be asked, such as which among a set of competing cleanup scenarios (including proposals for no action) would yield the greatest benefits. Another question is how much a community should be compensated for lost uses. Although the nature of these questions would not necessarily influence the outcome of a benefits assessment, they do influence the nature and outcome of the scoping exercise. In this example, we assume that the benefits information is needed for a cost-benefit analysis of the full cleanup scenario described above.

It is also important at the outset to know whether any particular benefits are of great concern to the study population and to identify any distributional parameters, such as whether policymakers are concerned with all the benefits that a project may generate (i.e. to all people) or just those that may accrue to the population paying for the study. For this study, we assume that an estimate of the total benefits is desired.

SCOPING THE BENEFITS

Preliminary scoping studies explore what can be learned easily about the potential benefits and costs of proposed projects. Such studies help economists make fundamental decisions about study design and even whether a study needs to be carried out at all. Scoping studies alone might show that the benefits of a specific project are in all likelihood greater than the costs, or vice versa. Alternatively, they may simply help to define what sorts of more detailed second-stage studies would be needed before judgments about the relative magnitudes of costs and benefits can be made. As we noted earlier in this guidebook, resource valuation tools often tackle a particular subset of benefits.

Step 1: Benchmark Minimum Benefits Necessary to Justify Costs

Although our focus is on the benefits of remediation, a rough cost estimate is a necessary ingredient of a scoping exercise. A cost figure can help economists understand whether an estimate of only a partial set of benefits will be adequate to determine whether benefits outweigh costs. If not, the study will have to cover a more comprehensive set of benefits to adequately answer the question.

From a scoping standpoint, a good starting point is to estimate how large the benefits would have to be in order to more than cover costs. This is typically determined on a per-household or per-person basis to place the dollar figures into perspective. Such cost figures, per household or per person, provide a benchmark for asking how plausible it is that benefits exceed costs. If such *benchmark benefits estimates* seem quite large, particularly when combined with values arrived at using informal benefits transfer, the economic justification for remediation would be more doubtful.

The Fox River-Green Bay example illustrates how this would work. For the Fox River and Green Bay, costs have yet to be fully estimated, but an often-mentioned figure is that more or less full cleanup could cost $100 million per year for 10 years. This cost estimate is based on the size of the sediment deposits and the cost of alternative technologies available to address them. Note that the cost figure can be as difficult to arrive at as the benefit. The University of Wisconsin Sea Grant Institute, in cooperation with several other organizations, is developing computer software that will add precision to the cost-estimating process. Due consideration should be given to the quality of the cost figures used for this exercise.

To arrive at a benchmark benefits estimate for Fox River sediment remediation, one must ask how much the benefits would have to be per household to equal or exceed the costs of $100 million per year for 10 years. Let's consider this question from several perspectives involving both the local or regional level and the state level.

If local or regional benefits already clearly offset costs, the work can stop there. Because a smaller study is less expensive, we will consider the local or regional level first. Eight counties comprising 246,000 households either touch the Fox River below Lake Winnebago (the portion of the river affected by PCBs) or border the Wisconsin waters of Green Bay, according to the 1990 Census. Assuming an annual compound interest rate corrected for inflation of 3 percent and assuming that benefits accrue for 50 years, we find that the benefits per household would have to be more than $138 per year before the benefits would exceed costs. This value would apply only under the assumption that there are no benefits outside the eight-county area and that population within the eight-county area is stable. In fact, benefits are likely to extend beyond the counties included in this part of the analysis, and their populations are likely to grow over the next 50 years. Hence, we can use the $138 per household per year value as a rather high benchmark in the sense that if we could be confident that benefits would be higher than that, we could be relatively sure that the benefits exceed the costs.

To get a rather different benchmark, consider that the number of households in the state of Wisconsin was 1.8 million in 1990. Thus, if the entire state would benefit from cleanup over a 50-year period, then the benefits per household per year would only have to be more than $19 on average before benefits would exceed costs. If we knew for sure that the whole state would benefit by this amount or more, then benefits would exceed costs. This can serve as another benchmark.

Next, spread the net a bit wider to include the state of Michigan. This might be justified because part of Michigan's population lives on or near Green Bay. Furthermore, although researchers are still considering the matter and have yet to reach definitive conclusions, PCB cleanup in the Fox River might improve the level of PCBs in the broader ecosystems of Lake Michigan as a whole or in a large share of the northern part of the lake. There were 3.4 million households in Michigan in 1990. Thus the total number of households in Wisconsin and Michigan combined would be 5.2 million, implying that benefits would have to exceed only about $7 per household per year before benefits would exceed costs.

These dollar figures were calculated using the formulas described here. Recall that the costs were assumed to be $100 million per year for 10 years. The discount rate was assumed to be 3 percent. Thus, the present value of costs, PVC, is given by

$$PVC = (\$100 \; million) \sum_{t=1}^{10} (1.03)^{-t} = \$853 \; million$$

Assume that B is the annual benefits of remediation, a fixed amount, accruing each year for T years. Then, the benchmark level for B for society as a whole is found by solving the following equation for B:

$$B \sum_{t=1}^{T} (1.03)^{-t} = PVC$$

If T is set at 50 years, as above, then B = $34.12 million per year. To get to a benchmark benefits estimate, this figure is simply divided by the population, 246,000 households for the eight-county region, 1.8 million households for Wisconsin as a whole, and 5.2 households for Wisconsin and Michigan combined.

Lump sums given in the text are found by simply dividing $853 million by the population sizes. This is equivalent to setting T equal to one year.

Step 2: Array Benefits Qualitatively

Contaminated sediments may contain sufficient concentrations of toxic substances to harm plants, animals, and people through direct contact, but more often harmful effects show up via the mechanisms of bioaccumulation. Fish, birds, and mammals high up on the food chain may accumulate body burdens sufficient to harm themselves or the people and predators that consume them. Economic losses occur as peoples' use and nonuse values for affected resources are reduced.

Although research on the effects of PCBs on Fox River and Green Bay resources continues, several potential benefits from remediation are already evident. Nearly all fish species of the system used by recreational anglers currently are subject to fish consumption advisories (FCAs) for PCBs. FCAs advise anglers and others who might eat the recreational catch that they should limit their consumption in order to minimize health risks. The primary emphasis of these advisories is on protecting the health of fetuses and children, but cancer also is a possible risk.

If sediment remediation would help reduce and eliminate FCAs, several economic benefits might arise. Some potential Green Bay and Fox River anglers may have decided not to fish there because of the FCAs. If so, then reducing or removing the FCAs would increase the number of angler-days of fishing on the river and bay, thus increasing angling benefits. Those who have continued to fish there may also be suffering losses because the quality of their fishing has been adversely affected. They may practice catch-and-release fishing more often than they would prefer or fish for different species or fish less often in response to the risks described in the FCAs. If contaminant remediation leads to lower risks from eating the fish, those who have continued to fish the river and bay despite the health risks may receive health benefits that would count as part of the benefits of remediation. Finally, even those who are not anglers or potential fish consumers may benefit if the fish become safer to eat, because they may hold nonuse values for reducing the risks to others from fish consumption. Though probably smaller in magnitude, similar benefits would probably accrue from reducing or eliminating existing consumption advisories for waterfowl taken by hunters in the area.

PCBs have been linked to other environmental problems in addition to fish contamination. Bald eagles have low nesting success along the bay, and scientists believe that PCBs are to blame. Similar effects are present for two species of terns, one of which is listed as endangered by the state of Wisconsin. Cormorant chicks have been found with deformed bills that limit their survival. Though other contaminants may also be contributing to these deformities, PCBs may be partly to blame. Other, subtler effects on other fish and wildlife may be identified in the future. A potentially important example is possible effects on lake trout. Native Lake Michigan and Green Bay lake trout were wiped out before the 1950s because of invasion of a parasite, the sea lamprey, and overfishing. Despite some success in controlling the lamprey and heavy stocking of lake trout, efforts to restore self-reproducing stocks have failed. Scientists are currently investigating whether the lack of natural reproduction of lake trout in Green Bay is linked to PCBs.

If remediation of Fox River sediments will reduce these effects, both use and nonuse benefits might be generated. These benefits include improved hunting and bird-watching, less need for fish stocking, and the existence value associated with a healthy eagle population. Additional benefits might accrue to those involved in water transportation of goods and raw materials. Such individuals are affected because of the need to periodically dredge shipping channels and harbors. Contaminated dredge spoils can be more expensive to dispose of because of the environmental hazards they pose. Cleaning up PCBs in the Fox River might eventually lead to cleaner sediments at the river mouth and in Green Bay, thus reducing the costs of disposal of spoils from dredging to maintain access to port facilities.

In sum, many of the benefits of sediment remediation are likely to be enjoyed by anglers as the FCAs are reduced or removed, but that is not the end of the story. Hunters, nonconsumptive users of wildlife (e.g., bird watchers), property owners, and those who bear the costs of dredging of shipping channels and harbors might also benefit. Nonuse values associated with reduced adverse impacts of PCBs on fish, wildlife, and people could also be present.

Step 3: Roughly Estimate Benefits Quantitatively

Given what is currently known, how plausible is it that benefits would exceed the benchmarks derived in Step 1? To gain some understanding, consider the Southern California Bight case study in Chapter 7. It involved the benefits to California households of capping a deposit of DDT and PCBs in the Pacific Ocean off the southern part of the state. This amounted to $55.61 per household as a lump sum. If people in the upper Midwest have values for sediment remediation roughly comparable to Californians, then this would leave one skeptical about whether the economic benefits of the Fox River cleanup exceed the costs. Converting the annual figures for the eight-county region, the state of Wisconsin, and Wisconsin and Michigan combined into lump sums and rounding would make them $3,500, $474, and $164, respectively. In contrast, it is worthwhile to consider the preliminary results from a contingent valuation study by John Stoll of the University of Wisconsin-Green Bay. These results indicate that Wisconsin households are willing to pay over $100 per year on average to implement a comprehensive water pollution control program for Green Bay, including various point and nonpoint source control projects targeted in the Green Bay Remedial Action Plan. Stoll's preliminary results appear also to show that many residents consider PCB cleanup to be a high priority among pollution control goals. Stoll's results, if they pan out under further analysis, make it quite plausible that the benefits of the Fox River cleanup exceed the costs.

Step 4: Draw Planning Conclusions

This scoping exercise indicates that more research will be needed to understand whether benefits exceed costs for the Fox River cleanup. This will not always be the result of scoping exercises, however. Had the costs been different (or should they change), the answer might have been clearer at this point. For example, if the costs had been only $10 million per year for 10 years, it would have been much more plausible that benefits would exceed costs. Statewide benefits would only have to be in the ballpark of the Southern California Bight results for this to be true. Benchmark benefits estimates would be well below the figures likely to come out of Stoll's study. Alternatively, had the costs been an order of magnitude larger than what the scoping analysis assumed, the prospects for benefits exceeding costs would have been dim indeed.

Given that scoping was not conclusive regarding the economic justification for the Fox River cleanup, we now use the scoping results to clarify what sorts of economic valuation studies would help to determine the relative magnitudes of benefits and costs.

SELECTING THE TOOL TO ANSWER THE QUESTION

By this point, the scoping study will have described what sorts of benefits might be present and perhaps a bit about how large those benefits might be. At this stage, those planning further studies must consider the prospects for successful application of alternative benefit valuation methods and the potential relevance of results in the decision-making process.

Most important, tough choices will have to be made about which methods to use to estimate benefits because any of the methods discussed in this guidebook will normally be capable of estimating only a portion of them. For example, a travel-cost study of recreational fishing values with and without FCAs will not reflect benefits of sediment cleanup to those who might otherwise have to deal with contaminated sediments dredged from shipping channels and harbors.

Choices among valuation methods will normally be based on the specific characteristics of the problem at hand, technical feasibility, and the size of the research budget. Specific characteristics will vary from site to site. For example, if the scoping study shows that shipping-related benefits are likely to be predominant, then market valuation methods may be called for. If recreational benefits appear to be paramount, then the travel-cost method might be more appropriate. To the extent that most tools yield partial estimates of benefits, it would not make sense to spend money to gain benefits estimates that even under optimistic expectations would not be large enough to matter in the overall comparison of benefits and costs. Furthermore, a method that can prove useful in one setting may not be feasible in another for technical reasons, as we will see in a moment for the Fox River cleanup. Finally, otherwise desirable benefit studies may simply be unaffordable.

Let us suppose that additional benefit studies are being considered for the Fox River cleanup and that we wish to decide among the alternative methods. It makes considerable sense to evaluate the potential of the least expensive and most noncontroversial approaches first. If they will not answer the question adequately, then other methods should be considered. In this scenario, the evaluation might look something like this:

Possibility 1: Benefits Transfer

When feasible, benefits transfer can be easy on budgets, but because too few valuation studies deal with the topic, the method does not seem promising for evaluating sediment remediation projects for the Fox River or elsewhere at this time. We used informal benefits transfer procedures when, as part of the scoping exercise, we compared benchmark benefit levels with benefit estimates for cleanup in the Southern California Bight and for water pollution control in the Green Bay watershed from Stoll's preliminary results. Without more such studies, benefits transfer efforts would lack the support they need to gain credibility.

Possibility 2: Market Valuation

The commercial fisheries of Green Bay are so small that any benefits to them from the Fox River cleanup would be of little consequence compared to costs. As we pointed out earlier, dredging is necessary to give Great Lakes ships access to the Port of Green Bay facilities. It is conceivable that the Fox River cleanup could eventually reduce PCB levels in dredge spoils and thus reduce the costs of spoils disposal. A more complete scoping study than the one presented in this chapter could consider this aspect further to see whether a detailed study to document these benefits would be worthwhile. This would be accomplished by examining the amount of dredging likely to be needed in the future and the extent of the possible cost savings if dredge spoils did not have to be disposed of in sites designed for contaminated sediments. If this initial scoping effort showed that substantial benefits might be present, further study could examine a number of issues that would determine how large the benefit would likely be. For example, sediment transport studies might be conducted to help estimate when it would no longer be necessary to take contaminant-related precautions in disposing of dredge spoils. Other efforts could evaluate whether port expansion might be feasible if dredge spoils disposal becomes cheaper. If so, then the benefits of regional economic expansion could be evaluated and included in the analysis.

Possibility 3: Hedonic Valuation

Unfortunately, the linkages between PCBs and property values appear to be too complex and subtle to make hedonic studies promising. Most hedonic studies have been performed when substantial variations in environmental quality exist within a relatively limited geographic area. Consider the hedonic valuation results for air quality in the Chicago metropolitan area case study (see Chapter 7). What made that study work was the substantial variation in airborne particulates and sulfur dioxide across the Chicago metropolitan area. Statistical methods could then be applied that in essence compared property values in areas with relatively dirty air with property values in areas with relatively clean air in order to assess how much the good air added to property values, other things held constant.

The effects of PCBs are much less localized and variable. For example, although FCAs are somewhat different for the Fox River than for Green Bay, within relatively large areas they are the same. To pick up the effects of PCBs on property values, it would be necessary to find another region of the state or nation that is more or less comparable to the Green Bay region except that the other area lacks the PCB problem. This is a tall order. Also, the areas of the Green Bay region where PCB contamination is the worst (i.e., in the Fox River and in Green Bay at the mouth of the Fox) also have other water quality problems such as high turbidity and algae blooms. Poor water quality from such nonpoint sources would not be affected by PCB cleanup. It could be hard to sort out the effect of PCBs on property values, if any, from the effects of these other forms of pollution. Furthermore, many of the benefits of cleanup, particularly those associated with nonuse values, would be overlooked by a hedonic study.

Possibility 4: Travel-Cost Method

Because PCBs affect fishing, waterfowl hunting, and other outdoor recreation activities, the travel-cost method appears applicable to the Fox River cleanup, at least in principle. However, to pursue a travel-cost study in this instance would not seem wise for a number of reasons. Technical feasibility is questionable for reasons that are in some ways comparable to the problems associated with hedonic methods. That is, the travel-cost method uses variations in environmental quality across recreation sites as a basis for teasing out the value of high-quality sites compared to low-quality sites. In essence, people reveal their values for high-quality recreation sites by spending extra money to get there rather than using lower quality sites. This would be difficult in the case of the Fox River cleanup because there is so little variation in PCB levels across sites. Even if this problem could be overcome, the travel-cost method is only capable of estimating recreational benefits of cleanup. Nonuse values would be completely neglected, which would be acceptable if recreational benefits alone were likely to exceed costs. Other benefits, such as nonuse benefits and benefits associated with reduced costs of dredge spoils disposal, could then be viewed as mere "frosting on the cake."

Unfortunately, recreational benefits alone are likely to fall far below costs. Consider fishing first. A rough estimate would be that Green Bay and the Fox River are supporting 300,000 angler-days per year. This number is based on Wisconsin Department of Natural Resources creel census data. Suppose that, by improving quality on existing fishing days, sediment remediation increases the value of existing fishing by $10 per angler-day. This would be $3 million in benefits. In addition, more anglers might be attracted to fishing the currently affected waters if the FCAs were reduced or eliminated. Suppose that there would be a 30 percent increase in angler-days and that these new angler-days are worth $30 each. That would be an additional $2.7 million. Such sums are certainly significant on their own terms. However, even if the hypothetical dollar figures given here are off by a wide margin from what an actual study would produce, it is hard to imagine that fishing benefits would come close to remediation costs in the hundreds of millions of dollars. Waterfowl hunting, bird-watching, and other benefits are likely to be substantially smaller than angling benefits simply because fewer people are involved in those activities.

Possibility 5: Contingent Valuation

Given the array of nonmarket environmental effects of PCBs in the Fox River and Green Bay and the potential for nonuse values associated with those effects, contingent valuation appears promising as a way to investigate the possible benefits of Fox River cleanup. Such a study would pick up nonuse benefits associated with effects on fish and birds, including endangered species, and other environmental assets along with recreation values of the affected resources. If decision-makers want or need cost-benefit comparisons and have sufficient budgets, a contingent valuation study appears to be the most promising avenue.

CONCLUSION

We have taken a hard-nosed stance toward economic studies in this chapter. If budgets for economic studies are tight, it may not make sense to do a full economic study. Instead, a three-stage approach based on the needs of decision-makers is appropriate. The first stage involves refinement of the policy question that must be answered. The second stage involves a simple scoping study based on easily acquired data, and studies done elsewhere may enable researchers to make a reasonably good judgment about whether benefits exceed costs or vice versa. If not, deeper investigation of benefits and costs can be conducted in the third stage, during which scoping study results should be helpful in judging which valuation methods are most promising for achieving useful practical results.

Contaminants in the environment will often separate citizens into two camps. On the one side will be environmentalists who will be certain that remediation should be carried out regardless of costs. From an economic perspective, they are assuming that benefits are very large or even infinite. On the other side will be economic interests who will be strongly oriented toward use values and particularly use values of market goods. This latter group will quickly come to the conclusion that benefits are small. A well-designed scoping study, followed when necessary by deeper third-stage studies tailored to the specific situation, will help arrive at economically sound decisions by providing more objective information about the magnitude of benefits of contaminant remediation projects.

References

Personal Communication. Richard Stoll, University of Wisconsin-Green Bay.

Chapter 9

Dealing with the Analytical Challenges of Valuation: Aquatic Nuisance Species Control[21]

When economists apply valuation methods in the real world, they frequently encounter complications that pose both theoretical and empirical challenges. These complicating factors, outlined in Chapter 4, include the complex interrelationships between environmental services, uncertainties pertaining to environmental impacts and their economic values, and the sometimes difficult to define magnitude and geographic scale of impacts. We can account for these concerns to some extent within the economic valuation framework described in this guidebook. However, in many cases, it will be necessary to account for these challenges through embedding the valuation exercise in a broader decision framework. Especially in the case of uncertainty, it may also be necessary to acknowledge what cannot be known or predicted, and if the potential environmental risk is high enough, place a high benefit value on the precautionary approach

In this chapter, we illustrate how economists might address the analytical challenges that accompany any benefits assessment. It includes strategies for overcoming these challenges, or, if necessary, to live with them. The context is a proposed project to discourage the spread of aquatic nuisance species between the Great Lakes and the Mississippi River basin.

BACKGROUND: CONTROLLING THE SPREAD OF AQUATIC NUISANCE SPECIES BETWEEN THE GREAT LAKES AND MISSISSIPPI RIVER WATERSHEDS

Although the zebra mussel invasion has garnered considerable attention, the Great Lakes have experienced a sequence of invasions before and after the mussel's arrival. The round goby is a recent invader that can interfere with the dynamics of domestic

---

[21] *Alan Randall and Hyma Gollamudi, Department of Agricultural, Environmental, and Development Economics, The Ohio State University.*

What substantial damage has been documented from the goby or the daphnid in the Great Lakes to justify an investment in control mechanisms?

species, affect recreational and commercial fishing, and possibly affect human health: The goby is known to eat zebra mussels (which accumulate toxicants deposited in the Great Lakes), thereby moving the toxics up the food chain, potentially to fish eaten by humans. Rainbow smelt, alewife, sea lamprey, and ruffe are other examples of aquatic nuisance species that have invaded the Great Lakes and are causing problems. One can understand the desire of local communities, policymakers, and other concerned parties to prevent future invasions and to limit the spread of invaders that have already achieved a toehold in U.S. waters.

The zebra mussel has already spread from the Great Lakes to the Mississippi River basin, and six additional species are poised to invade the Mississippi system through the Illinois ship canal system. This invasion may result in decreased game fishing, loss of native bivalve species, and increased cost of production for electricity and water utilities (Sparks et al. 1995). In the other direction, some nonnative species, such as daphnid, striped bass, and Asian carp (big head and black), may invade the Great Lakes from the Mississippi River basin. Nonnative daphnids have a competitive edge over native daphnids because of their spines (Stoeckel et al. 1997) and were spotted as far north as Ohio and Illinois in 1996 (Stoeckel et al. 1996).

The futures of these two ecosystems are intertwined because they are connected through the Illinois ship canal system. Thus, any Mississippi River basin species, native or nonnative, can potentially come upstream and enter the Great Lakes, and vice versa. In order to prevent this problem, a current proposal calls for a barrier in the Illinois ship canal system, using an electric filter as the first line of defense, backed up by chemical agents for use if necessary (Keppner and Theriot 1997). Although the initial impetus for this strategy was the need to prevent the goby from spreading from the Great Lakes into the Mississippi River system, this system would act as a two-way barrier to prevent susceptible species in either water body from invading the other. The barrier would be built in three phases (personal communication with Phil Moy of the Army Corps of Engineers): In phase 1, two electric barriers, five or six feet from the canal bottom, would be constructed at an estimated cost of $750,000. This is expected to be more than 99 percent effective in intercepting goby and similar fish. In phase 2, an electric apparatus (with an estimated cost anywhere from $1.5 million to $6 million, depending on modifications and safety requirements, and with an annual operating cost of $80,000) would be installed. This apparatus is claimed to deter all marine species, including fish. A proposed phase 3, expected to cost more than the first two phases, would provide even greater protection.

Concerns have been raised about the need for this investment. For example, what substantial damage has been documented from the goby or the daphnid in the Great Lakes to justify such an investment? No economic studies have yet been conducted for either species.

More is known in the case of the zebra mussel. For instance, a single power plant spends $40,000 per year in operation costs (in addition to $1 million in fixed costs) to control the zebra mussel; and the Mississippi River commercial shelling industry, which exports cultured pearls and has a worldwide market of $3 billion, has been halted (Sparks et al. 1995). Surveys conducted by researchers at the Ohio Sea Grant College Program found that 160 municipal and industrial water users reported detecting zebra mussels in their facilities and spending over $60.2 million during the 1989-1994 period for monitoring and control expenses (Hushak and Deng 1996). Various public and private agencies spent an additional $18.7 million during the same period for zebra mussel research. These reported expenditures for zebra mussel monitoring, control, and research omit respondents' expenditures since 1994 and all expenditures by nonrespondents to the surveys (Hushak and Deng 1996).

Furthermore, controversy exists about the control technology selected. The electric barrier was chosen because it satisfies the conditions specified by the Illinois water system authorities: (1) the barrier should not disturb the navigation of ships, (2) only one-time use of chemicals is permitted, and (3) no changes in the volume and flow of water are permitted. The electric barrier shocks the fish but does not kill them. The intent is to repel invading fish, but some people have expressed concern that stunned fish may be carried through the barrier with the water flow. Even with the barrier in place, the goby may be carried in ships' ballast water or by fishermen going back and forth between the two water systems and using goby as bait. Studies of zebra mussel spread show that education and inspection have been more effective deterrents than quarantines and controls (Schneider et al., 1998).

COMPLEXITIES

When the environment is disturbed by the establishment of an invasive species, a mix of environmental services is changed, sometimes quite drastically. The negative effects of such invasions offset any positive effects, thus diminishing the value of the baseline environment. If an effective barrier on the Illinois ship canal system is built, it would protect against adverse impacts to businesses, outdoor recreationists, and the like, thus providing use values of various kinds. These values include protecting resource-based industries and fishing and hunting opportunities. Nonuse values (such as ones derived from knowing an ecosystem is healthy) are nonrival (i.e., nonusers do not compete with each other for the benefit) and can be large in cases such as the barrier system. The barrier would also protect the uniqueness of the Great Lakes and Mississippi River basin ecosystems, providing a full range of nonuse values enjoyed by those who appreciate the uniqueness of the Mississippi's ecological community, regardless of their personal contact with it. The individuals who do not use the Mississippi's unique biota currently, but are willing to pay a premium to ensure that future use is available, place option value on protection of the resource. Quasi-option value reflects the desire of others to preserve the unique biota because some component of it may provide some unforeseen use value in future (e.g., a cure to a disease).

Summing these values, however, is not simple, with practically all the analytical challenges outlined in Chapter 4 standing in the way. An ecosystem like the Mississippi or the Great Lakes — baseline or modified — is an especially complex good, service, or amenity. In some ways, it is all of these things. It might be most appropriate to think of an ecosystem as a state of the world. As befits the attempt to value what is basically a state of the world, nonuse values, nonmarket use values, and values arising from uncertain future uses of various kinds loom large in the analysis. Some of the sources of complexity associated with this case are complex outcomes, substitution, and complementary relationships that can become complicated when many environmental services are affected by a single project.

The need to anticipate the complex outcomes of changes resulting from an environmental disturbance such as an aquatic nuisance species invasion stretches the capacity of the natural sciences. Moreover, many of the environmental services and amenities may be unfamiliar to ordinary citizens, whose willingness to pay to prevent such disturbances is fundamental to valuation. For example, many recreational users of the Mississippi River might view the zebra mussel as an asset because of its ability to reduce turbidity. These users may be unaware that the reduced turbidity could in the end curtail their fishing opportunities by reducing the sources of nourishment for forage fish. Moreover, a valid valuation framework must accommodate substitution and complementarity relationships among ecosystem services as well as real resource constraints.

Additivity is another source of complexity. Installation of the aquatic nuisance species barrier proposed for the Illinois ship canal system will no doubt be accompanied both by public education regarding the need to clean trailered recreational boats and by an initiative to stop the use of gobies as a bait fish. Which benefits can be attributed to the barrier and which to the other initiatives?

One approach to dealing with complexity is to simplify the problem by narrowing the scope of the study to a very specific change and set of impacts. Although we should be ever mindful of the inherent complexity of ecosystems, not all valuation tasks call on us to address the full extent of that complexity. Often, we are asked to value not ecosystems in the large, but the benefits and costs of actions or disturbances that would make relatively modest changes in ecosystems, for example, disturbing just a few species in a particular place, or modifying a particular small section of habitat. The challenge of valuing modest changes in ecosystems is not trivial, but the task is more manageable than valuing large changes in complex ecosystems. Any decision to reduce the extent of the complexity by narrowing the scope of the problem should be clearly stated at the outset and with the results of the study.

As befits the attempt to value what is basically a state of the world, nonuse values, nonmarket use values, and values arising from uncertain future uses of various kinds looms large in the analysis.

If an estimate of total benefits is the goal, however, valid approaches to meeting these challenges are limited to two options. One is sequential *piece-wise valuation* in which each successive component is valued, assuming budgets have been adjusted for willingness to pay of all components valued earlier in the sequence. There are by necessity some stringent requirements on the design of the sequential piece-wise approach, and published valuation efforts using the piece-wise strategy typically are susceptible to criticism for failure to satisfy these requirements. What difference does this make to the results of the valuation exercise? There is no general rule when the number of environmental services involved is relatively small, but as the number of components grows large, the error becomes systematic. Economists employ a total value framework to address these analytical challenges (Randall 1987, 1992).

The second option is *holistic total valuation* (e.g., one-shot willingness to pay for the proposed change in the state of the world) (Randall et al. 1990; Randall 1992). Holistic total valuation tends to tilt the choice of methods toward contingent valuation (CV), because other methods are unlikely to capture the full array of values involved, especially the nonuse values.

In this case, we are dealing with a complex of ecosystem disturbances, both known and unknown, that may be prevented by a barrier in the Illinois ship canal system, or caused perhaps by unintended consequences of that project. As a result, a total value framework will be essential. CV is at least in principle capable of valuing nonmarket use values, nonuse values, and total economic value. Of the more than 2,000 publications to date involving CV, relatively few have addressed nonuse values such as biodiversity, habitats, or endangered species, questions related to our case example. Nevertheless, many (perhaps most) of the existing studies dealing with use values of various kinds have implemented CV, as have all of the studies dealing with nonuse values. In light of the complexities of the barrier example, CV is our best choice. However, citizen knowledge of the details of any particular ecosystem modification case is likely to be quite slim, so the researcher will need to provide a good deal of case-specific information.

RISK AND UNCERTAINTY

Ecosystem disturbances have uncertain outcomes. Uncertainty pertains both to the impacts of the disturbance on ecosystem services and to the magnitude of the resulting benefits and costs. We may define various levels of uncertainty: *risk* refers to situations where we know in advance the probabilities of the possible outcomes, *uncertainty* to situations where the outcomes can be defined but their probabilities are unknown, and *gross ignorance* to cases where it is impossible to define in advance the array of possible outcomes or their probabilities. It makes sense to divide the effects of potential disturbances into insurable and uninsurable categories. Risk is usually insurable; the exception is catastrophic risk, and drastic environmental disturbance may be catastrophic and therefore uninsurable. Uncertainty and gross ignorance are typically uninsurable.

In this scenario, there is uncertainty about the effectiveness of the proposed barrier. The prevention strategy may fail to prevent the spread of the target species or may have unintended effects on other species. Even if the barrier performs as planned, the payoffs are complex and include a variety of potential impacts, both beneficial and adverse. To take the goby as an example, its ecosystemic effects are not completely known, but it is known to eat zebra mussels. An effective barrier would inhibit this effect in the Mississippi River basin. However, this outcome is not necessarily an adverse one. Gobies could, by eating the zebra mussel, move accumulated toxicants up the food chain toward humans (personal communications with Phil Moy and Edwin Theriot of the US Army Corps of Engineers, Marg Dahoda of Great Lakes Fisheries, and Richard Sparks of Illinois Natural History Survey). We also may have to plead gross ignorance regarding the types of organisms that could enter the Great Lakes and then the Mississippi River basin in the future and their potential impacts, which a dispersal barrier may be able to prevent over time.

Formal decision tools are best adapted to the case of insurable risk. However, in the case of ecosystem disturbances, the problem is often best characterized as gross ignorance, which calls for a quite different set of strategies.

To evaluate alternatives under risk, the conventional expected utility criterion may be adopted, leading to an emphasis on expected net benefits, which is appropriate for risk-neutral individuals and governments. Risk-aversion suggests an emphasis on insurance and hedging arrangements. In the case of ordinary goods, a risk-averse individual can completely insure himself or herself against any loss if insurance can be purchased at an actuarially fair premium (i.e., a premium equal to the expected value of the loss). This result is less impressive than it sounds, because it is costly to run an insurance business, and these costs typically are recouped by charging premiums greater than the expected value of losses.

Individuals may seek hedging contracts, insurance, and so on, to protect against insurable risks, whereas government, being a large and diverse enterprise, may choose to self-insure. Standard cost-benefit approaches implicitly assume expected utility maximization, which is appropriate for insurable risks. If intuition suggests that risk-aversion is the proper stance, and a piece-wise total valuation scheme is used, the analyst can take pains to include option and existence values. Holistic total valuation by CV will include these values as a matter of course.

When facing serious uncertainty, gross ignorance, or uninsurable risks, even the large size of government offers little protection, and the public may seek security in *precautionary decision protocols*. The cost-benefit approach alone may seem thoroughly inadequate, and the decision-maker may seek risk-averse strategies. One approach is to back-stop the cost-benefit analysis with decision rules based on some version of the precautionary principle (e.g., the safe minimum standard of conservation, by which a sufficient reserve of the species and habitat etc. is maintained to ensure its continued survival). Another precautionary approach is to maximize the revocability of an action so that, if it turns out badly, we can revoke the action and return to the status quo.

> An ecosystem like the Mississippi or the Great Lakes is an especially complex good, service, or amenity.... It might be most appropriate to think of an ecosystem as a state of the world.

One way to maximize revocability is to proceed in baby steps, so that we can reverse course at the first sign of danger, before real harm is done.

In the case of the proposed barrier in the Illinois ship canal system, the application of these approaches presents an interesting challenge for decision rules under uncertainty. The barrier is intended to prevent ecosystem disturbance, so the safe minimum standard approach would suggest implementing it right away to minimize the chance of aquatic nuisance species spread, and baby steps make little sense. However, the possibility of unintended consequences suggests that precautions are best provided by a baby-steps approach: Move ahead cautiously, and be prepared to retreat at the first sign of unintended adverse effects.

The precautionary principle would focus on avoiding the worst outcomes, but suppose that these exposures are opposite and symmetrical: If we do not build it (or it turns out to be ineffective), there is a chance of damage from invasions; if we build it, there is an equally great exposure to possible unintended adverse consequences. In that case, the precautionary principle cannot suggest what to do. Precaution with respect to one of these fears entails exposure to the other. So, the planner must make some judgments about the magnitudes of the countervailing exposures. In the case of the proposed barrier, we would guess that the greater risk lies in taking no action, continuing the exposure to spread of aquatic nuisance species. If we are right about that, the precautionary principle would support the barrier proposal.

THE EXPECTED UTILITY CRITERION AND RISK AVERSION

The expected utility criterion may be interpreted in the context of potential ecosystem disturbance as follows: Suppose an ecosystem may take configuration x or y, with probabilities p and $(1-p)$ respectively (the analysis can readily be modified to include more than two outcomes). Let society's expected utility be:

$$E(Usociety) = p.u\ (x) + (1-p).u\ (y).$$

We can analyze society's behavior under such circumstances only if we know its risk attitude. If society prefers to get the expected value $U[p.x + (1-p).y]$ for sure rather than take its chances, $[p.u(x) + (1-p).u(y)]$, it is risk averse. If the opposite holds, society is risk-seeking. The expected utility hypothesis — that people act as expected utility maximizers — assumes that society is indifferent between getting $E(U)$ for sure and taking its chances; this hypothesis underpins the standard cost-benefit analysis practice of calculating expected value to society.

MAGNITUDE AND GEOGRAPHIC SCALE

If the impacts of ecosystem disturbance are of large geographic and economic scale, a general, rather than partial, equilibrium analysis may be required. *Partial equilibrium analysis* addresses changes in a single sector, assuming that prices (i.e., values) of goods and services in other sectors remain unaffected. In contrast, *general equilibrium analysis* arrives at market-clearing equilibrium by assuming that prices of all goods and services adjust to changes precipitated by the disturbance. Thus general equilibrium analysis accounts more completely for the interactions among various goods and environmental services.

General equilibrium analysis increases the complexity of the valuation exercise. Where circumstances warrant the extra effort, general equilibrium methods are available that incorporate market and nonmarket values, and their application is feasible (Böhringer and Rutherford 1996; Jorgenson 1998). Nevertheless, general equilibrium analysis is recommended only when there is reason to believe that a partial equilibrium analysis would produce misleading results.

CONCLUSION

In the context of ecosystem disturbances, three major factors complicate economic valuation: the complex suite of environmental services affected, the uncertain consequences of action or inaction, and the magnitude and geographic scale of impacts. For each of these problems, there is a solution that, to paraphrase H.L. Mencken, is simple, obvious, and wrong: just add up the values of all components in a complex suite of services; just assume the risks are insurable, and use expected values for uncertain outcomes; and just use partial equilibrium analysis even when the scale of impacts suggests general equilibrium analysis. In this chapter, we have suggested methods which, while they complicate the analysis, avoid these errors of oversimplification. However, the use of these more sophisticated methods – e.g., valid valuation schemes, and general equilibrium analysis – is justified only when there are good reasons to believe that the simple and obvious methods would be seriously misleading.

When serious uncertainty or gross ignorance pertains to the effects of ecosystem disturbance, this problem cannot be addressed adequately by standard benefit cost methods. A more promising approach is to embed the cost-benefit analysis in a decision framework that includes precautionary principles. Examples include a safe minimum standard of conversation and a focus on revocable strategies that can be reversed should bad outcomes appear on the horizon.

References

Böhringer, Christoph, and Thomas F. Rutherford. 1996. Carbon taxes with exemptions in an open economy: a general equilibrium analysis of the German tax initiative. *Journal of Environmental Economics and Management*. 31: 189-203.

Hushak, Leroy, and Yuming Deng. 1996. *Costs of Alternative Zebra Mussel Control Strategies: The Case of Great lakes Surface Water Users.* Ohio Sea Grant College Program, The Ohio State University.

Jorgenson, Dale W. 1998. *Econometric General Equilibrium Modeling.* Cambridge, MA: MIT Press.

Keppner, Sandra, and Theriot Edwin. March1997. *A Recommended Control Strategy for Round Goby, Negobius melanostomus, in the Illinios Waterway System.* Prepared for the Aquatic Nuisance Task Force.

Randall, A. 1987. Total economic value as a basis for policy. *Transactions of the American Fisheries Society* 116:325-335.

Randall, A. 1992. 'A total value framework for benefit estimation' in *Valuing Wildlife Resources in Alaska.* Edited by G. L. Peterson, C.S. Swanson, D.W. Mccollum and M.H. Thomas. Boulder, CO: Westview Press.

Randall, A., J. Hoehn, and C. S. Swanson. 1990. *Estimating the Recreational, Visual, Habitat, and Quality of Life Benefits of Tongass National Forest.* General Technical Report RM-192. Fort Collins, CO: USDA Forest Service.

Schneider, D.W., C.D. Ellis and K.S. Cummings. 1998. A transportation model assessment of the risk to native mussel communities from zebra mussel spread. Conservation Biology 12: 788-800.

Sparks, Richard and Ellen Marsden. 1995. *Invasive Species in the Mississippi River.* Northeast-Midwest Economic Review, June.

Stoeckel, James, et al. 1996. *Establishment of Daphnia lumholtzi (an exotic zooplankter) in the Illinois River.* Journal of Freshwater Ecology 11:3.

Stoeckel, James, Schneider, Soeken, Blodgett and Sparks. 1997. Larval dynamics of a riverine metapopulation: implications for zebra mussel recruitment, dispersal, and control in a large-river system. Journal of North American Benthology Society 16(3):586-601.

Chapter 10

Measuring the Value of Health Improvements From Great Lakes Cleanup[22]

e xposure to pollutants in the Great Lakes region can have significant effects on human health. Some forms of pollution affect humans directly, through the air we breathe and the water we drink. Other forms of pollution affect humans indirectly, for example, through consumption of contaminated fish. Indeed, the weight of evidence is that persistent toxic substances, such as polychlorinated biphenols (PCBs) and dioxin-like substances found in Great Lakes fish, can cause neurobehavioral and developmental problems.

All individuals would agree that decreasing exposure to potentially harmful pollution is beneficial, but there is significant disagreement about how to measure the benefits, and specifically whether to measure benefits in monetary terms or express it in physical terms only. Economists point out that monetary valuation is an appropriate way to measure the strength of individual preferences and a convenient way to compare very dissimilar benefit categories, and to compare benefits with costs, which are usually already denominated in monetary terms. Others argue that it is demeaning to try to value human health because they feel health (like the environment) should not be subjected to sacrifice or compromise. However, just as in the case of natural resource issues in the Great Lakes, we face scarce resources and competing priorities for controlling pollution and its effects on health. When tradeoffs are necessary, economics seems particularly well suited to provide some guidance about how this can be best accomplished.

Tradeoffs do not always need to be expressed in monetary terms. One example is when the effectiveness of a policy or course of action is to be measured according to a single criterion, such as the reduction in exposure to a specific pollutant. Then cost-effectiveness analysis is appropriate. This approach allows comparisons among alternative

---

[22] *Dallas Burtraw, Senior Fellow, and Alan Krupnick, Senior Fellow and Division Director in the Quality of the Environment Division at Resources for the Future in Washington DC.*

courses of action by measuring the improvement that can be achieved in nonmonetary terms per dollar of cost (i.e., exposures per dollar). Other things being equal, those actions that can deliver the biggest bang for the buck should be pursued first.

In other cases, one may wish to compare dissimilar improvements, such as a reduction in exposure to air pollution with a reduction in exposure to water pollution, that can be achieved for a specific cost. This type of analysis also can be done in nonmonetary terms, but some means must be found for comparing potentially quite different risks associated with the different types of exposures. One example is triage, practiced in the hospital or the battlefield, wherein scarce resources (i.e., physician time and emergency room space) are allocated on the basis of expected risks of death and the risk reduction that intervention can bring. Less dramatic tradeoffs involving health but made entirely in nonmonetary terms are an everyday fact of life.

Another type of analysis could involve decisions about the level of expenditures or the level of environmental protection that will be pursued. When the level of the budget is variable, the decision involves a comparison with the cost of increasing the budget. Setting the level of the budget, or alternatively setting the level of protection for the environment or public health, introduces the realm of cost-benefit analysis.

In this chapter, we describe methods to measure health benefits in monetary and nonmonetary terms in the context of reductions in pollutants as part of a program to improve the environment in the Great Lakes. Freeman (1993) offers more in-depth treatment of valuation for environmental improvements. Kopp et al. (1997) take a close look at issues related to cost-benefit analysis. Johnson et al. (1998) provide a good survey of the toxicological and epidemiological literature relevant to persistent toxic substances affecting the Great Lakes.

PRINCIPLES OF VALUATION

Two ideas are central to the valuation of changes in human health. First, because a given public policy decision rarely leads to major changes in health status, the data that economists need in order to estimate values are only for small changes in health status or in the risk of a major change in health status. For example, an incident of the flu with its associated symptoms may be thought of as a small change in health status; a 1 in 10,000 change in the risk of death is a small change in risk of a major change in health status (given that the baseline risk of death is 80 in 10,000). Individuals rarely face decisions about major changes in health status, and observed behavior cannot provide data on how to value such changes. But individuals regularly make decisions reflected in their behavior that reveals their willingness to accept health risk, and this provides the data economists need to estimate the value of changes in risk.

Second, the economic notion of value is a measure of how an individual or group would trade one thing for another. The notion of a numerical value per se does not exist, and there is no meaning to "economic value" outside the context in which trade-offs have to be made. The data that economists use to assess value come from the choices that individuals make in such contexts. Absent a meaningful choice, there is no meaningful notion of economic value.

These two ideas are important because they help to dispel a common misperception that economics places value on human life (or health). Indeed, an economist is no more capable of assessing the value of a human life than is any other individual, and to suggest that public policy does so is unacceptable in democratic society.

Instead, economists collect and interpret data about how the choices individuals make reflect those individuals' attitudes toward risks. Individuals (and society) regularly make decisions that affect relative health risks. In doing so, we make a choice about the probability of one outcome or another.

We describe methods to measure health benefits in monetary and nonmonetary terms in the context of reductions in pollutants as part of a program to improve the environment in the Great Lakes.

For instance, sidewalks always can be constructed to be wider and with curbs cut higher to provide additional margins of safety for pedestrians. Current standards may be deemed acceptable, but they do not entirely eliminate the risk of a runaway automobile striking a pedestrian. By assessing the probability of such an unfortunate event, and considering the cost of changing that probability through wider sidewalks or higher curbs, one can infer the value society (or at least the Department of Public Works) places on avoiding accidents, including accidental death. Similar choices are made by individuals, in deciding the level of risks that are acceptable in various contexts, such as speeding up on a highway to save time. These choices offer data for the consideration of policies to reduce pollution and their effect on health through changes in the incidence of morbidity (disease) and premature mortality (death).

The notion of value that is useful in economic analysis is the individual's willingness to pay for small reductions in risk (or small changes in health status). In technical terms, this measure should reflect the maximum amount of money that could be subtracted from an individual's income while providing for an environmental improvement, such that one is just indifferent between this outcome and the prior situation with more income but without the environmental improvement. Because this is a maximum amount, any environmental improvement that costs the individual less than this amount would actually leave him or her better off. Often it is not possible to identify this perfect measure, and in practice one must cobble together estimates.

TECHNIQUES FOR VALUATION

The techniques for measuring the benefits of improvements in health fall into two general categories. The *stated preference technique* involves asking people questions in surveys to elicit, either directly or indirectly, estimates of the willingness to pay for the improvement in question. Examples include contingent valuation (CV) methods, which are structured surveys meant to elicit preferences in monetary terms when confronted with a choice, and conjoint analysis, an approach used extensively to elicit preferences for particular combinations of attributes that describe health status and alternatives.

The second category is the *revealed preference technique*. In this case, economists collect data about actual behavior either in the marketplace or elsewhere to discern willingness to pay for improvements in risk or health status.

When properly applied, the stated or revealed preference analyses are generally acknowledged to produce valid results, but both techniques are subject to limitations. In response to the constructed nature of stated preference surveys, respondents might provide inaccurate information due to poorly understood questions or poorly designed questions that invite strategic behavior on the part of those surveyed. Revealed preference techniques, though based on actual consumer behavior, are restricted to the observed market conditions. As a result, they may be of limited value in situations where the conditions to be analyzed differ substantially from current markets. An analysis based on a combination of revealed and stated preference data can draw from the strengths of each of the two methods.

One type of revealed preference data, though at best a weak proxy for willingness to pay, is the measure of cost of illness. This approach involves accounting for out-of-pocket and in-kind expenses associated with specific health effects. These could include doctor visits, medicine, hospital admissions, and lost work days as well as information not reflected by consumers' actions, such as charges paid by insurance companies. The approach is inadequate because it fails to account for the discomfort and inconvenience of an illness. Obviously, individuals would be willing to pay in excess of their cost of an illness, sometimes substantially so, in order to avoid the illness altogether. Also, the availability of insurance can affect individuals' actions and the level of care taken to avoid harm to themselves or others, thereby distorting the measure of cost. The distribution of income also affects this measure of cost because the limitation on the ability to pay imparts a limit on the measure of cost of illness. Typically this aspect of income distribution is addressed by using a measure that represents the average for the population (across all income groups), but when a harm or illness befalls a low-income group disproportionately, the measure of cost of illness will reflect the distribution of income.

Extended to the consideration of premature mortality, a cost of illness approach translates into the measure of lost earnings. This old-fashioned approach to valuation relies on a calculation of the present discounted value of future earnings that were lost due to premature mortality. Sometimes this approach has been used as the basis for actual compensation for job-related fatalities, with the result that the death of individuals who differ only in their annual income would lead to different levels of compensation. Consequently this approach is found to be offensive on both equity and efficiency grounds.

More complete willingness-to-pay estimates for morbidity and mortality sometimes can be drawn from observed behavior in product markets, the workplace, or other settings. This approach may be called the *averting behavior approach*. In product markets, economists observe individuals making decisions about products with differing safety attributes and different prices. From this data, one can infer willingness to pay for small reductions in risk. Values can be placed on any steps individuals take to avoid some bad outcome as a proxy of the willingness to pay to avoid that outcome.

For instance, if someone purchases bottled water to reduce the potential for consumption of pollutants in the local water supply, the added costs of their water bill may have some relationship to their willingness to pay to avoid the health effect. A problem with this approach concerns separating out the joint effects of a given product. For instance, bottled water may taste better, and some of the full willingness to pay may be due to this attribute. Similarly, the purchase of a smoke detector affects multi-

Obviously, individuals would be willing to pay in excess of their cost of an illness, sometimes substantially so, in order to avoid the illness altogether.

ple risks such as the risk of death, injury, and expected losses of property; as a result, its value cannot be applied to just one of these risks.

In the workplace, a variety of attributes — including workplace safety — distinguish among jobs. When it is possible to control for all the other distinctions, one can look at differences in workplace safety and differences in wages to calculate the compensating wage differential between relatively safer or more dangerous jobs or occupations. This differential reflects the additional wages that are required to entice an average worker to accept additional risk. Under the assumption that individuals are well-informed of such risk differences and are free to choose among employment alternatives (assumptions that often do not hold), then one can infer a willingness to pay to avoid such risks. The outcome of a process of valuation typically is an estimate of the willingness to pay in monetary terms for a small reduction in risk.

THE VALUE OF A STATISTICAL LIFE

The policy analyst can extrapolate from these data to provide an estimate of the value of a statistical event. Often workers have the opportunity to make choices about activities in the workplace or their job classification. Part of that choice may reflect considerations about relative safety risks and the relative wages in different jobs. The compensating wage differential is defined as the difference in wage that is sufficient to entice a worker to accept a less desirable job, such as one with a greater risk to worker safety. Economists sometimes rely on this kind of data from occupational choices to calculate the value of statistical life. This technique is referred to as the hedonic labor market approach.

Imagine that we observe two occupational categories, and we are able to control statistically for all the non-safety related differences between these jobs to find the difference in wage associated with differences in safety. We find the difference to be $500 per year and to be associated with an increase in the risk of a fatal accident of 1 in 10,000 per year. We can divide the difference in wage by the difference in risk to obtain the implicit value of a statistical life in the following way:

Though conceptually simple, this type of calculation has plenty of practical problems when used as a measure of preferences for reducing mortality risks. Workers may not have the economic freedom to choose among occupational alternatives. Further, it is not easy to control for all the differences in occupational categories unrelated to safety that may be contributing to differences in wages. Also, one must account for the risk of injury separately from accounting for the risk of mortality. Other factors can complicate the statistics, including differences in age and sex, and there is evidence that workers sort themselves by a willingness-to-accept risk. If the least risk-averse individuals chose dangerous jobs then there would be a bias in applying the relevant wage differential that would understate the compensating wage differential among the entire population.

COMPARISONS WITHOUT VALUATION

For a variety of reasons, a nonmonetary measure of environmental benefits may be preferred in public policy discussions. One reason may be that participants feel it "cheapens" the intrinsic value of health to place a value on it. Another reason may be that monetary values cannot be estimated when one cannot identify or construct meaningful choices that reveal how people view risk tradeoffs in monetary terms. The relation between health risk and monetary values is an abstract and difficult one. Psychologists find that individuals typically have an easier time and provide more replicable answers in making comparisons between more similar objects or concepts. In psychology this is known as the *compatibility hypothesis*, which suggests that calculation of and consistent judgment about tradeoffs is facilitated when comparing risks or outcomes with similar attributes. Furthermore, values may be more acceptable in the policy context if they are expressed in terms of relative risks rather than in monetary terms.

Conjoint analysis is a stated preference method designed to elicit choices among alternatives without necessarily relating those alternatives to a money value. For example, in one study, individuals with family members who had chronic lung disease were asked to make choices over living in one of two cities: one with a greater chance of dying in an auto accident, the other with a greater chance of developing chronic bronchitis. The result was a measure of willingness to trade a risk of a chronic condition for a risk of accidental death. The authors went further by translating these measures to monetary terms by asking for the tradeoff between the risk of chronic bronchitis and the cost of living in the cities (Krupnick and Cropper 1992). Another ongoing effort is using conjoint analysis to ask individuals to compare and rank episodes of various types of health impairments, in order to analyze attitudes toward disease that can result from exposure to air pollution (Desvousges et al. 1996).

The comparison of one type of impairment to health with another may seem difficult, at best. However, surprising evidence indicates that individuals, at least trained health professionals, from different cultures and different parts of the world have consistent attitudes toward the relative severity of dissimilar diseases. An ongoing study by the World Health Organization (WHO) and the Harvard School of Public Health is exploring attitudes toward disease in attempting to assess priorities for public health expenditures around the world (Murray and Lopez 1996). The study convened focus groups of health professionals from a number of countries. In order to establish a ranking for expenditures of funds for assistance, these groups were asked to deliberate over the severity of diseases. The groups arrived at remarkably similar results even when representing large cultural diversity, suggesting that trained health professionals from different cultures can make consistent decisions involving difficult choices about health effects when the choice context is meaningful and well-informed. Whether this consistency would extend to society in general is a matter for future study. In addition, the study focused on ranking public health outcomes as opposed to private risk rankings, which is the more relevant measure for cost-benefit analysis.

VALUATION OF POTENTIAL HEALTH EFFECTS OF POLLUTION IN THE GREAT LAKES

The uncertainties implicit in analyzing health risks pose especially difficult challenges for public policy, but much of the difficulty lies outside of economic analysis. In order for economists to estimate the willingness to pay for changes in health risk, individuals need only to have a fairly precise idea of health status alternatives. However, to relate this willingness to pay for changes in risk (i.e., changes in health status) to a willingness to pay for changes in pollution emissions or discharges one needs a great deal more information from disciplines other than economics. The identification of risks requires knowledge about:

- Changes in emissions or discharges,
- How these affect changes in concentrations of pollutants in various environmental media (e.g., water, air, soils),
- How these affect changes in exposure, and
- How health status responds to changes in exposure.

With this information in place, one can apply economic estimates of changes in health status to changes upstream in the causal chain relating emissions and health status.

An issue of particular interest to the Great Lakes region is the health risk associated with consumption of fish that is potentially contaminated with various pollutants. Although an environmental pathway relating how changes in emissions would lead to changes in health effects is well established in qualitative terms, the quantitative relationships are uncertain.

Another type of health effect we consider in this chapter is that resulting from exposure to a conventional air pollutant such as particulate matter that has a less uncertain effect on health than, say, the effect of mercury operating through fish consumption. Air pollution is of general interest across the country, but it also has a special relationship to the Great Lakes because control of conventional air pollutants can simultaneously lead to reduced emissions of hazardous air pollutants that are thought to contribute to contamination of sport fish. Conversely, we may find that policies designed to reduce emissions and contamination of sport fish lead to direct benefits that are difficult to quantify; but they may simultaneously produce indirect benefits such as reduced exposure to conventional air pollutants that can be quantified and valued with greater confidence.

Fish Consumption

The discovery of contaminated sport fish in the Great Lakes in the early 1970s prompted the health agencies in the Great Lakes states and in Canada to advise that individuals reduce or eliminate consumption of the most contaminated fish. Today all of the Great Lakes states issue consumption advisories for Great Lakes sport fish. Consumption advisories for sport fish are triggered by mercury and certain halogenated organic compounds such as PCBs, DDT and its metabolites (DDD and DDE), dieldrin, dioxins, and chlordane. These chemicals are labeled persistent toxic substances because they do not biodegrade in the environment. Unless sequestered in sediment deposits or elsewhere, they remain available for biological uptake through different pathways of exposure, and they bioaccumulate at the top levels of the food chain, including in fish populations in the Great Lakes. Fish consumption has been identified as the major route of exposure to these chemicals. The weight of evidence clearly indicates populations continue to be exposed to persistent toxic substances in the Great Lakes basin and that health consequences are associated with these exposures. The health implications are summarized in Johnson et al. (1998).

The U.S. Environmental Protection Agency (EPA 1996) has identified fifteen pollutants that are of concern, including pesticides, metal compounds, chlorinated organic compounds, and nitrogen compounds. Most are bioaccumulative and persistent in the environment. Concentrations of these compounds are especially high in tissues of large, predatory species such as lake trout and salmon. Tissue concentrations of these compounds can run as high as 100,000 times the concentrations in surrounding water. These concentrations can then be passed on to humans who eat the fish. Schantz et al. (1996) found that individuals who consumed Great Lakes sport fish for more than 15 years had two to four times more pollutants in their blood serum than did those who did not eat fish. Jensen (1987) found that PCBs in blood serum increased with age and with the number of meals in which fish was consumed per year.

These pollutants are associated with deleterious effects on many target organs in humans and animals, including the liver, kidney, nervous system, endocrine system, reproductive organs, and immunological system. Because humans do not metabolize these compounds easily, they are stored in body tissues. When a woman becomes pregnant, these compounds are readily transferred across the placenta to the developing fetus. In addition, as a result of consumption of contaminated fish, high levels of PCBs and DDT have occurred and been measured in the breast milk of some Great Lakes residents. Hence, children of exposed mothers are especially susceptible.

Some of these substances may be developmental toxics. Subtle abnormalities (e.g., poorer motor reflex, impaired visual recognition) as well as lower birth weight and smaller head circumference have been reported in the children of women exposed to PCBs on the job (Taylor et al. 1989) as well as to DDT and mercury from environmental exposures. These abnormalities have also been reported in children of women who were regular consumers of Great Lake sport fish prior to and during pregnancies, compared to a nonexposed group (Fein et al. 1984; Jacobson et al. 1990). They are also confirmed by differences in the level of PCBs measured in umbilical cord blood. A recent re-examination of children participating in one of the largest studies (Lake Michigan Maternal/Infant Cohort Study) found that the neurodevelopmental deficits observed in infancy persisted through age 11 years (Jacobson and Jacobson 1996), in the form of lower intelligence quotient (IQ) scores and reading level, and poorer memory and attention span.

Humphrey (1988) found that higher blood serum PCBs in pregnant women were associated with a greater rate of infectious illnesses in their infants, and Tryphonas (1995) found a correlation between infection incidence and fish consumption in pregnancy. Within the past several years, studies published in medical journals indicated a decline in the male sperm count and fertility over time, and shorter menstrual cycles associated with more frequent fish consumption (Mendola et al. 1997). Studies have indicated a direct effect of reduced conception success as a result of larger Great Lakes fish consumption in male partners (Courval et al. 1997). Some studies have identified certain chemicals — termed endocrine disrupters — as one culprit (Colborn et al. 1996), although this issue is highly contentious and EPA has convened a special panel to consider it. Exposure to certain chemicals prior to or during pregnancy may affect the development of the reproductive system of the fetus, leading to reproductive impairments later in life. Consequences of exposure thus occur in generations following the generation exposed to the chemicals.

Finally, several types of cancer have been associated with occupational exposure to PCBs, although causality has not been established. Several limited epidemiological studies have indicated a possible association of pesticide exposure with cancer. In discussing valuation of health effects, we focus first on reproductive issues and then turn to cancer.

Valuation of Reproductive Effects

In this section, we describe the capability of economics to value changes in health status of the type that have been described above. First we discuss affects on fertility and then effects on child development. The section draws in part on Cannon et al. (1996).

Fertility. The benefits associated with a reduction in exposure to these chemicals depend on how the chemicals affect the reproductive process. The value placed on current fertility can be represented by potential parents' willingness to pay for an increased probability of a successful pregnancy. Similarly, the value placed on future fertility can be estimated by parents' willingness to pay for normal reproductive ability in their children.

Different techniques are required to estimate different willingness to pay values. Estimation of the willingness to pay to reduce the probability that one's children will experience reproductive difficulties is limited to stated preference techniques. Estimation of the welfare change associated with a change in exposure to chemicals is best estimated through methods such as conjoint analysis or CV surveys that elicit information concerning how much individuals would be willing to pay to reduce the probability that their children would have reproductive impairments. In the sense that the conditions are long-term and have large perceived costs, such a survey might be similar to stated preference methods used to determine willingness to pay to reduce the likelihood of low birth weight or birth defects.

When estimating the willingness to pay to reduce current reproductive impairment, information based on couples' actions in addition to stated responses may be utilized. One source of data is expenditures by infertile couples on infertility treatments that reflect the value placed on moving from a state of infertility to fertility. Infertility is defined as the inability to conceive after 12 months of intercourse without contracep-

Few existing studies have used stated preference techniques to directly estimate the benefits associated with a reduction in the health effects under consideration. Estimation of the willingness to pay to reduce the probability that one's children will experience reproductive difficulties is limited to stated preference techniques.

tion. Using this definition, the rate of infertility for U.S. couples between the ages of 15 and 44 was about 7.9 percent, or 1 couple in 12 in 1988.

Few existing studies have used stated preference techniques to directly estimate the benefits associated with a reduction in the health effects under consideration. Existing analyses of revealed preference have estimated willingness to pay for in vitro fertilization (IVF) infertility treatments. Charges for a single episode of IVF have been estimated to be roughly $8,000. (The literature has not examined willingness to pay for more common infertility treatment procedures.) A couple's expended effort on infertility treatments includes both money and any number of nonpecuniary items, including the couple's time. The opportunity cost of the couple's time can be objectively estimated based on wage rates and time estimates. Other indirect costs such as physical discomfort and psychological stress are more difficult to quantify and may change over time as the couple progresses through the treatment.

Due to the uncertainty associated with the success of infertility treatments, the perceived benefits and costs of treatment are important in determining whether treatment will result in a net benefit to the couple. A couple that elects to begin infertility treatment is aware of the underlying common probability of success in the general population but not to themselves. Heterogeneous preferences for childbearing result in different perceived benefits of treatment across couples. Although success rates vary by the treatment procedure, it is not likely that a treatment will be successful after the first episode, and many couples undergo multiple episodes of infertility treatment.

One study used stated preference methods through a CV survey in which respondents were asked several different hypothetical questions related to IVF treatment (Neumann and Johannesson 1994). On average, conditional on the knowledge that they were infertile, respondents were willing to pay $17,730 for IVF treatment having a 10 percent chance of success. Across all individuals and without knowledge of their fertility status, individuals were willing to make a one-time payment of $865 for insurance providing IVF if needed. The study also found that individuals would be willing to pay $32 per year in taxes for a public program giving 1,200 couples per year a 10 percent chance of successful fertilization.

In addition, survey respondents were asked to compare infertility risk reduction with mortality risk reduction by choosing between two uses of public funds: providing IVF coverage for state residents or reducing highway fatalities. The respondents identified a program resulting in 300 IVF babies as equivalent to one reducing auto deaths by 35 per year. This comparison illustrates one way of estimating an economic value without using dollar values.

Child and embryo development. Although child development may be affected by exposure to the same pollutants that invite concern about infertility, substantial differences exist with regard to the factors determining the proper valuation methodology. For example, although many infertile couples desire a successful pregnancy, few are willing to obtain this goal irrespective of cost. A portion of infertile couples choose not to incur the costs of treatment and remain childless or choose an alternative such as adoption, and others drop out of treatment before obtaining a successful outcome. It is not likely, however, that a couple having a child that is low birth weight or that has birth defects will choose not to provide the needed treatment for that child. One would expect that the demand curves for treatment of low birth weight and birth defects are much less sensitive to cost than the demand curves for infertility treatments.

The two types of effects also differ with regard to the question of whose welfare is relevant to the analysis. Although infertility can be modeled in terms of the effect on the welfare of a couple, child development has an impact on the child and the parents, and hence benefits are best framed in terms of the family. In addition to the obvious costs incurred by the child, medical costs, lost time, and emotional distress are all costs borne by the parents for at least a portion of the child's life. In some cases, costs may be borne by the parents after the child has reached adulthood.

Unfortunately, the studies that are available to establish the benefits of reducing risks of these health effects have concentrated on the incidence of low birth weight and birth defects. Low birth weight is defined as 2500 g or less, very low birth weight as 1500 g or less, and extremely low birth weight as 1000 g or less. Low birth weight is a major cause of neonatal and infant mortality in the United States. Low birth weight survivors are more likely to have health problems than those born at a heavier birth weight. In addition, they are more likely to experience preschool developmental delays and additional adverse effects later in life (Chaikind and Corman 1991).

Table 10.1.

INCREMENTAL DIRECT COSTS OF LOW BIRTH WEIGHT AMONG CHILDREN FROM BIRTH TO AGE 15 IN 1988.

Age Group	Cost Type	Mean Cost per Low Birth Weight Child ($)	Number of Low Birth Weight Children	Total Cost ($)
Infancy	Health Care	15,000	271,000	4,000,000,000
1 to 2 years	All	not estimated	500,000	not estimated
3 to 5 years	Health Care	290	820,000	240,000,000
3 to 5 years	Child Care	180	820,000	150,000,000
6 to 10 years	Health Care	470	1,300,000	610,000,000
6 to 15 years	Special Education	150	2,400,000	360,000,000
11 to 15 years	Grade Repetition	45	1,100,000	50,000,000
Total			*4,000,000*	*5,410,000,000*

Source: Lewit et al. (1995)

The studies that have estimated the cost of low birth weight are limited to cost-of-illness analyses. One study estimated the incremental health care, education, and child care cost of the 3.5 to 4 million children aged 0 to 15 years who were born at low birth weight (about 7 percent of all children in that age group) between $5.5 and $6 billion (Lewit et al. 1995). This study is summarized in Table 10.1.[23]

Using similar methods, the cost of 17 major birth defects and cerebral palsy was estimated by another study to be $8 billion in 1992 (Waitzman et al. 1996). Cost estimates were based on direct medical and special service costs, and indirect costs of increased mortality and morbidity. Medical costs included inpatient, outpatient, and long-term care costs. Special services included developmental services such as day care centers, counseling, and special education. Mortality and morbidity costs were represented by lost productivity. The total cost of a birth defect was defined as the discounted sum of all of the component incremental direct and indirect costs, assuming a 5 percent discount rate. As noted, however, these studies can provide only a lower bound estimate of the true costs associated with the incidence of these effects.

[23] *The difference between the total in the table and in the text reflects an estimate for the missing 1 to 2 years age group.*

Another study examined the cost of mercury exposure by using estimates of the cost of compensating education and IQ loss (in terms of lower earnings and labor market participation), plus medical costs (Rowe et al. 1995). There are no studies that relate fetal mercury studies to IQ loss, although IQ deficits are likely to be associated with psychomotor retardation observed from mercury exposure. The study assumed a relationship between predicted psychomotor retardation and IQ loss, and calculated the present-value costs at a 3 percent discount rate associated with IQ point loss. Finally, it applied a willingness to pay to cost-of-illness ratio of 2 in order to reflect unmeasured aspects in calculating total damages form mercury. The central estimate per case was $289,000 (1992 dollars).

Valuation of Cancer Effects

As with other health effects, one can draw on several methods for valuation of reduced incidence of cancer. The traditional approach is to apply a willingness-to-pay estimate associated with accidental deaths to an estimate of the reduced annual deaths associated with a change in pollution exposure. Several problems with this approach should be considered. First, there is a long latency period for cancer between exposure to potential carcinogens and the manifestation of disease and deaths. If people value current health more than future health, this suggests that the willingness-to-pay estimates from accidental death studies should be revised downward for cancer fatalities. A related concern is that older people with fewer years of life expectancy are primarily the people affected by cancer (about 70% of cancer mortality occurs in individuals over age 65 years). Studies of the willingness to pay to avoid accidental death at work and elsewhere apply to individuals who average about 40 years old. Several studies indicate that the value of a statistical life falls somewhat for older individuals.

In contrast, work by psychologists on risk rankings suggests that people might be more willing to pay to avoid death from a "dreaded" disease, like cancer, than one involving a more familiar cause (like an auto accident). In addition, we are here abstracting from the willingness to pay to avoid the morbidity associated with cancer, which can be treated as a separate issue.

To value morbidity associated with cancer, researchers have relied primarily on cost-of-illness approaches. Hartunian et al. (1981) estimated average direct costs per cancer patient to be $49,000, including medical and administrative costs. Indirect costs including change in earnings, and the provision of household services associated with nonfatal cancers was estimated by Rowe et al. (1995) to be $87,000. The total cost of illness for nonfatal cancers is the sum, or approximately $136,000. Rowe et al. (1995) amend this by applying a willingness to pay to cost-of-illness ratio of 1.5, resulting in an estimate of $204,000 per case. Other approaches are possible, however. For example, in principle, the conjoint analyses discussed above could be used to obtain the willingness to pay to avoid a statistical case of cancer.

Air Pathways

Valuation of health effects associated with air pollution is somewhat more straightforward than valuation of health effects associated with fish consumption. In addition to uncertainties that apply to air pollutants, the prediction of changes in health effects with respect to fish consumption is complicated by the role of the aquatic ecological system. Also, health effects from air pollution are thought to be more prominent, have been more widely studied, and are better understood.

To illustrate valuation of health effects from air pollutants we focus on the suspected effects of particulate matter, one of six so-called "criteria" air pollutants regulated primarily for their effects on health under the Clean Air Act and its Amendments. EPA has authored Criteria Documents for each pollutant that contain thousands of pages evaluating toxicological, clinical, and epidemiological studies that relate particular criteria pollutants to a variety of health endpoints.

Mortality Effects

Strong evidence indicates that exposure to particulate air pollution is associated with premature mortality, but there continues to be significant controversy over its precise measure. Concentration-response functions can be drawn from the literature that estimate the change in risk of premature mortality that results from a small change in particulate concentrations, although one can have much more confidence in the efficacy of these functions with respect to small changes than for large changes.

The most common approach to valuation is to apply a value of a statistical life to the change in the number of statistical deaths predicted to result from a change in particulate concentrations. A key choice is the value to apply. Estimates drawn from labor market studies yield values ranging from $1 million to $9 million, the upper end exceeding values drawn from CV studies of accidental death risks. CV studies may be somewhat more appropriate for valuing mortality risks in the environmental health context. For example, Jones-Lee et al. (1985) asked about willingness to pay for riding with a bus company with a better safety record than another bus company. They identified that an adjustment that would lower the value of a statistical life is appropriate for individuals in older age groups, who are the primary subjects of premature mortality resulting from particulates. They show a declining ratio of willingness to pay with age, from age 70 years to age 40 years, of about 80 percent. Moore and Viscusi (1988) show a steeper decline in willingness to pay, with a ratio of about 40%. Accounting for these considerations in a recent examination focused specifically on particulates, Burtraw et al. (1998) used a probability distribution to indicate the range of possible values, with a mean of $3.1 million.

In the recent Regulatory Impact Analysis (RIA) for Ozone and Particulate National Ambient Air Quality Standards (1997), EPA used a value of $4.8 million (1990 dollars) for the high value of a statistical life applied to deaths related to particulate exposure. However, they have also identified an adjustment to account for the age of the affected population and other problems with the underlying basis of the $4.8 million figure, suggesting a low value of $2 million might be more appropriate. EPA's RIA used a discounted life-year approach, working with the estimate of $2 million per statistical life to derive a value of a life-year of $120,000.

The obvious mismatch between accidental deaths and deaths from cancer or particulate exposures has raised serious concerns about the appropriateness of using the traditional valuation techniques (Thurston et al. 1997; Krupnick et al. 1998). The research frontier involves expressing excess deaths in terms of changes in life expectancy and using survey research to estimate people's willingness to pay today to increase their life expectancy (mostly from risk reductions late in life). A controversial study has estimated that the willingness to pay today for a treatment that increases life expectancy by one year beginning at age 75 (where life expectancy is 10 years normally but would be extended in this scenario to 11 years) is about $1,500 over the adult population in Sweden. According to Johannesson and Johansson (1997) and for their particular case only, this implies a value of statistical life of $70,000 to $130,000. Until this literature matures, the preferable approach is to treat these values as probability distributions and to explore the sensitivity of results to alternative values in these distributions.

Morbidity Effects
Dozens of morbidity effects have been identified with particulate pollution, including acute and chronic cardiopulmonary and respiratory effects, and prevalence of chronic illness. Health endpoints that can be valued separately include changes in chronic bronchitis risk, respiratory hospital admissions, emergency room visits, asthma attacks, restricted activity days, and many others. To apply values to these endpoints is conceptually simple. Unit values for various endpoints are drawn from the literature and multiplied by the expected change in the incidence of that effect.

Table 10.2.

A SAMPLING OF VALUES USED IN HEALTH BENEFITS VALUATION.

Endpoint	Monetary Value	Original Study or Source	Referenced in
Cardiac hospital admission	in 1992 $14,000		Chestnut (1995)
Respiratory hospital admission	in 1989 $6,306	Krupnick and Cropper (1989)	Lee et al. (1995)
Restricted activity day	in 1990 $51.38	Krupnick and Kopp (1989)	Lee et al. (1995)
Adult chronic bronchitis	in 1989 $210,000	Viscusi et al. (1991) Krupnick and Cropper (1992)	Lee et al. (1995)
Acute cough	in 1990 $1.26 (33%) 7 (34%) 13.84 (33%)	Dickie et al. (1987) Tolley et al. (1986) Loehman et al. (1979)	EPA (1996)
Phlegm day	in 1990 $3.77 (33%) 10 (34%) 36.44 (33%)	Dickie et al. (1987) Tolley et al. (1986)	EPA (1996)
Eye irritation day	in 1990 $15.72 (33%) 15.72 (34%) 34.88 (33%)	Tolley et al. (1986)	EPA (1996)
Child chronic bronchitis	in 1989 $132	Krupnick and Cropper (1989)	Lee et al. (1995)
Minor respiratory-related restricted activity day	in 1990 $22 (central estimate)	Krupnick and Kopp (1989)	Chestnut (1994)
Respiratory restricted activity day	in 1990 $45 (central estimate)	Harrison and Nichols (1990)	NERA (1994)
Asthma attack	in 1990 $31 (central estimate)	Rowe and Chestnut (1985)	EPA (1996)

Source: Bloyd et al. 1996.

Willingness-to-pay (as opposed to cost-of-illness) estimates are available for only about half of identified endpoints. Also, these estimates characteristically have relied on small sample sizes; there is limited variation in the health effect studied; and few studies that have tried to replicate previous results. However, they have been widely reviewed; there is some consistency across outcomes; and these reviews provide accessible interpretations of the results. Where the willingness-to-pay studies are weak, valuation must rely on cost-of-illness estimates. A summary of values used for a few illustrative endpoints are provided in Table 10.2.

EQUITY CONSIDERATIONS IN ECONOMIC VALUATION

A crucial step in valuation is the aggregation from measures of individual willingness to pay to a measure for society. In the most common applications, individuals are treated anonymously. No person's welfare is weighted more heavily than anyone else's, and health effects that are valued are treated consistently without regard to an individual's income or social status. In this sense, valuation methods are equitable, and most people find this a desirable feature.

Adjusting for Quality of Life and Life Expectancy

In some applications, equity considerations might suggest that differences among individuals should matter in valuation. In particular, the age and prior health status of individuals are factors that decision-makers might want to consider in accounting for the benefits of reduced pollution. These factors are relevant for efficiency as much as for equity.

Age at time of an incidence of disease (and sex, due to differing life expectancy) is an important equity consideration. The earlier example of triage is a case where a preference for allocating resources toward saving relatively younger lives is readily apparent. Age is also the one factor that distinguishes individuals in the WHO study described previously (Murray and Lopez 1996). In that study, diseases affecting different age groups were viewed differently by the health professionals in the study. A disease that struck a 23-year-old would be viewed differently than a disease that struck a 65-year-old, for two reasons. First, a higher number of healthy life-years would be lost in the former case; and, second, many of those years are viewed as especially precious in part because of responsibilities in child-rearing. The study coupled the relative ranking of the severity of disease with information about the number of healthy years that would be lost due to the disease. Comparing a healthy 23-year-old with a 65-year-old who already has an impaired health status and shortened life-expectancy would make these considerations even more poignant.

These equity considerations are not particular to the exercise of monetary valuation or even to the consideration of environmentally related exposure. Even if one stops short of valuation and restricts oneself to comparisons among types of health effects in order to prioritize the use of resources, as did the WHO study, one cannot escape a consideration of the equity issues.

Involuntary Exposures

To assess the possible tradeoffs in environmental protection, decision-makers also need information about the manner in which individuals are affected because many decision-makers and members of society feel involuntary exposures should be considered differently from voluntary ones. For example, the decision whether to wear a seat belt or to smoke cigarettes is perceived as an individual decision. However, inadvertent exposure to reckless drivers or second-hand cigarette smoke is a different matter, in the minds of many individuals, because risks are imposed on third parties without their consent and therefore should be given greater weight than risks that are accepted voluntarily. Although environmental exposures can be of either kind, often they are involuntary.

Effects on Sensitive Populations

Important equity considerations also emerge from the knowledge of who specifically will experience a change in health status as a result of pollution. An example from economic philosophy illuminates this distinction. Imagine yourself in a room of 1,000 persons. You are informed that with equal probability one of you will suffer a severe disease unless the group acts to prevent it. Imagine that the moderator has an envelope in his hand with the name of the affected individual. Presumably everyone in the room would report a positive willingness to pay to prevent this disease.

Now imagine that the moderator opens the envelope and identifies the individual before eliciting the willingness to pay to prevent this disease. Assuredly, the outcome would be different. The affected individual would be willing to pay substantially more, and others would have no selfish incentive to pay to prevent the disease. However, some would have an altruistic motive, lacking in the first scenario, to prevent the disease. By analogy, if a subpopulation is particularly sensitive to exposure from an environmental contaminant (whether because of some inherent trait or through circumstances beyond their control), the economic measure of society's willingness to pay may be larger. This could be attributable to the existence of an altruistic motive that adds to the economic efficiency measure of willingness to pay for statistical events.

For example, in the decision to consume sport fish from an area with a fish advisory recommending against consumption of fish caught, there is to some degree a voluntary risk-taking, which works against making special equity considerations. However, many would view consumption of contaminated fish by some populations to be an involuntary form of exposure, due to social and economic factors that limit the options that these individuals have available. Because Native American and lower income populations often have diets that include unusually high levels of fish consumption, special economic considerations emerge for public policy. Similar considerations apply to policies to regulate air pollution, where subpopulations have been identified to be particularly susceptible. When specific subpopulations can be identified to be at special risk, then an altruistic motive may emerge for addressing environmental problems.

CONCLUSION

Exposure to pollutants in the Great Lakes region can have direct effects on human health, through the air we breathe and the water we drink, and indirectly through consumption of contaminated fish. All individuals would agree that decreasing exposure to potentially harmful pollution is beneficial, but there is significant disagreement about how to measure the benefits, and specifically whether to measure benefits in monetary terms or express them in physical terms only.

When tradeoffs are necessary in making public policy, these tradeoffs do not always need to be expressed in monetary terms. The analysis of cost-effectiveness can be expressed as nonmonetary terms per dollar of cost (i.e., exposures per dollar) with the goal being to deliver the biggest bang for the buck should be pursued first. However, in other cases one may wish to compare dissimilar improvements, such as a reduction in exposure to air pollution with a reduction in exposure to water pollution, that can be achieved for a specific cost. This can be done in nonmonetary terms, but some means must be found for comparing potentially quite different risks associated with the different types of exposures. Finally, when the level of the budget is variable, the decision involves a comparison of benefits with the cost of increasing the budget. Setting the level of the budget, or alternatively setting the level of protection for the environment or public health, introduces the realm of cost-benefit analysis.

In this chapter we review methods to measure health benefits in monetary and nonmonetary terms in the context of reductions in pollutants as part of a program to improve the environment in the Great Lakes. The appropriate means of analysis depends on the type of policy question being addressed, and each approach has its limitations. However, taken together, these tools provide important input to public debate.

References

Bloyd, Cary, et al. 1996. *Tracking and Analysis Framework (TAF) Model Documentation and User's Guide*. ANL/DIS/TM-36. Illinois: Argonne National Laboratory.

Burtraw, Dallas, et al. 1998. Costs and benefits of reducing air pollutants related to acid rain. *Contemporary Economic Policy* 16:379-400.

Cannon, Matt, Raymond Kopp, and Alan Krupnick. 1996. Valuation of developmental and reproductive effects: a scoping study. Unpublished report. Washington, DC: Resources for the Future.

Chaikind, S., and H. Corman. 1991. The impact of low birth weight on special education costs. *Journal of Health Economics* 10(3):291-311.

Colborn, T., J. Myers, and D. Dumanoski. 1996. Our Stolen Future; *How We Are Threatening Our Fertility, Intelligence, and Survival; A Scientific Detective Story*. New York: Dutton.

Courval, J. M., et al. 1997. *Sport Caught Fish Consumption and Conception Failure in Michigan Anglers*. Health Conference '97 Great Lakes and St. Lawrence. Montreal, Quebec, Canada.

Desvousges, William H., et al. 1996. Using conjoint analysis and health-state classifications to estimate the value of health effects of air pollution: pilot test results and implications. *Triangle Economic Research*, December 20.

Fein, G. G., et al. 1984. Prenatal exposure to PCBs: effects on birth size and gestation age. *Journal of Pediatrics* 105:315-320.

Freeman, A. Myrick. 1993. *The Measurement of Environmental and Resource Values: Theory and Methods*. Washington, DC: Resources for the Future.

Hartunian, N. S., et al. 1981. "Cancer." Chapter 5 in *The Incidence and Economic Cost of Major Health Impairments*. Eds. N.S. Hartunian, S.N. Smart, and M.S. Thompson. Lexington, MA: D.C. Heath.

Humphrey, H. E. B. 1988. Chemical contaminants in the Great Lakes: the human health aspect. In *Toxic Contaminants and Ecosystem Health: A Great Lakes Focus*. Edited by Evans M. S. New York: Wiley, pp. 153-165.

Jacobson, J. L., and S. W. Jacobson. 1996. Intellectual impairment in children exposed to PCBs in utero. *New England Journal of Medicine* 335(11):783-789.

Jacobson, J.L., et al. 1990. Effects of in utero exposure to PCBs and related contaminants on cognitive functioning in young children. *Journal of Pediatrics* 116:38-45.

Jensen, A. A. 1987. PCBs, PCDDs, PCDFs in human milk, blood, and adipose tissue. *Science of the Total Environment* 64:259-293.

Johannesson, Magnus, and Per-Olov Johansson. 1997. Quality of life and the WTP for an increased life expectancy at an advanced age. *Journal of Public Economics* 65:219-228.

Johnson, B., et al. 1998. Public health implications of persistent toxic substances in the Great Lakes and St. Lawrence Basins. *Journal of Great Lakes Research* 24(2):698-722.

Jones-Lee, M. W., M. Hammerton, and P. R. Philips. 1985. The value of safety: results of a national sample survey. *The Economic Journal* 95:49-72.

Kopp, Raymond J., Alan J. Krupnick, and Michael Toman. 1997. *Cost-Benefit Analysis and Regulatory Reform: An Assessment of the Science and the Art*. Discussion Paper 97-19. Washington, DC: Resources for the Future.

Krupnick, Alan J., and Maureen Cropper. 1992. The effect of information on health risk valuation. *Journal of Risk and Uncertainty* 5: 29-48.

Krupnick, Alan, et al. 1998. *New Directions in Mortality Risk Valuation and Stated Preference Methods: Preliminary Results*. Paper presented at the First World Congress of Environmental and Natural Resource Economists, Venice, Italy.

Lewit, Eugene M., et al. 1995. The direct cost of low birth weight. *The Future of Children* 5(1):35-56.

Mendola, P., et al. 1997. Consumption of PCB-contaminated freshwater fish and shortened menstrual cycle. *American Journal of Epidemiology* 146(11):955-960.

Moore, M. J., and W. K. Viscusi. 1988. The quantity-adjusted value of life. *Economic Inquiry* 26:369-388.

Murray, Christopher, and Alan Lopez. 1996. *The Global Burden of Disease*. Cambridge, MA: Harvard University Press.

Neumann, Peter J., and Magnus Johannesson. 1994. Willingness to pay for in vitro fertilization: a pilot test using contingent valuation. *Medical Care* 32(7):686-699.

Rowe, Robert, et al. 1995. *New York State Environmental Externalities Cost Study*, prepared for ESEERCO. Project EP91-50. Prepared by RCG/Hagler, Bailly.

Schantz, S. L., et al. 1996. Neuropsychological assessment of an aging population of Great Lakes fisheaters. *Toxicology and Industrial Health* 12:403-417.

Taylor, P. R., et al. 1989. The relation of PCBs to birth weight and gestational age in the offspring of occupationally exposed mothers. *American Journal of Epidemiology* 129:395-406.

Thurston, George, et al. 1997. *Health and Environmental Impact Assessment Panel Report: The Health Benefits of Reducing Sulfur in Gasoline and Diesel Fuels*. Joint Industry/Government Study, Canadian Government, Ottawa, Canada.

Tryphonas, H. 1995. Immunotoxicity of PCBs in relation to Great Lakes. *Environmental Health Perspectives* 103(Suppl 9):35-46.

U.S. Environmental Protection Agency (EPA). 1996. *Regulatory Impact Analysis for Proposed Particulate Matter National Ambient Air Quality Standard (Draft)*. Research Triangle Park, NC: Innovative Strategies and Economics Group, Office of Air Quality Planning and Standards, EPA.

Waitzman, N. J., P. S. Romano, and R. M. Scheffler. 1996. *The Costs of Birth Defects: Estimates of the Value of Prevention*. Lanham, MD: University Press of America.

part IV:
Appendices

Great Lakes Web Sites and Valuation References

WEB SITES

Environment Canada, Environment and Economy
web site: http://www.cciw.ca/green-lane/env-econ/

Environmental Damage Valuation and Cost Benefit News Links
web site: http://people.delphi.com/kenacks/links.htm

Integrated Ecological Economic Modeling and Valuation of Watersheds
web site: http://kabir.cbl.umces.edu/PLM/

National Oceanic and Atmospheric Administration, Damage Assessment and Restoration Program
web site: http://www-orca.nos.noaa.gov/darp/

National Oceanic and Atmospheric Administration, National Sea Grant Office,
Coastal Environmental Economics Extention Network
web site: http://www.mdsg.umd.edu:80/MDSG/Extension/valuation/

Northeast-Midwest Institute
web site: http://www.nemw.org/

U.S. Environmental Protection Agency, Economy and Environment
web site: http://www.epa.gov/oppe/eaed/eedhmpg.htm

VALUATION REFERENCES FOR THE GREAT LAKES REGION

Air Quality
Chattopadhyay, Sudip. 1999. Forthcoming. Estimating the Demand for Air Quality: New Evidence Based on the Chicago Housing Market. Land Economics 75(1).

Aquatic Nuisance Species
Hushak, Leroy. 1997. Economics of Ruffe in the Great Lakes. Proceedings of the International Symposium on Biology and Management of Ruffe, March 21-23, 1997. (http://www.ansc.purdue.edu/sgnis/)

Hushak, L.J. and Y. Deng. 1997. Costs of Alternative Zebra Mussel Control Strategies: The Case of Great Lakes Surface Water Users. The Seventh International Zebra Mussel and Other Aquatic Nuisance Species Conference, New Orleans, Louisiana, January, 1997.

Leigh, Peter. 1997. Benefits and Costs of the Ruffe Control Program for the Great Lakes Fishery. Proceedings of the International Symposium on Biology and Management of Ruffe, March 21-23, 1997. (http://www.ansc.purdue.edu/sgnis/)

Meyer, Fred P. 1992. Potential for Economic Damage. Ruffe in the Great Lakes: A Threat to North American Fisheries. The Great Lakes Fishery Commission Ruffe Task Force Report.

O'Neill, Charles R. Jr. 1997. Economic Impact of Zebra Mussels—Results of the 1995 National Zebra Mussel Information Clearinghouse Study. Great Lakes Research Review. (http://www.ansc.purdue.edu/sgnis/)

Sun, Jian Feng. 1994. The Evaluation of Impacts of Colonization of Zebra Mussels on the Recreation Demand in Lake Erie. Proceedings of The Fourth International Zebra Mussel Conference, Madison, Wisconsin. (http://www.ansc.purdue.edu/sgnis/)

Beaches/Shoreline

Sohngen, Brent, Frank Lichtkoppler, and Mary Bielen. Forthcoming. The Value of Day Trips to Lake Erie Beaches. Technical Bulletin. The Ohio State University Sea Grant. (http://www-agecon.ag.ohio-state.edu/Faculty/bsohngen/beach/beachin.htm)

Sohngen, Brent, Frank Lichtkoppler, and Mary Bielen. Forthcoming. Valuing Great Lakes Beach Recreation: An Economic Assessment of the Recreational Value of Freshwater Beaches.
(http://www-agecon.ag.ohio-state.edu/Faculty/bsohngen/beach/beachin.htm)

Environmental Restoration and Quality

Environment Canada. 1998. Restoring Great Lakes Watersheds: Adding Up the Economic Benefits. Burlington, Ontario: Environment Canada.
(http://www.cciw.ca/green-lane/env-econ/)

Fraser, Noel C., ed. 1997. The McMaster Eco-Research Program for Hamilton Harbour. Hamilton, Ontario: McMaster University. Funded by Environment Canada's Green Plan through the Tri-Council Eco-Research Program.
(http://www.mcmaster.ca/ecowise)

Hickling Corporation. 1993. Development Potential and Other Benefits from Restoration, Enhancement and Protection of Great Lakes Basin Watersheds. Burlington, Ontario: Environment Canada.

Lyke, Audrey J. 1993. Discrete Choice Models to Value Changes in Environmental Quality: A Great Lakes Case Study. Unpublished Doctoral Dissertation, Department of Agricultural and Applied Economics, University of Wisconsin, Madison.

Ontario Ministry of Environment and Energy, The Economic Services Branch. 1995. Benefit-Cost Analysis Framework for the Evaluation of Contaminated Site Remediation Projects in Ontario. Toronto: Ontario Ministry of Environment and Energy.

Sustainable Futures. 1996. Economic Development Capacity and Other Benefits of Restoration, Enhancement and Protection of Metro Toronto Watersheds with Emphasis on the Humber River. Prepared for Environment Canada-Ontario Region.

Sustainable Futures. 1996. Economic Development Capacity and Other Benefits of Rehabilitation of the Northern Wood Preservers Site and Adjacent Waterfront in the Thunder Bay Area of Concern. Prepared for Environment Canada-Ontario Region.

Sustainable Futures. 1995. Development Potential and Other Benefits from Restoration, Enhancement and Protection of the Thunder Bay Area of Concern. Prepared for Environment Canada-Ontario Region.

Sustainable Futures. 1995. Development Potential and Other Benefits from Restoration, Enhancement and Protection of the St. Lawrence (Cornwall) Area of Concern. Prepared for Environment Canada-Ontario Region.

Sustainable Futures. 1995. Development Potential and Other Benefits from Restoration, Enhancement and Protection of the Metropolitan Toronto Watersheds. Prepared for Environment Canada-Ontario Region.

Sustainable Futures. 1995. Development Potential and Other Benefits from Restoration, Enhancement and Protection of the the Nipigon Bay Area of Concern. Prepared for Environment Canada-Ontario Region.

Zegarac, M., and T. Muir. 1998. The Effects of RAP Related Restoration and Parkland Development on Residential Property Values: A Hamilton Harbour Case Study. Burlington, Ontario: Environment Canada.

Zegarac, M., and T. Muir. 1998. The Cleanup of Nipigon Bay: Adding Up the Economic Impacts and Benefits of Restoration Activities. Burlington, Ontario: Environment Canada.

Zegarac, M., and T. Muir. 1998. The Cleanup of Collingwood Harbour: Adding Up the Economic Impacts and Benefits of Restoration Activities. Burlington, Ontario: Environment Canada.

Filter Strips

Nakao, Megumi, and Brent Sohngen. 1998. The Cost of Riparian Forest Filter Strips for Soil Erosion Control. Fact Sheet. Department of Agricultural, Environmental and Development Economics, The Ohio State University. (http://www-agecon.ag.ohio-state.edu/Faculty/bsohngen/maumee/maum_sed.htm)

Nakao, Megumi, and Brent Sohngen. 1999. The Effect of Site Quality on the Costs of Reducing Soil Erosion with Filter Strips. Mimeo. Department of Agricultural, Environmental, and Development Economics, The Ohio State University. (http://www-age-con.ag.ohio-state.edu/Faculty/bsohngen/maumee/maum_sed.htm)

Fisheries

Anderson, Lee G. 1994. An Introduction to Economic Valuation Principles for Fisheries Management. Great Lakes Fishery Comission. Special Publication 94-2.

Bishop, Richard C., Kevin J. Boyle, and Michael P. Welsh. 1987. Toward Total Economic Valuation of Great Lakes Fishery Resources. Transactions of the American Fisheries Society 116:339-345.

Cochrane, Jeffrey A., Richard C. Bishop, and David B. Ives. 1992. Lake Michigan Salmonid Stocking Costs in Wisconsin. Marine Resource Economics 7:169-185.

Gould, Brian W., and Richard C. Bishop. 1989. Costs of Fisheries Rehabilitation in Green Bay and the Bay of Quinte. Ann Arbor, MI: Great Lakes Fishery Commisstion. Completion Report.

Gunderson, Jeff, and Glenn Kreag. 1991. Estimated Economic Impact of Recreational Fishing on Minnesota Waters of Lake Superior. (http://www.d.umn.edu/seagr/index2.html

Hoehn, John P., Theodore Tomasi, Frank Lupi, and Heng Z. Chen. December 1996. An Economic Model for Valuing Recreational Angling Resources in Michigan. Report Submitted to Michigan Department of Natural Resources and Michigan Department of Environmental Quality. Department of Agricultural Economics, Michigan State University.

Hushak, Leroy J., George W. Morse, and Kofi Apraku. 1986. Regional Impacts of Fishery Allocation to Sport and Commercial Interests: A Case Study of Ohio's Portion of Lake Erie. North American Journal of Fisheries Management 6:472-480.

Hushak, L.J., J.M. Winslow, and N. Dutta. 1988. Economic Value of Great Lakes Sport Fishing: The Case of Private-Boat Fishing in Ohio's Lake Erie. Transactions of the American Fisheries Society 117(4):363-373.

Kikuchi, Hideo. 1986. Segmenting Michigan's Sport Fishing Market: Evaluation of Two Approaches. Unpublished Doctoral Dissertation, Michigan State University.

Krieger, Douglas J. 1994. The Economic Value of Environmental Risk Information: Theory and Application to the Michigan Sport Fishery. Unpublished Doctoral Dissertation, Department of Agricultural Economics, Michigan State University.

Lupi, Frank, and John P. Hoehn. October 1997. A Preliminary Valuation of Lake Trout Using the Michigan Recreational Angling Demand Model. Draft report to the Great Lakes Fishery Commission. Department of Agricultural Economics, Michigan State University.

Milliman, Scott, Barry L. Johnson, Richard C. Bishop, and Kevin j. Boyle. 1992. The Bioeconomics of Resource Rehabilitation: A Commercial-Sport Analysis for a Great Lakes Fishery. *Land Economics* 68(2):191-210.

Provencher, Bill, and Richard C. Bishop. 1997. An Estimable Dynamic Model of Recreation Behavior with an Application to Great Lakes Angling. Journal of Environmental Economics and Management 33:107-127.

Samples, Karl C., and Richard C. Bishop. 1985. Estimating the Value of Variations in Anglers' Success Rates: An Application of the Multiple-Site Travel Cost Method. Journal of Marine Resource Economics 2(1):55-74.

Talhelm, D.R. 1988. Economics of Great Lakes Fisheries: A 1985 Assessment. Great Lakes Fishery Commission. Technical Report No. 54.

Greenspace

Zegarac, Mike. 1996. A Catalogue of Benefits Associated with Greenspaces and An Analysis of the Effects of Greenspaces on Residential Property Values: A Windsor Case Study. Prepared for Environment Canada-Ontario Region.

Groundwater

Troyak, Marg. October 1996. An Assessment of the Ecological and Economic Value of Groundwater: Town of Caledon Case Study. Prepared for Environment Canada-Ontario Region in partnership with The Metro Toronto Remedial Action Plan and the Humber Watershed Task Force.

Human Health

Desvousges, William H., F. Reed Johnson, Sara P. Hudson, Alicia R. Gable, Melissa C. Ruby. 1996. Using Conjoint Analysis and Health-State Classifications to Estimate the Value of Health Effects of Air Pollution: Pilot Test Results and Implications. Triangel Economic Research.

Krieger, Douglas J., John P. Hoehn. Health Risk Advisories for Sport Anglers: The Economic Value of Having a Choice. Michigan Sea Grant College Program.

Recreation

The DPA Group Inc. 1987. Recreation Benefits Arising from Lake Reclamation in Ontario. Toronto: Ontario Ministry of the Environment.

Jones, Carol Adair, and Yusen D. Sung. September 1993. Valuation of Environmental Quality at Michigan Recreational Sites: Methodological Issues and Policy Applications. Final Report. EPA Contract No. CR-816247-01-2.

Sediment Remediation
Keilor, P. 1996. An Economic Decision Framework for Estimating Benefits and Costs of Sediment Remediation. Presented at the Western Dredging Association Conference XVI. Minneapolis, Minnesota, May 22-26, 1996.

Soil Conservation
Nakao, Megumi, and Brent Sohngen. 1999. The Effect of Site Quality on the Costs of Reducing Soil Erosion with Filter Strips. Mimeo. The Ohio State University. (http://www-agecon.ag.ohio-state.edu/Faculty/bsohngen/maumee/maum_sed.htm)

Water Quality
DeZoysa, A. Damitha. 1996. A Benefit Evaluation of Programs to Enhance Groundwater Quality, Surface Water Quality, and Wetland Habitat in Northwest Ohio. Unpublished Doctoral Dissertation. The Ohio State University.

DRI/McGraw-Hill. 1995. Great Lakes Water Quality Initiative: Cost Effectiveness Update. Prepared for the Council of Great Lakes Governors.

U.S. Environmental Protection Agency. 1995. Protection the Great Lakes: The Costs and Benefits of Reducing Toxic Pollution in Three Communities. EPA Office of Water. EPA-820-F-95-004.

Wetlands
Bardecki, M.J. 1998. Wetlands and Economics: An Annotated Review of the Literature, 1988-1998, with special reference to the wetlands of the Great Lakes. Prepared for Environment Canada, Ontario Region.

Environment Canada, Ontario Region. Forthcoming. The Economic Value of Great Lakes Wetlands. [Short factsheet targeted at planners, consultants, environmental assessment officers, etc. to improve profile of wetlands and highlight their economic importance.]

Jaworski, Eugene, and C. Nicholas Raphael. 1978. Fish, Wildlife, and Recreational Values of Michigan's Coastal Wetlands. Prepared for Michigan Department of Natural Resources, Division of Land Resource Programs, Great Lakes Shorelands Section.

LMSOFT. August 1995. Valuing the Economic Benefit of Wetlands: Case Studies in Ontario. Prepared for Environment Canada, Ontario Region, and Canada Centre for Inland Waters, Burlington, Ontario.

Resources for Performing Great Lakes Environmental Valuations

POTENTIAL FUNDING OPPORTUNITIES

Environmental Protection Agency's Great Lakes National Program Office
USEPA — GLNPO (G-17J)
77 West Jackson Boulevard, Chicago, IL 60604-3590
phone: (312) 886-4013
http://www.epa.gov/glnpo/fund/glf.html

Environmental Protection Agency and National Science Foundation
Annual RFP: "Decision-Making and Valuation for Environmental Policy"
U.S. National Science Foundation
4201 Wilson Boulevard, Arlington, VA 22230
phone: (703) 306-1118
http://www.nsf.gov/home/grants.htm

Great Lakes Protection Fund
35 E. Wacker Drive, Suite 1880, Chicago, IL 60601
phone: (312) 201-0660
http://www.glpf.org/

Lake Erie Protection Fund
Ohio Lake Erie Office
One Maritime Plaza, Toledo, OH 43604
phone: (419) 245-2514, fax: (419) 245-2519
http://www.epa.state.oh.us/oleo/lepf1.htm

Michigan Great Lakes Protection Fund
Michigan Department of Environmental Quality, Office of the Great Lakes
P.O. Box 30473 , Lansing, MI 48909-7973
phone: (517) 335-4056
http://www.deq.state.mi.us/ogl/

ACADEMIC INSTITUTIONS IN GREAT LAKES STATES WITH RESOURCE ECONOMICS DEPARTMENTS

University of Illinois, Urbana-Champaign, Department of Agriculture and Consumer Economics, Environmental and Natural Resource Management Research Area
The Department performs research on land values, ownership, and control; and pollution in agriculture, ranging from preventing pollution of surface and ground water to assessing the effects of climate changes and air pollution on agriculture. Production economics emphasizes both microeconomic and macroeconomic forces that shape the way food and fiber are produced. Researchers are studying climate change, crop insurance, and other production-related topics.

    Department of Agricultural and Consumer Economics, University of Illinois
    332 Mumford Hall , 1301 W. Gregory Dr., Urbana, IL 61801
    phone: (217) 333-8859, fax: (217) 333-5538
    email: ace-aces@uiuc.edu
    http://w3.aces.uiuc.edu/ACE/

Michigan State University, Department of Agricultural Economics
The Department emphasizes applied and disciplinary contributions especially to the economic and managerial effectiveness of firms in the food and agricultural sector, and to the sustainability of agricultural production, environmental resources, and rural communities.

    Department of Agricultural Economics. Michigan State University
    202 Agriculture Hall, East Lansing, MI 48824
    phone: (517) 355-4563, fax: (517) 432-1800
    email: anraec@msu.edu
    http://www.aec.msu.edu/agecon/

The Ohio State University, Department of Agricultural, Environmental, and Development Economics
The Department disseminates information through application of economic and business principles to the challenges of food, agriculture, the environment, and rural communities. The activities in the Department fall within four major subject matter areas: commercial agriculture, international development, community economics, and environmental economics.

    Department of Agricultural, Environmental, and Development Economics
    The Ohio State University
    2120 Fyffe Rd.. Columbus, OH 43210
    phone: (614) 292-7911, fax: (614) 292-4749
    email: sheller.1@osu.edu
    http://www-agecon.ag.ohio-state.edu/

Pennsylvania State University, Department of Agricultural Economics and Rural Sociology
The Department offers programs in basic and applied research and public service that support private and public decision-making in the areas of: food and agricultural production, processing and marketing; environmental and resource management; economic and community development; and rural social change and demography.

Department of Agricultural Economics and Rural Sociology
Pennsylvania State University
103 Armsby Building, University Park, PA 16802
phone: (814) 865-5461, fax: (814) 865-3746
http://www.aers.psu.edu/

Purdue University, Department of Agricultural Economics
The Department is recognized for its strengths in marketing and agribusiness management, international trade and agricultural development, production and farm management, and agricultural and resource policy analysis.

Department of Agricultural Economics. Purdue University
1145 Krannert Building, West Lafayette, IN 47907-1145
phone: 765 494-4191, fax: 765 494-9176
http://www.agecon.purdue.edu/

University of Wisconsin-Madison, Department of Agricultural and Applied Economics
The Department focuses its research and extension efforts in the areas of: environmental and resource economics; growth and development in low-income economies; agricultural production and technical change; State and local economics; global markets and trade; resources and the environment in economic development; and markets and prices in the food system.

Department of Agricultural and Applied Economics
University of Wisconsin-Madison
Taylor Hall, 427 Lorch St., Madison, WI 53706
phone: (608) 262-9489
email: Info@aae.wisc.edu
http://www.wisc.edu/aae/

PROFESSIONAL RESOURCE ECONOMICS ASSOCIATIONS

American Agricultural Economics Association
415 South Duff Ave., Suite C, Ames, IA 50010-6600
phone: (515) 233-3202
http://www.aaea.org/

Association of Environmental and Resource Economists
1616 P Street, N.W. Room 507, Washington, DC 20036
http://www.ecu.edu/econ/aere/

Canadian Society for Ecological Economics
http://socserv2.socsci.mcmaster.ca/~cansee/

ORGANIZATIONS WITH RESOURCE ECONOMICS EXPERTISE

Canadian Resource and Environmental Economics Study Group
http://socserv2.socsci.mcmaster.ca/~cree/

Centre for the Economics and Managment of Aquatic Resources
Department of Economics, University of Portsmouth
Milton Campus, Locksway Road, Portsmouth PO4 8JF United Kingdom
http://www.pbs.port.ac.uk/econ/cemare/

Northeast-Midwest Institute
218 D Street, SE, Washington, DC 20003
phone: (202) 544-5200, fax: (202) 544-0043
http://www.nemw.org

Resources for the Future
1616 P Street, NW, Washington, DC 20036

World Resources Institute
1709 New York Avenue, NW, Washington, DC 20006
http://www.wri.org/wri/

PRIVATE CONSULTANTS AND INDIVIDUALS WITH EXPERTISE[24]

David R. Alldardice, Senior Vice President and William Bergman
Federal Reserve Bank of Chicago, Detroit Branch
160 West Ford Street, Detroit, MI 48231
phone: (313) 961-6880
http://www.frbchi.org/
(submitted by Martha Waszak, MI Department of Environmental Quality, Office of
the Great Lakes; WASZAKM@state.mi.us; (517) 355-4112)

Richard C. Bishop, Ph.D.
Department of Agricultural and Applied Economics, University of Wisconsin
Taylor Hall, Room 334, 427 Lorch Street, Madison, WI 53706-1513
phone: (608) 262-8966, fax: (608) 262-4376
email: bishop@aae.wisc.edu

---

[24] *These sources were compiled from responses to an e-mail request to the the Great Lakes community.*

Gale A. Boyd, Ph.D.
Economist, Decision and Information Sciences Division
Argonne National Laboratory, DIS-900
9700 S. Cass Ave., Argonne IL 60439-4832
phone: (630) 252-5393, fax: (630) 252-4498
email: gboyd@anl.gov
http://www.dis.anl.gov/
(submitted self after information referred from Tom Brody at EPA)

John B. Braden, Ph.D.
Department of Agricultural and Consumer Economics, University of Illinois
601 E. John Street, Room 204, Champaign, IL 61820
phone: (217) 333-8159, fax: (217) 244-5639
e-mail: j-braden@uiuc.edu

Sudip Chattopadhyay, Ph.D.
Department of Economics, Kansas State University
Manhattan, KS 66506
phone: (785) 532-4578, fax: (785) 532-6919
email: sudip@ksu.edu

Roger L. Gauthier
Senior Hydrologist, Chief, Watershed Hydrology Section
Great Lakes Hydraulics and Hydrology Branch
U.S. Army Corps of Engineers, Detroit District
P.O. Box 1027, Detroit, MI 48231-1027
phone: (313) 226-3054, fax: (313) 226-2398
email: Roger.L.Gauthier@LRE01.usace.army.mil
http://sparky.nce.usace.army.mil/hmpghh.html
(submitted self)

Leroy J. Hushak, Ph.D.
Department of Agricultural, Environmental, and Development Economics
The Ohio State University
2120 Fyffe Road, Columbus, OH 43210-1066
phone: (614) 292-3548, fax: (614) 292-7710
email: hushak.1@osu.edu

Ray Rivers
Chief Economist, Environment Canada, Ontario Region
867 Lakeshore Road, PO Box 5050, Burlington, Ontario L7R4A6 Canada
phone: (905) 336-4949, fax: (905) 336-8901
email: Ray.Rivers@ec.gc.ca
http://www.cciw.ca/green-lane/or-home.html
(submitted self)

Brent Sohngen, Ph.D.
Agricultural, Environmental, and Development Economics, The Ohio State University
2120 Fyffe Road, Columbus, OH 43210-1067
phone: (614) 688-4640, fax: (614) 292-0078
email: sohngen.1@osu.edu

Peter K. Stokoe, Ph.D.
ECOSTRATEGIES
9 Hazelwood Avenue, Toronto, Ontario M4J 1K4 Canada
phone: (416)-463-5907, fax: (416)-463-3680
email: p.stokoe@utoronto.ca
http://www.ecostrategies.com/
(submitted self)

Mike Welsh
Senior Associate, Hagler Bailly, Inc.
455 Science Drive, Madison, WI 53711
phone: (608) 232-2800, fax: (608) 232-2858
email: mwelsh@habaco.com
http://www.haglerbailly.com/
(submitted self after referral from Rich Bishop)

John Wolfe, Ph.D., M.S.E.
Limno-Tech, Inc.
501 Avis Drive, Ann Arbor, MI 48108
phone: (313) 332-1200, fax: (313) 332-1212
email: jwolfe@limno.com
http://www.limno.com/
(submitted self)

Resources for Economic Valuation of Environmental Benefit Studies

Performing an economic valuation study of environmental benefits can be a large undertaking. Before anyone begins a new study from scratch it is worthwhile to determine if similar studies have been done or if the necessary data has already been collected. While it would be impossible to compile all the resources available related to these types of studies, this chapter is intended to provide many of the major databases and research centers regionally and nationally.

CONTENTS:

Ecological Data and Software 206
    EPA's Practitioner's Tools 206
    Agriculture / Soils 206
        State NRCS / NRI Programs 208
    Air Quality 210
    Biodiversity 212
    Chemicals / Toxics 213
    Contaminated Sediments 216
    Fish 217
    Forestry 218
    Geographic / Mapping 219
    Nonindigenous Species 220
    Physical Attributes 221
    Water 222
        Great Lakes Regional NAWQA Study Units 222
    Wetlands 224
Environmental Economic / Social Data and Laws 224
Major Research Centers in the Great Lakes Region 226
State, Canadian, and Indian Natural Resources Offices 232

ECOLOGICAL DATA AND SOFTWARE

These are resources that are readily available, particularly to those with Internet access. Many of the databases can provide the ecological data to form the basis for an economic benefits study, or can be used as models for acquiring similar data in different geographic areas.

EPA's Practitioner's Tools

The EPA webpage provides access to software, databases, and modeling tools for those interested in studying the areas of air; prevention, pesticides, and toxic substances; solid wastes and emergency response; water; and geographic information systems tools. Contact information: (http://www.epa.gov/epahome/Data.html

Agriculture/Soils

Data available through these sources can be used in studies involving agricultural products, soil erosion, and land use.

Agriculture Network Information Center (AgNIC)
AgNIC is an electronic source of agricultural information in electronic form over an international network of networks. Agricultural information includes basic, applied, and developmental research, extension, and teaching activities in the food, agricultural, renewable natural resources, forestry, and physical and social sciences.

The mission of AgNIC is to facilitate and advance electronic access to people, agricultural information, and other resources for use by the public (academia, researchers, experiment stations, extension service, and other government users) and private (producers, agribusiness, suppliers and customers) components of agriculture, as well as private citizens.

The AgNIC will provide a wide array of value-added information services uniquely related to agriculture:

AgDesk: Use the capabilities of the Internet to provide assistance in using Internet resources through a distributed virtual Help Desk environment.

Reference Desk: Provide mediated assistance, with librarians and subject area specialists through a distributed system in combination with virtual information services.

Database Activities: Facilitate collaborative development, description of, use, and archiving of distributed agricultural on-line databases.

Directory Activities: Provide, in coordination with InterNIC and other information providers, pointers to agriculture resources available on the Internet.

Educational Services: Provide training in use of AgNIC resources and participate in outreach activities to promote the use of electronic networks.

Liaison Activities: Share information and coordinate with national and international user groups, network organizations, and professional organizations.

Contact information:
Richard E. Thompson
National Agricultural Library
Information Systems Division, Room 204
US Department of Agriculture, ARS
10301 Baltimore Boulevard, Beltsville, MD 20705-2351
phone: (301) 504-5018, fax: (301) 504-5472
email: rthompson@nal.usda.gov
http://www.agnic.org/

Database of Soils within the 88 counties of Ohio

The soil resources within the 88 counties of Ohio have been progressively evaluated since the early 1950's as part of the National Cooperative Soil Survey. This survey also included an intensive, pedon (soil profile)-level sampling program that was under-taken concurrently with field mapping. Over 3,000 sampling sites, representing 40,000 soil samples, were studied in each county with the number of sites per county ranging from 5 to nearly 100. Over two-thirds of these sites were sampled and ana-lyzed prior to 1965 and, therefore, pre-date the introduction of modern BMP's. About 10% of these sites are located in forested areas. These samples are archived at The Ohio State University.

Field data for each site include the date described and sampled; the exact location by section, township and range, and by latitude-longitude (update ongoing); physiogra-phy; internal drainage; slope; land-use at the time of sampling; thickness; color; tex-ture; structure and consistance by soil horizon; depth to carbonates; and other impor-tant information.

Laboratory data includes texture, pH in water, and organic carbon percentage. More detailed data for most sites includes cation exchange capacity (CEC), exchangeable bases (Ca, Mg, K & Na), acidity (H & Al), bulk density, water retention characteristics, clay mineralogy, and total elemental analysis of selected size fractions.

Morphology of soil horizons for sample sites formated in soil survey style have been completed for most sample sites.

Contact information:
Ohio State University, Department of Soil Science
Williams Hall, Wooster, OH 44691
http://flashman.ag.ohio-state.edu/pedology/soilindex.html

NRCS National Resources Inventories Technical Resources

Links to NRCS base map coverages, status maps, the National Resources Inventory (NRI) database, and data bases on soil, water and climate, plants for conservation, and other subjects. This site is a node of the National Spatial Data Infrastructure. The web page also has links to:

National Resources Inventory (NRI): Comprehensive data collected by NRCS on the state of natural resources in the US.

Resource Analysis and Assessment: Maps, facts, and figures about the "State of the Land" — analysis and insight on the health of America's private lands.

National PLANTS Database: Provides a single source of standardized information about plants. PLANTS provides standardized plant names, symbols, and other plant attribute information.

Soils Data: Access, query, analyze, download, and report the various national soils databases. Includes the NSDAF national MUIR, OSD, SC, and soil characterization databases.

Technical Notes/Briefs: Not just for professionals, a wide-ranging collection of NRCS documents on technical application and program direction.

Technical Tools: For conservation professionals, downloadable or interactive software for such tasks as animal waste management, urban hydrology, and conservation buffer selection and sizing.

Technical References: The Soil Survey Manual, Conservation Practice Standards, and other major references for professionals in natural resource conservation.

Contact information:
Natural Resource Conservation Service
Mid West Region2820 Walton Commons West, Suite 123
Madison, WI 53718-6797
phone: (608) 224-3000, fax: (608) 224-3010
http://www.nrcs.usda.gov/TechRes.html

STATE NRCS/NRI PROGRAMS:
Every five years, NRCS conducts the National Resources Inventory (NRI) on nonfederal rural land in the United States. This inventory shows natural resource trends, such as land cover and use, soil erosion, prime farmland, and wetlands. The 1992 NRI, for example, shows that farmers are dramatically reducing soil erosion on cropland. From 1982 to 1992, erosion on all cropland declined by about one-third, going from 3.1 billion to 2.1 billion tons a year. NRI data are statistically reliable for national, regional, state, and substate analysis. The NRI was scientifically designed and conducted and is based on recognized statistical sampling methods.

The data are used in national, state, and local planning, university research, and private sector analysis. They help shape major environmental and land-use decisions.

Illinois Natural Resources Conservation Service
Contact information:
USDA-NRCS
1902 Fox Drive, Champaign, IL 61820
phone: (217) 398-5267, fax: (217) 398-5310
http://www.il.nrcs.usda.gov/default.htm

Indiana Natural Resources Conservation Service
Contact information:
Robert L. Eddleman, State Conservationist
Indiana Natural Resources Conservation Service
6013 Lakeside Blvd., Indianapolis, IN 46278
phone: (317) 290-3200
http://www.in.nrcs.usda.gov/

Michigan Natural Resources Conservation Service
Contact information:
Bill Frederick, National Resources Inventory
phone: 517-337-6701 ext. 1229
http://www.mi.nrcs.usda.gov/

Midwest Regional Natural Resources Conservation Service
The Midwest Regional Office is located in Madison, Wisconsin and is one of six
regional offices that was established as a result of the Agency Reorganization/Reinven-
tion Plan of November 1994 and the Agriculture Reorganization Act of December
1994. The Midwest Region encompasses about 458,000 square miles and includes the
following eight states: Illinois, Indiana, Iowa, Michigan, Minnesota, Missouri, Ohio,
and Wisconsin.
Contact information:
Charles Whitmore, Regional Conservationist
Natural Resources Conservation Service
2820 Walton Commons West, Suite 123, Madison, WI 53718
phone: (608) 224-3001, fax: (608) 224-3010
email: Charles.Whitmore@mw.nrcs.usda.gov
http://www.mw.nrcs.usda.gov/

Minnesota National Resources Inventory
Contact information:
USDA — Natural Resources Conservation Service
375 Jackson St., Suite 600, St. Paul, Minnesota 55101-1854
phone: (612) 290-3679
email: nri@mn.nrcs.usda.gov
http://www.mn.nrcs.usda.gov/nri/nri.html

Ohio Natural Resources Conservation Service
Contact information:
Pat Wolf, State Conservationist
Ohio Natural Resources Conservation Service
200 N. High St. Rm. 522, Columbus Ohio 43215
phone: (614) 469-6962
email: Pat.Wolf@oh.nrcs.usda.gov
http://www.oh.nrcs.usda.gov/

Pennsylvania Natural Resources Conservation Service
Contact information:
Janet L.Oertly, State Conservationist
One Credit Union Place, Suite 340, Harrisburg, Pennsylvania 17110
phone: (717)782-2202, fax: (717) 782-4469
email: joertly@pa.nrcs.usda.gov
http://www.pa.nrcs.usda.gov/

Wisconsin National Resources Inventory
Contact information:
Patricia Leavenworth, State Conservationist
Wisconsin Natural Resources Conservation Service
6515 Watts Rd., Suite 200, Madison, WI 53719
phone: (608) 264-5341, fax: (608) 264-5483
email: randerso@wi.nrcs.usda.gov
http://www.wi.nrcs.usda.gov/

Air Quality
Data available through these sources can be used in studies involving general air quality and air toxics.

Great Lakes Regional Air Toxics Emissions Inventory
This inventory will assist in the successful implementation of key provisions of the Great Lakes Toxic Substances Control Agreement, signed by the Great Lakes governors in 1986. In addition, this work is consistent with the state activities for the implementation of the Urban Area Source Program required under sections 112(c) and 112(k) under the Clean Air Act Amendments of 1990 and the assessment of atmospheric deposition to the Great Lakes under the efforts of U.S. EPA's Great Waters Program. Specifically, the program's goal is to establish a baseline using 1993 data on point and area source emissions of 49 toxic air pollutants that have been identified as significant contributors to the contamination of the Great Lakes. Contact information:

Michael J. Donahue, Executive Director
Great Lakes Commission
400 Fourth St., Ann Arbor, MI 48103-4816
phone: (313) 665-9135, fax: (313) 665-4370
email: glc@great-lakes.net
http://www.glc.org/projects/air/regdbase.html

Michigan Air Pollution Reporting System (MAPRS)

The objectives of the MAPRS are to provide needed information for estimating emissions of air contaminants or pollutants from commercial, industrial, and governmental sources. The information collected from the Michigan Air Pollution Reporting System is used for a variety of air quality planning purposes. Federal regulations require submittal of emissions data to the U.S. Environmental Protection Agency so that it can be added to the national data bank. The data is used to: track air pollution trends; determine the effectiveness of State air pollution control programs; serve as the basis for future year projections of air quality; track source compliance; provide information for permit review and open market emissions trading; and to calculate the emissions portion of the air quality fee.

By State law, information on the amount and type of air contaminants emitted from a facility is available to the general public. Access to the data and further information may be obtained by contacting the Emissions Reporting & Assessment Unit of the Air Quality Division. Contact information:

Rick Dalebout
Michigan Department of Environmental Quality
phone: (517) 373-7047, fax: (517) 335-3122
e-mail: dalebout@deq.state.mi.us
http://www.deq.state.mi.us/aqd/eval/maprs/maprs.html

Support Technology for Environmental, Water, and Agricultural Resource Decisions (STEWARD)

STEWARD is an integrated knowledge, GIS, and model based software application for the selection, evaluation, siting, and design of nonpoint source control systems. A single site (non-GIS) version is also accessible online through the World Wide Web. The targeted user group is nonpoint source watershed project managers and technical staff. Contact information:

David W. Lehning, World Wide Web Programmer
Center for Artificial Intelligence Applications in Water Quality
001 Land and Water Research Building
The Pennsylvania State University, University Park, PA 16802
phone: (814) 865-9753, fax: (814) 865-3378
email: dwl6@psu.edu
http://rcwpsun.cas.psu.edu/steward/

U.S. State Air Quality Resources
A webpage with links to sources of data and regulatory information from all 50 states, where available. Contact information:

> http://homepage.interaccess.com/~scotte/apr/states/statesmi.htm

Biodiversity
Data available through these sources can be used in studies involving species diversity, ecosystem values, existence values, and the effects of human activity on species diversity and distribution.

Species of Illinois Database
A searchable database of plant and animal species in Illinois maintained by the Illinois Natural History Survey. Contact information:

> Illinois Department of Natural Resources
> Illinois Natural History Survey
> 524 South Second Street, Springfield, IL 62701-1787
> http://www.inhs.uiuc.edu/databases/datahome.html

Wisconsin Cooperative Park Studies Unit
A cooperative research unit that helps organizations pool their capabilities in the collection, analysis and dissemination of scientific information about the nation's biological resources. Includes databases on flora of midwestern National Parks and lichens of the entire National Park System. Contact information:

> Dr. James P. Bennett
> University of Wisconsin-Madison , Cooperative Park Studies Unit
> Institute for Environmental Studies
> 610 Walnut Street, 1007 WARF Building, Madison, WI 53705
> phone: (608) 262-9937, fax: (608) 262-0339
> email: jpbennett@macc.wisc.edu
> http://www.emtc.nbs.gov/wicpsu.html

Canadian Biodiversity Information Network (CBIN)
This website was developed in support of the Convention on Biological Diversity, Agenda 21 and BIN21. It includes links to Canadian organizations involved in the conservation of biodiversity, maps and other educational products, and databases from the Canadian Forest Service, Canadian Centre for Biodiversity, and Canadian Museum of Nature, among others. Contact information:

> email: mark.cantwell@ec.gc.ca
> http://www.doe.ca/ecs/biodiv/biodiv.html

Chemicals/Toxics

Data available through these sources can be used in studies involving hazardous waste, Superfund sites, release of toxics, human health affects of toxics, transport and fate of toxics, and behavior of toxics in the environment

Envirofacts Warehouse

The Envirofacts Warehouse allows you to retrieve environmental information from EPA databases on Superfund sites, drinking water, toxic releases, air releases, hazardous waste, water discharge permits, and grants information. Use on line queries to retrieve data or generate maps of environmental information by choosing from several mapping applications available through EPA's Maps On Demand. Envirofacts is a relational database that integrates data extracted monthly from five facility (or site) based EPA program systems including Superfund, Hazardous Waste, Water Discharge Permits, and the Toxics Release Inventory. Envirofacts contains data that are available under the Freedom of Information Act (FOIA). No enforcement, budget-sensitive, or proprietary business information is contained in this database. Contact information:

Pranas Pranckevicius
U.S. EPA Great Lakes National Program Office, US EPA, G-9J
77 West Jackson Blvd., Chicago, IL. 60604-3590
phone: (312) 353-3437. fax: (312) 353-2018
email: Pranckevicius.pranas@epamail.epa.gov or enviromail@epamail.epa.gov
http://www.epa.gov/enviro/html/ef_home.html

The Effects of Great Lakes Contaminants on Human Health (Report to Congress)

In accordance with the responsibilities under the Great Lakes Critical Programs Act of 1990, the USEPA transferred funds to the Agency for Toxic Substances and Disease Registry (ATSDR), which has developed a research program to address human health effects from exposure to contaminants in the Great Lakes. Much of the historical data used in this report was obtained from information and prior research performed by state health departments and universities. Federal agencies other than the USEPA and ATSDR, such as the Centers for Disease Control and Prevention (CDC), National Institute for Occupational Safety and Health, and state agencies have all participated in preliminary reviews of this report. This report reflects comments made by those agencies as well as those made by the principal researchers whose work is contained within the report. Contact information:

Diane Dennis-Flagler
United States Environmental Protection Agency
Great Lakes National Program Office
77 West Jackson Boulevard, Chicago, Illinois 60604
phone: (312) 886-4040, fax: (312) 353-2018
email: dennis.flagler.diane@epamail.epa.gov
http://www.epa.gov/glnpo/health/atsdr.htm)

ATSDR's Hazardous Substance Release/Health Effects Database (HazDat)
This scientific and administrative database was developed to provide access to information on the release of hazardous substances from Superfund sites or from emergency events and on the effects of hazardous substances on the health of human populations. The following information is included in HazDat: site characteristics, activities and site events, contaminants found, contaminant media and maximum concentration levels, impact on population, community health concerns, ATSDR public health threat categorization, ATSDR recommendations, environmental fate of hazardous substances, exposure routes, and physical hazards at the site/event. In addition, HazDat contains substance-specific information such as the ATSDR Priority List of Hazardous Substances, health effects by route and duration of exposure, metabolites, interactions of substances, susceptible populations, and biomarkers of exposure and effects. HazDat also contains data from the U.S. Environmental Protection Agency (EPA) Comprehensive Environmental Response, Compensation, and Liability Information System (CERCLIS) database, including site CERCLIS number, site description, latitude/longitude, operable units, and additional site information. Contact information:

Dr. Sandra Susten, Principal Scientist
ATSDR/OAA
1600 Clifton Road (E28), Atlanta, GA 30333
phone: (404) 639-0700, fax: (404) 639-0744
email: sss2@cdc.gov
http://atsdr1.atsdr.cdc.gov:8080/hazdat.html

Green Bay Mass Balance Data
This study was conducted in 1989-90 to pilot the technique of mass balance analysis in understanding the sources and effects of toxic pollutants in the Great Lakes' food chain. The study, headed by EPA's Great Lakes National Program Office (GLNPO) and the Wisconsin Department of Natural Resources, had many participants from the Federal, state, interagency, and academic communities. The study focused on four representative chemicals or chemical classes: PCBs, dieldrin, cadmium, and lead. Contact information:

Dave DeVault
Minnesota Pollution Control Agency
520 Lafayette Road, St. Paul, MN 55155-4194
phone: 612-296-7253, fax: 612-297-8683
email: dave.devault@pca.state.mn.us
http://www.epa.gov/glnpo/gbdata/

The Lake Michigan Mass Balance Project

This project began in 1994 and will be concluded in 1999. Four major chemicals are being studied including mercury, polychlorinated biphenyls (PCBs), atrazine (an agricultural herbicide), and trans-nonachlor (a pesticide). The Lake Michigan Mass Balance Project is aiding in the understanding of where these chemicals are entering the lake and what happens to them as they move through the ecosystem. This study will identify relative pollutant loads from rivers, air deposition, and sediment resuspension, and will allow for the prediction of the benefits associated with reducing loads. Online data is coming soon. Contact information:

Glenn Warren
United States Environmental Protection Agency
Great Lakes National Program Office
77 West Jackson Boulevard, Chicago, Illinois 60604
phone: (312) 886-4040, fax: (312) 353-2018
email: warren.glenn@epamail.epa.gov
http://www.epa.gov/glnpo/lmmb/)

University of Minnesota Biocatalysis/Biodegradation Database

This database contains information on microbial biocatalytic reactions and biodegradation pathways for primarily xenobiotic chemical compounds. The goal of the UM-BBD is to provide information on microbial enzyme-catalyzed reactions that are important for biotechnology. Contact information:

Lynda Ellis
email: lynda@umnhcs.labmed.umn.edu
or
Larry Wackett
email: wackett@biosci.cbs.umn.edu.
http://dragon.labmed.umn.edu/~lynda/index.html

The Pesticide Properties Database

This database is a compendium of chemical and physical properties of 230 widely used pesticides, focusing on 16 important properties that affect pesticide characteristics. New pesticides and data are added as they become available. A steering committee that represents database users gives advice on the form and content of the database. Contact information:

Dr. Vangimalla R. Reddy, Research Leader
phone: (301) 504-5806, fax: (301) 504-5823
email:VREDDY@ASRR.ARSUSDA.GOV
http://www.arsusda.gov/rsml/ppdb.html

The Hormone Disrupting Toxicity Website
These pages provide an introduction to the effects of hormone disrupting chemicals on man and the environment. Other terms used to describe these chemicals include xenoestrogens, oestrogenic (estrogenic), hormone mimicking and endocrine disrupting chemicals. The chemicals involved include pesticides such as DDT, lindane and atrazine, the food packaging chemicals, phthalates and bisphenol A, alkylphenol ethoxylate detergents and the chemical industry by-products, dioxins. These pages are aimed at anyone interested in the subject, and include references to other research and reviews for those interested in investigating the field further. The pages focus particularly on those chemicals which are not organochlorines, but some information is also provided on organochlorines. The material in these pages has been written by Dr. Michael Warhurst, an Environmental Chemist who works for Friends of the Earth, London, UK. This site is currently a personal project, and does not necessarily reflect Friends of the Earth policy. Contact information:

Dr. Michael Warhurst
Friends of the Earth, London, UK
email: michaelw@foe.co.uk
http://easyweb.easynet.co.uk/~mwarhurst/oestrogenic.html

Contaminated Sediments
Data available through these sources can be used in studies involving the remediation of contaminated sediments and the recycling of toxics from sediment-water interactions.

Assessment and Remediation of Contaminated Sediments (ARCS) Reports
The 1987 amendments to the Clean Water Act, in Section 118(c)(3), authorized the U.S. Environmental Protection Agency's (EPA) Great Lakes National Program Office (GLNPO) to coordinate and conduct a 5-year study and demonstration project relating to the appropriate treatment of toxic pollutants in bottom sediments. Five areas were specified in the Act as requiring priority consideration in conducting demonstration projects: Saginaw Bay, Michigan; Sheboygan Harbor, Wisconsin; Grand Calumet River, Indiana; Ashtabula River, Ohio; and Buffalo River, New York. To fulfill the requirements of the Act, GLNPO initiated the Assessment and Remediation of Contaminated Sediments (ARCS) Program. In addition, the Great Lakes Critical Programs Act of 1990 amended the Section, now 118(c)(7), by extending the Program by one year and specifying completion dates for certain interim activities. Information available from this source includes technical reports containing results of assessments and

other studies of contaminated sediments by the Great Lakes National Program Office of the U.S. EPA between 1988 and 1994. The focus of these studies is on the five priority areas of concern (AOC) in five of the Great Lake states (see above). Contact information:

Marc Tuchman, Program Manager
Great Lakes National Program Office/EPA G-9J
77 West Jackson Blvd., Chicago, IL 60604-3590
phone: (312) 353-1369, fax: (312) 353-2018
http://www.epa.gov/glnpo/arcs/arcsguide.html

Detroit District Operations Technical Support

The U.S. Army Corps of Engineers Detroit District's database of Great Lakes dredging projects, costs, cubic yards removed and more. Contact information:

Mr. Douglas Zande, Chief
Operations Technical Support Branch
phone: (313) 226-6796
or
Mr. Wayne Schloop, Chief
Project Operations Section
phone: (313) 226-6797, fax: (313) 226-3519
http://sparky.nce.usace.army.mil/OandM/o&m.html

Fish

Data available through these sources can be used in studies involving fisheries assessment, angler surveys, and habitat quality and restoration.

Great Lakes Fish Stocking Database

The core of the fish stocking database (1950-1988) may be viewed on the Great Lakes Fishery Commission's Web Page. The database is held and formatted primarily for use by technical committees and researchers in models and assessment. Another important objective is meeting information needs of fishery managers, but is served as much as possible in a manner accessible and useful to other government agencies and the public. Data gathering began with 1996 and is collected from hatchery administrators. Data are available for the following species: brook trout, brown trout, chinook salmon, coho salmon, lake trout, and rainbow trout. Contact information:

Mr. Shawn Sitar
Great Lakes Fishery Analyst Fisheries Resource Office, U.S. Fish and Wildlife Service
1015 Challenger Ct., Green Bay, WI 54311-8331
phone: (414) 465-7440, fax: (414) 465-7410
email: shawn_sitar@mail.fws.gov
http://www.glfc.org/dbfs.htm)

Michigan Fisheries Information System (MFINS)

The Michigan Fisheries Information System (MFINS) is a computerized information system designed to provide users with access to computerized databases coupled with a user-friendly Geographic Information System (GIS) — ArcView. This combination will allow access to and integration of fisheries information, county and watershed basemaps, and statewide data, the capability to query and link databases, and the ability to make maps and graphs from the data. MFINS consists of five major modules: Data, Geoview, Graph, Model, and Help. The current datasets include: Dam, USGS Streamflow, Historical Fish Distributions, and River Inventory. Contact information:

Yung-Tsung Kang and Lois Wolfson
Institute of Water Research, Michigan State University
115 Manly Miles Building, 1405 S. Harrison Road, East Lansing, MI 48823-5243
phone: (517)353-3742, fax: (517)353-1812
http://www.iwr.msu.edu/mfins.html

U.S. Fish and Wildlife Service Alpena Fishery Resources Office (FRO)

Alpena Fishery Resources Office activities support U.S. Fish and Wildlife Service goals regarding native species, nonindigenous species, federal lands, Native American trust responsibilities, and fishery assistance. The Lake Huron lake trout restoration effort is a large component of the station's annual work schedule. Restoration activities for lake sturgeon in Lake Huron, the St. Clair system, and Western Lake Erie are also a major focus of the FRO. Monitoring of nonindigenous aquatic species continues as these species threaten the Great Lakes ecosystem. The FRO has assumed responsibility for monitoring Lake Huron waters for Eurasian ruffe and goby. Ecosystem restoration projects are conducted in the western basin of Lake Erie. The office is sensitive to it's trust responsibilities to Native American Tribes and is involved in tribal issues. The office frequently provides assistance to state and federal agencies with fisheries projects. Contact information:

Alpena Fishery Resources Office, U.S. Fish and Wildlife Service
Federal Building Room 204, 145 Waters St., Alpena, MI 49707
phone: (517) 356-5102, fax: (517) 356-4651
http://www.fws.gov/~r3pao/alpena/

Forestry

Data available through these sources can be used in studies involving forest products, land use and biodiversity.

USDA Forest Service Software and Databases

This webpage includes links to a multitude of software and databases for use in forestry assessment and management. Contact information:

http://www.fs.fed.us/database/)

Geographic/Mapping and Land Use

Data available through these sources can be used in studies involving land use, and large scale geographic and social features.

Great Lakes Map Server

This prototype map server allows the user to interactively compose a map with select EPA site datasets and feature coverages for any local U.S. area within the Great Lakes region. In the future, additional features, datasets and functions will be added. Contact information:

United States Environmental Protection Agency
Great Lakes National Program Office
77 West Jackson Boulevard, Chicago, IL 60604
http://epawww.ciesin.org/arc/map-home.html

Illinois Critical Trends Assessment Program Land Cover Mapping

Using Landsat satellite imagery, DNR scientists have compiled a comprehensive database of the state's surface cover. The data delineates natural features and artificial structures at a level of detail appropriate for regional analyses. CTAP staff have analyzed this data and published it in Illinois Land Cover, An Atlas. The report inventories land cover on both the state and the county level, and includes maps and county rankings for each of the seven land cover categories: cropland, open water, forest/woodland, grassland, wetland, barren/exposed land and urban/built-up land. Contact information:

Brent Manning, Director
Illinois Department of Natural Resources
524 South Street, Springfield, IL 62701-1787
ctap2@dnrmail.state.il.us
http://dnr.state.il.us/ctap/map/landmap.htm

Illinois Natural Resources NSDI Geospatial Data Clearinghouse Node

This site is a gateway to GIS data and imagery for Illinois geology, hydrology, natural history, conservation, environment, land use, Public Land Survey, and infrastructure. These data have been made available by several divisions of the Illinois DNR and address such topics as groundwater, wells, mines, geologic materials, nature preserves, wildlife areas, administrative and political boundaries, roads, census information, and many others. Contact information:

Illinois State Geological Survey
615 E. Peabody, Champaign, IL 61820
phone: (217) 333-4747
email: denhart@nomad.isgs.uiuc.edu
http://www.inhs.uiuc.edu/nsdihome/ISGSindex.html

Minnesota Land Management Information Center
A division of Minnesota Planning. LMI. It was established in 1977 by the Minnesota legislature to promote the use of geographic information and analysis in government. Contact information:

> Minnesota Land Management Information Center
> Room 330, Centennial Office Building, 658 Cedar St., St. Paul, MN 55155
> phone: (612) 296-1211, fax: (612) 296-1212
> http://www.lmic.state.mn.us/

Surf Your Watershed
Both a database of urls to world wide web pages associated with the watershed approach of environmental management and also data sets of relevant environmental information that can be queried. It is designed for citizens and decision makers across the country who are active and interested in the watershed-based environmental movement.

> http://www.epa.gov/surf/

Nonindigenous Species

Data available through these sources can be used in studies involving the past or potential introduction of nonindigenous species.

Sea Grant Nonindigenous Species Site
A project of the National Sea Grant College Program, produced by the Great Lakes Sea Grant Network. It is a national information center that contains a comprehensive collection of research publications and education materials produced by Sea Grant programs and other research institutions across the country on zebra mussels and other aquatic nuisance species. All materials available through this home page have either appeared in professional science journals or have been through a rigorous scientific review to ensure the quality of the information provided. Detailed information is provided about species including zebra mussel, spiny water flea, round goby, ruffe, and the sea lamprey. Links are provided to other sites that also focus on nonindigenous species. Contact information:

> Al Miller, Nonindigenous Species Project
> Illinois-Indiana Sea Grant Program
> 211 Forestry Bldg., Purdue University, West Lafayette, IN 47907
> phone: (317) 494-3593, fax: (317) 494-0409
> email: ahmiller@seagrant.wisc.edu
> http://www.ansc.purdue.edu/sgnis/)

Invasive Plants of Canada (IPCAN)
This project grew out of an initiative in 1991 by the Habitat Conservation Division, Canadian Wildlife Service (CWS) to compile information on invasive exotic plants of

wetland and upland habitats. IPCAN was established for compiling information on the biology, range and control of invasive exotic plants and for developing databases for computer mapping and analysis. Data for inclusion in these national databases are derived from specimen records in national collections, from sight records made by naturalists and professional botanists and from published reports. These databases not only provide a historical perspective on the origins and rate of spread of invasives but also allow for the determination of possible correlations with climatic and other environmental and land use factors using geographic information systems (GIS). Information about many aquatic and terrestrial plants is provided, including garlic mustard, purple loosestrife, leafy spurge, and Eurasian watermilfoil. Contact information:

Erich Haber
National Botanical Services
604 Wavell Avenue, Ottawa, ON, Canada
email:ehaber@magi.com
http://infoweb.magi.com./~ehaber/ipcan.html

Physical Attributes

Data available through these sources can be used in studies in which information is needed about weather, physical limnology, hydrography and hydraulics, and geological and geophysical attributes of the Great Lakes.

Canadian Great Lakes Coastal Zone Database

The database is housed in a Geographic Information System (GIS) and was developed in support of Phase I of the International Joint Commission Water Levels Reference Study. The purpose of the database was to view the Great Lakes environment in an integrative manner to identify and analyze those areas susceptible to fluctuating water levels, flooding and erosion. This database was never fully completed, but is primarily complete for Lake Ontario, Lake Erie and Lake St. Clair; incomplete for Lake Huron, Superior and the St. Lawrence River. Contact information:

Wendy Leger
Water Issues Division, Environmental Services Branch, Environment Canada
867 Lakeshore Road, Burlington, Ontario L7R 4A6
phone: (905) 336-4630, fax: (905) 336-8901
email: Wendy.Leger@cciw.ca
http://www.cciw.ca/glimr/metadata/coastal-zone-database/intro.html

Great Lakes Hydraulics & Hydrology

The U.S. Army Corps of Engineers provides historical and current data on water levels, outflows, weather, precipitation, and coastal engineering on all the Great Lakes. Contact information:

Roger L. Gauthier, Senior Hydrologist
Great Lakes Hydraulics and Hydrology Branch
U.S. Army Corps of Engineers, Detroit District
P.O. Box 1027, Detroit, MI 48231-1027
phone: (313) 226-3054, fax: (313) 226-2398
email: Roger.L.Gauthier@LRE01.usace.army.mil
http://sparky.nce.usace.army.mil/hmpghh.html

Great Lakes Data Rescue

The National Oceanographic and Atmospheric Administration (NOAA) is actively engaged in a program to Rescue Great Lakes seismic reflection, bathymetric, and sediment-sample data and place them in established marine geological and geophysical data repositories at the NOAA National Geophysical Data Center (NGDC). To the extent possible, NOAA will "rescue" Great Lakes geological and geophysical data and make them readily available to anyone, but especially the communities concerned with Great Lakes science, pollution, coastal erosion, response to climate changes, threats to lake ecosystems, and health of the fishing industry. An important element of this program is the rescue of bathymetric data and the compilation of new bathymetry for the Great Lakes, being carried out cooperatively between NOAA and the Canadian Hydrographic Service. Contact information:

Troy L. Holcombe
NOAA/NGDC
Mail Code E/GC3, 325 Broadway, Boulder, CO USA 80303
phone: (303) 497-6390
email: tholcombe@ngdc.noaa.gov
or
David F. Reid
NOAA/GLERL
2205 Commonwealth Blvd, R/E/GL, Ann Arbor, MI 48105-1593
phone (313)741-2019
email: reid@glerl.noaa.gov
http://www.ngdc.noaa.gov/mgg/greatlakes/greatlakes.html

Water

Data available through these sources can be used in studies in which information is needed about the effects of water levels on shoreline erosion, water quality and distribution.

GREAT LAKES REGIONAL NAWQA STUDY UNITS:

Lake Erie-Lake St. Clair Basin study unit

The study unit drains a 22,300 square mile area of northern Ohio (62 percent of the study unit), southeastern Michigan (27 percent), northeastern Indiana (6 percent), the northern tip of Pennsylvania, and southwestern New York (5 percent). The study unit represents all of the Lake Erie Basin in the United States and is about two-thirds of the total 30,140 square mile area of the Lake Erie Basin in the United States and Canada. The study unit drains to the St. Clair River (starting at the outflow of Lake Huron) and to Lake St. Clair, the Detroit River, and Lake Erie. The study unit ends at the Niagara River, the outflow of Lake Erie. Principal streams in the study unit include the Maumee River in Ohio and Indiana, the Sandusky River in Ohio, the River Raisin in Michigan, and Cattaraugus Creek in New York. Contact information:

Project Chief
Lake Erie—Lake St. Clair Basin NAWQA Study, U.S. Geological Survey
975 West Third Avenue, Columbus, OH 43212-3192
phone: (614) 469-5553
email: dnmyers@dohclb.er.usgs.gov
http://www-oh.er.usgs.gov/nawqa/index.html

Western Lake Michigan study unit

The study unit drains a 20,000 square mile area located in eastern Wisconsin and upper peninsula of Michigan. The unit is comprised of Lake Michigan, the Fox-Wolf River, and the Menominee-Oconto-Peshtigo River basins in Wisconsin, and the Ford and Escanaba basins in Michigan. Contact information:

District Chief, Water Resources Division
U.S. Geological Survey
6417 Normandy Lane, Madison, Wisconsin 53719
http://wwwdwimdn.er.usgs.gov/nawqa/fact.html

Upper Illinois River Basin study unit

The Upper Illinois River Basin Study Unit encompasses 10,949 square miles in parts of northeastern Illinois (62%), northwestern Indiana (28%), southeastern Wisconsin (10%), and southwestern Michigan (<1%). Major cities within study unit are Chicago, Illinois; and Kankakee, Illinois. The basin is drained by three principal rivers-the Kankakee, Des Plaines, and Fox Rivers. Contact information:

Michael J. Friedel, Project Chief
phone: (217) 344-0037 x 3020
e-mail: mfriedel@usgs.gov
http://wwwdwimdn.er.usgs.gov/nawqa/uirb/index.html

Upper Mississippi study unit

The Upper Mississippi River Basin NAWQA study area encompasses more than 48,000 square miles in five states and includes three major drainage basins--those of the Mississippi, Minnesota, and St. Croix Rivers. Contact information:

Upper Mississippi River Basin NAWQA, Project Chief
U.S. Geological Survey
2280 Woodale Drive, Mounds View, MN 55112-4900
phone: (612) 783-3100
email: wandrews@usgs.gov
http://wwwmn.cr.usgs.gov/umis/descript.html

Wetlands

Data available through these sources can be used in studies in which information is needed about the location and condition of wetland areas.

National Wetlands Inventory

The U.S. Fish and Wildlife Service's National Wetlands Inventory plans, directs, coordinates, and monitors the gathering, analysis, dissemination, and evaluation of information relating to the location, quantity, and ecological importance of the Nation's wetlands. Contact information:

United States Department of the Interior
Fish and Wildlife Service, National Wetlands Inventory
9720 Executive Center Drive, Suite 101, Monroe Building, St. Petersburg, FL 33702
phone: (813) 570-5412, fax: (813) 570-5420
http://www.nwi.fws.gov/

Nonmarket Values and Freshwater Wetlands Research

The site provides information on wetland valuation studies being conducted at Michigan State University. The site also serves as a clearinghouse for previous wetland valuation studies and information on Great Lakes wetlands. Contact information:

Gwyn Heyboer
Michigan State University
416 Agriculture Hall
East Lansing, MI 48824-1039
heyboerg@msu.edu
http://wetland.rd.msu.edu/

ENVIRONMENTAL ECONOMIC/SOCIAL DATA AND LAWS

These are readily available sources of information about economic and social data and trends (e.g., demographic, housing starts, employment rates, etc.) and state and federal laws pertaining to the natural resources of the Great Lakes region.

The U.S. Census Bureau

Census Customer Services (Data products & ordering information for computer tapes, CD-ROM's, microfiche, & some publications) Contact information:

phone: (301) 457-4100
Chicago, IL regional office phone: (708) 562-1723
Detroit, MI regional office phone: (313) 259-1875
http://www.census.gov

The Summary of Environmental Law in North America Website
The Commission for Environmental Cooperation created this summary of Environmental Law in North America to improve public access to the environmental law of the three parties to the North American Free Trade Agreement (NAFTA), i.e., Canada, Mexico and the United States. The summary is also designed to serve as a research tool for any person or organization interested in the environmental legislation of the three countries. For each country there is a list of legal instruments statutes, regulations, laws, norms, etc. These lists enable viewers to get a sense of the entire body of environmental law of a country. Each list also includes a short description of how to get copies of the laws and regulations, and where available, links to other relevant information sources on the Internet. Contact information:

Commission for Environmental Cooperation
393, rue St-Jacques Ouest , Bureau 200, Montréal (Québec) Canada H2Y 1N9
phone: (514) 350-4300, fax : (514) 350-4314
email : mpaquin@cec.org.
http://www.cec.org/infobases/law/index.cfm?lan

Michigan Information Center
The Michigan Information Center (MIC) is a unit within the Department of Management and Budget. MIC provides user consultation regarding data availability and applicability as well as training activities for its Michigan State Data Center Program (MSDCP) statewide affiliate network. Although MIC focuses primarily on Michigan data, it receives and archives census data for the region, other states, and the nation. Most information is available in both tabular printed reports and digital format on tape or diskette. Data extracts, Geographic Information Systems (GIS), and computer mapping are used extensively for creating standard products and for completing custom projects. Types of data available include demographic, economic, geographic, and education. Contact information:

Trina Williams
phone: (517) 373-7910
email: williamst1@state.mi.us
http://www.michigan.state.mi.us/michome/mic.html-ssi)

Minnesota State Demographer's Office
A variety of data and information is available from the State Demographer's Office, part of Minnesota Planning. Contact information:
State Demographer's Office, Minnesota Planning
658 Cedar, St. Paul, MN 55155
phone: (612) 296-2557, fax: (612) 296-1754
helpline@mnplan.state.mn.us
http://www.winterweb.com/mnplan/demography/)

Northeast-Midwest Economic Data
Provides information about major economic indicators in the Northeast-Midwest region, broken down by state. Contact information:
Dick Munson, Director
Northeast-Midwest Institute
218 D Street, SE, Washington, D.C. 20003
phone: (202) 544-5200, fax: (202) 544-0043
email: dickmunson@nemw.org
http://www.nemw.org/data.htm)

The U.S. House of Representatives Internet Law Library U.S. Code (searchable)
The United States Code contains the text of current public laws enacted by Congress. The U.S. Code does not include regulations issued by executive branch agencies, decisions of the federal courts, or treaties. Links are provided to the states which have online searchable Codes of Statutes. The database includes all official U.S. Code notes and appendices, as well as the Table of Popular Names.
http://law.house.gov/usc.htm

Thomas
Acting under the directive of the leadership of the 104th Congress to make Federal legislative information freely available to the Internet public, a Library of Congress team brought the THOMAS World Wide Web system online in January 1995, at the inception of the 104th Congress. Through this service, members of the public can search for information about current bills, bills from previous Congresses, access the Congressional Record, and search other historical documents related to the Congress. The data base is constantly updated as information becomes available. Contact information:
http://thomas.loc.gov/

MAJOR RESEARCH CENTERS IN THE GREAT LAKES REGION

These centers are major loci for research on topics related to the natural resources of the Great Lakes region. All of these have ongoing research programs and house data and personnel which could be of use to those involved in studies of the economic valuation of environmental benefits.

U.S. Fish and Wildlife Service

A bureau within the Department of the Interior. Its mission, working with others, is to conserve, protect, and enhance fish and wildlife and their habitats for the continuing benefit of the American people. Its major responsibilities are: migratory birds, endangered species, certain marine mammals, freshwater and anadromous fish, the National Wildlife Refuge System, wetlands, conserving habitat, and environmental contaminants. USFWS is divided into seven geographic regions, and its headquarters is located in Washington, DC. Regional Offices are involved in regional and local activities. Headquarters offices are involved in nationwide activities. Contact information:

Jamie Rappaport Clark, Director
U.S. Fish and Wildlife Service
3256 Interior Building, 1849 C St., NW, Washington, D.C. 20240
phone: 202/208-4717
http://www.fws.gov

Fish and Wildlife Service Region 3 (Great Lakes-Big Rivers Region)

The Great Lakes-Big Rivers Region includes the states of Illinois, Indiana, Iowa, Michigan, Minnesota, Missouri, Ohio, and Wisconsin. The Region manages 1.2 million acres in refuge land and water on 46 national wildlife refuges and 9 wetland management districts, including more than 240,000 acres in waterfowl production areas. The region also manages 6 national fish hatcheries, 9 other fisheries stations, 10 ecological services field offices, and 18 law enforcement field offices. Contact information:

Bill Hartwig, Regional Director
U.S. Fish and Wildlife Service Region 3
1 Federal Drive, BHW Federal Building, Fort Snelling, MN 55111
phone: (612) 725-3520
http://www.fws.gov/~r3pao/

National Water Research Institute

The National Water Research Institute is Canada's largest freshwater establishment. It conducts a comprehensive progam of research and development in the aquatic sciences, in partnership with the Canadian and international science communities. NWRI research provides a sound basis for actions to sustain Canada's natural resources and freshwater ecosystems. Contact information:

National Water Research Institute
P.O. Box 5050, 867 Lakeshore Road, Burlington, Ontario, Canada, L7R 4A6
phone: (905) 336-4912, fax: (905) 336-6230
http://www.cciw.ca/nwri-e/intro.html

Indiana Business Research Center at Indiana University Purdue University Indianapolis
The Center conducts and facilitates economic and demographic research which contributes to the understanding and development of Indiana. It is a central source of information and data for and about Indiana. The four main online information sources are:

1) Economy — Economic data consists of the 1996 Business Outlook, Economic Trends, and Metropolitan Service Area data.

2) Population — Population contains information on federal and state population trends.

3) EDIN — The Economic Development Information Network provides direct computer access for information about Indiana counties and cities and the 50 states. County and city profiles, telnet and ftp options, and factbook ordering information can be found here.

4) Indiana Business Review (IBR) — Monthly trends and in-depth articles for Indiana can be found in this monthly publication.

Contact information:
Morton J. Marcus, Director
Indiana Business Research Center
email: marcus@indiana.edu
http://www.IUPUI.edu/it/ibrc/ibrc.html

Institute for Water Research (IWR) at Michigan State University (MSU)

The IWR provides timely information for addressing contemporary land and water resource issues through coordinated multidisciplinary efforts using advanced information and networking systems. The IWR endeavors to strengthen MSU's efforts in non-traditional education, outreach, and interdisciplinary studies utilizing available advanced technology, and partnerships with local, state, regional, and federal organizations and individuals. Activities include coordinating education and training programs on surface and ground water protection, land use and watershed management, and many others. Contact information:

John Bartholic, Director
115 Manly Miles Building, 1405 S. Harrison Road, East Lansing, MI 48823-5243
bartholi@pilot.msu.edu
phone: (517)353-3742, fax: (517)353-1812

The Great Lakes Environmental Research Laboratory (GLERL)

The lab, located in Ann Arbor, Michigan, is a U.S. Department of Commerce (DOC) facility operated by the National Oceanic and Atmospheric Administration (NOAA), Office of Oceanic and Atmospheric Research (OAR), through the NOAA Environmental Research Laboratories (ERL). GLERL's mission is to conduct integrated, interdisciplinary environmental research in support of resource management and environmental services in coastal and estuarine water, with special emphasis on the Great Lakes.

GLERL's research provides Federal, State, and international decision and policy makers with scientific understanding of:

- sources, pathways, fates, and effects of toxicants in the Great Lakes;
- natural hazards such as severe waves, storm surges, and ice;
- ecosystems and their interactions, including the implications of invasion by nuisance species;
- the hydrology and water levels of the Great Lakes; and
- regional effects related to global climate change.

Contact information:

Dr. Stephen Brandt, Director
NOAA Great Lakes Environmental Research Laboratory
2205 Commonwealth Blvd., Ann Arbor, MI 48105-2945
phone: (313) 741-2235, fax: (313) 741-2055
email: director@glerl.noaa.gov
http://www.glerl.noaa.gov/

GLERL Data Sets

A variety of data sets collected at GLERL are available for access. Unless noted otherwise in the description of the data set, you may inquire for detailed information on data access to:

Cathy M. Darnell
Information Services, Great Lakes Environmental Research Laboratory
2205 Commonwealth Blvd., Ann Arbor, MI 48105-1593
phone: (313) 741-2262
email: Darnell@glerl.noaa.gov
http://www.glerl.noaa.gov/data/data.html

Great Lakes Commission

The Commission has three principal functions: 1) information sharing among the Great Lakes States; 2) coordination of state positions on issues of regional concern; and 3) advocacy of those positions on which the States agree. The Commission provides services ranging from policy development and regional advocacy, to communications, coordination and research. Contact information:

Michael J. Donahue, Executive Director
Great Lakes Commission
400 Fourth St., Ann Arbor, MI 48103-4816
phone: (313) 665-9135, fax: (313) 665-4370
email: glc@great-lakes.net
http://www.glc.org/)

U.S. Geological Survey's Biological Resources Division
The BRD mission is to work with others to provide the scientific understanding and technologies needed to support the sound management and conservation of our nation's biological resources. Contact information:

Dennis B. Fenn, Chief Biologist
Biological Resources Division — USGS
U.S. Department of the Interior, Office of Public Affairs
12201 Sunrise Valley Drive, Reston, VA 20192
phone: (703) 648-4050
email: denny_fenn@nbs.gov
http://www.nbs.gov/

Great Lakes Science Center
The Center is dedicated to providing scientific information for the management of our nation's biological resources. The Center is headquartered in Ann Arbor, Michigan, and has biological stations and research vessels located throughout the Great Lakes Basin. The precursor to the current Center's programs began in 1927 when investigations of the collapse of the Lake Erie cisco population were initiated by the Center's first director, Dr. John Van Oosten. Its research spans a range of studies including fish populations and communities, aquatic habitats, terrestrial ecology, nearshore and coastal communities and the biological processes that occur in the complex ecosystem of the Great Lakes.
Contact information:

U.S. Geological Survey, Biological Resources Division
Great Lakes Science Center, 1451 Green Road, Ann Arbor, MI 48105
phone: (313)994-3331, fax: (313) 994-8780
http://www.glsc.nbs.gov/)

The Great Lakes Sea Grant Network
Through its network of Advisory Service agents and its use of modern communications and education techniques, the Great Lakes Sea Grant Network plays a central role in supplying the region and the nation with usable solutions to pressing problems and providing the basic information needed to better manage Great Lakes resources for present and future generations of Americans. Contact information:

Anders W. Andren, Institute Director
University of Wisconsin Sea Grant Institute
1800 University Avenue, Madison, Wisconsin 53705-4094
phone: (608)262-0905, fax: (608)263-2063
email address: awandren@seagrant.wisc.edu
http://www.seagrant.wisc.edu/GreatLakes/glnetwork/glnetwork.html

The Lake Erie Soil and Water Research and Education Center at the University of Toledo
The Center is an interdisciplinary center dedicated to environmental research. The goal of the Center is to assemble within a single facility programs in agricultural management, environmental chemistry, geography and land use planning, remote sensing and environmental monitoring, aquatic and terrestrial ecology, and aquatic ecosystem management to create a multidisciplinary center exploring the linkages between land use and water quality in the western catchment of Lake Erie. The Center is located in the northwestern corner of Ohio's Maumee Bay State Park. Contact information:

Lake Erie Center, The University of Toledo
2801 W. Bancroft Street, Toledo, Ohio 43606
phone: (419)530-5503, fax: (419)530-7737
email the secretary, Patricia Uzmann: puzmann@uoft02.utoledo.edu
http://www.utoledo.edu/www/lake-erie-center/

U.S. EPA Region 5
Includes Illinois, Indiana, Michigan, Minnesota, Ohio, and Wisconsin. The EPA conducts research and provides information regarding important environmental issues in regions throughout the United States. Contact information:

David Ullrich, Regional Administrator
U.S. EPA, Region 5
77 West Jackson Blvd., Chicago, IL 60604
phone: (312) 886-3000
http://www.epa.gov/region5/

U.S. EPA Great Lakes National Program Office (GLNPO)
GLNPO was created administratively in 1978 to oversee fulfillment of the U.S. commitment under the Great Lakes Water Quality Agreement with Canada to restore and maintain the physical, chemical, and biological integrity of the Great Lakes basin ecosystem. GLNPO carries out a program which combines research and monitoring with education and outreach, and supports grants for specific activities to enhance and protect the Great Lakes environment.

Contact information:
Gary Gulezian, Director
United States Environmental Protection Agency
Great Lakes National Program Office
77 West Jackson Boulevard, Chicago, Illinois 60604
phone: (312) 886-4040, fax: (312) 353-2018
http://www.epa.gov/glnpo/)

STATE, CANADIAN, AND INDIAN NATURAL RESOURCES OFFICES

Great Lakes Indian Fish and Wildlife Commission
P.O. Box 9
Odanah, WI 54861
phone: (715) 682-6619, fax: (715) 682-9294

Canada Department of Fisheries and Oceans
Fisheries and Oceans, Central and Arctic Region
501 University Crescent, Winnipeg,Manitoba R3T 2N6 Canada
phone: (204) 983-5000, fax: (204) 984-2401
http://www.ncr.dfo.ca/home_e.htm

Environment Canada
Inquiry Centre
351 St. Joseph Boulevard, Hull, Quebec, K1A 0H3
phone (819) 997-2800 or 1-800-668-6767, fax: (819) 953-2225
EnviroFax: (819) 953-0966
email: enviroinfo@cpgsv1.am.doe.ca
http://www.ec.gc.ca/

Province of Ontario, Ministry of Natural Resources
Natural Resources Information Centre, in Toronto:
General Inquiry 416-314-2000
French Inquiry 416-314-1665

Regional Office - Thunder Bay
435 S. James St., Suite 221, Thunder Bay, Ontario P7E 6S8 Canada
phone: (807) 473-3023

Regional Office - Sault Ste. Marie
875 Queen Street, Sault Ste. Marie, Ontario P6A 2B3Canada
phone: (705) 949-1231
http://www.mnr.gov.on.ca/MNR/

State of Illinois, Department of Natural Resources
Brent Manning, Director
Illinois Department of Natural Resources
524 South Second Street, Springfield, IL 62701-1705
phone: (217) 785-6302, fax: (217) 524-4639
http://dnr.state.il.us/

State of Indiana, Department of Natural Resources
Larry D. Macklin, Director
402 W. Washington Street, Indianapolis, IN 46204
phone: 317-232-4020, fax: 317-232-8036
http://www.state.in.us/dnr/index.html

State of Michigan, Department of Natural Resources
K. L. Cool, Director
Michigan Department of Natural Resources
Box 30028, Lansing MI 48909
phone: (517) 373-2329
http://www.dnr.state.mi.us/

Michigan DNR, Institute for Fisheries Research
A research station of Fisheries Division, Michigan Department of Natural Resources
(MDNR). Contact information:
Institute for Fisheries Research
1109 N. University Ave., 212 Museums Annex Bldg. 1084, Ann Arbor, MI 48109-1084
phone: (313) 663-3554, fax: (313) 663-9399
http://www.dnr.state.mi.us/www/ifr/ifrhome/index.htm)

Office of the Great Lakes, Michigan Department of Environmental Quality
The Office of the Great Lakes was created by the Michigan Legislature in 1985 to provide Michigan State Government offices, and the public, with a single information
center on issues affecting or involving the Great Lakes, and to guide the development
of government policies, programs and procedures that will protect, enhance, and provide wise management of Great Lakes resources.

It provides advice and assistance to the Governor's office, members and staff of the
Michigan Legislature and Congressional delegation, Directors and staff of the DNR,
Public Health, Agriculture, Transportation and other State offices. It participates in
regional policy discussions and forums such as the Great Lakes Commission, International Joint Commission, Council of Great Lakes Governors and the Binational Executive Committee. Contact information:
G. Tracy Mehan, Director
Michigan Department of Environmental Quality
P.O. Box 30473 , Lansing, MI 48909-4053
phone: (517) 335-4056
http://www.deq.state.mi.us/ogl/

State of Minnesota, Department of Natural Resources
500 Lafayette Road, St. Paul, MN 55155-4001
phone: (612) 296-6157, toll free phone: 1-800-766-6000
e-mail: info@dnr.state.mn.us
http://www.dnr.state.mn.us/toc/toc.htm

State of New York, Department of Environmental Conservation
John P. Cahill, Acting DEC Commissioner
50 Wolf Road, Albany, New York ????
phone: (518) 457-3446
http://www.dec.state.ny.us/

State of Ohio, Department of Natural Resources
Ohio Department of Natural Resources
Publications Center, 1952 Belcher Drive, Bldg. C-1, Columbus, OH 43224
phone: (614)265-6565, fax: (614)268-1943
email: Infomail@dnr.state.oh.us
http://www.dnr.ohio.gov/

State of Pennsylvania, Fish and Boat Commission
Executive Director, Peter A. Colangelo
State Headquarters: 3532 Walnut Street, Harrisburg, PA 17109
phone: (717) 657-4515
Mailing Address: P.O. Box 67000, Harrisburg, PA 17106-7000
http://www.state.pa.us/PA_Exec/Fish_Boat/

State of Wisconsin, Department of Natural Resources
George Meyer, DNR Secretary
Information center phone: (608) 266-2621
http://www.dnr.state.wi.us/

Project Collaborators

PANEL OF ECONOMISTS

Sandra Archibald
Associate Professor
Hubert H. Humphrey Institute of
    Public Affairs
University of Minnesota
255 Humphrey Center, 301 19th Ave., South
Minneapolis, MN 55455
612/625-3533 fax: 612/625-6351
sarch@hhh.umn.edu

Richard Bishop
Professor
Dept. of Agricultural & Applied Economics
University of Wisconsin-Madison
Taylor Hall, Room 334, 427 Lorch Street
Madison, WI 53706-1513
608/262-8966, fax: 608/262-4376
bishop@aae.wisc.edu

John B. Braden
Professor of Environmental and
    Natural Resource Economics
Director of Illinois Water Resources Center
University of Illinois
1101 W. Peabody Drive, Room 278
Urbana, IL 61801
217/333-0536 or 217/333-8159
fax: 217/244-8583
j-braden@uiuc.edu

Dallas Burtraw
Resources for the Future
1616 P St., NW
Washington, DC 20036
202/328-5087, fax: 202/939-3460
burtraw@rff.org

Jay Coggins
Department of Applied Economics
University of Minnesota-St. Paul
1994 Buford Ave.
St. Paul, MN 55108
612/625-6232, fax: 612/625-2729
jcoggins@dept.agecon.umn.edu

Paul Faeth
World Resources Institute
1709 New York Ave., NW
Washington, DC 20006
202/638-6300, fax: 202/638-0036
paul@wri.org

John Hoehn
Professor
Department of Agricultural Economics,
Michigan State University
East Lansing, MI 48824
517/353-6735, fax: 517/432-1800
hoehn@pilot.msu.edu

Leroy Hushak
Ohio State University Extension
2120 Fyffe Road
Columbus, OH 43210-1066
614/292-3548, fax: 614/292-7710
hushak.1@osu.edu

Mike Klepinger
Sea Grant Extension Specialist
Michigan Sea Grant
334 Natural Resources Building
East Lansing, MI 48824
517/353-5508, fax: 517/353-6496
klep@pilot.msu.edu

Doug Lipton
Department of Agricultural and
    Resource Economics
University of Maryland-College Park
Room 2200, Symons Hall
College Park, MD 20742
301/405-1280, fax: 301/314-9032
dlipton@arec.umd.edu

Frank Lupi
Assistant Professor
Department of Agricultural Economics
Michigan State University
East Lansing, MI 48824-1039
517/432-3883, fax: 517/432-1800
lupi@pilot.msu.edu

Brian Miller
Ext. Wildlife Specialist
Coordinator of Marine Advisory Services
IL-IN Sea Grant Program
1159 Forestry Building
West Lafayette, IN 47907-1159
765/494-3586, fax: 765/496-2422
brian_miller@acn.purdue.edu

Tom Muir
Senior Economist
Economics Section
Great Lakes Environment and
    Economics Office
Great Lakes and Corporate Affairs
Environment Canada-Ontario Region
867 Lakeshore Road
Burlington, Ontario, Canada L7R 1Y7
905/336-4951, fax: 905/336-8901
tom.muir@ec.gc.ca

Alan Randall
Department of Agricultural,
    Environmental, and Development
    Economics
The Ohio State University
2120 Fyffe Road
Columbus, OH 43210
614/292-6423, fax: 614/292-0078
arandall@magnus.acs.ohio-state.edu

Karl Schaefer
Great Lakes and Corporate Affairs Office
Environment Canada — Ontario Region
867 Lakeshore Road, P.O. Box 5050
Burlington, Ontario, Canada L7R 4A6
905/336-4950, fax: 905/336-8901
karl.schaefer@ec.gc.ca

Brent Sohngen
Department of Agricultural,
    Environmental, and Development
    Economics
The Ohio State University
2120 Fyffe Road
Columbus, OH 43210-1067
614/688-4640, fax: 614/292-0078
sohngen.1@osu.edu

ADVISORY BOARD

Virginia Aveni
Manager, Environmental Planning
Cuyahoga County Planning Commission
323 Lakeside Ave.
Cleveland, OH 44113
216/443-3716, fax: 216/443-3737

Ron Baird
Director
National Sea Grant College Program
National Oceanic & Atmospheric Admin.
1315 East West Highway
Silver Spring, MD 20910
301/713-2448, fax: 301/713-1031

Stephen Brandt
Director
Great Lakes Environmental Research Lab.
2205 Commonwealth Blvd.
Ann Arbor, MI 48105-1593
734/741-2244, fax: 734/741-2003
brandt@glerl.noaa.gov

Jim Chandler
International Joint Commission
1250 23rd St., NW, Suite 100
Washington, D.C. 20440
202/736-9000, fax: 202/736-9015
chandlerj@ijc.achilles.net

Mike Donahue
Executive Director
Great Lakes Commission
The Argus II Building
400 S. Fourth Street
Ann Arbor, MI 48103-4816
734/665-9135, fax: 734/665-4370
mdonahue@glc.org

Tim Eder
National Wildlife Federation
Great Lakes Natural Resource Center
506 East Liberty, 2nd Floor
Ann Arbor, MI 48104-2210
734/769-3351, fax: 734/769-1449
eder@nwf.org

Maggie Grant
Executive Director
Council of Great Lakes Governors
35 East Wacker Drive, Suite 1850
Chicago, IL 60601
312/407-0177, fax: 312/407-0038

Greg Hill
Great Lakes Program Leader
Wisconsin Department of Natural
    Resources
101 S. Webster St.
P.O. Box 7921
Madison, WI 53707
608/267-9352, fax: 608/267-2800
HILLG@dnr.state.wi.us

John Jackson
Great Lakes United
17 Major Street
Kitchener, Ontario N2H 4R1 Canada
519/744-7503, fax: 519/744-1546
jjackson@web.net

George Kuper
President and Chief Executive Officer
Council of Great Lakes Industries
P.O. Box 134006
Ann Arbor, MI 48113-4006
734/663-1944, fax: 734/663-2424
ghk@iti.org

Sheila Tooze
Environmental Affairs Officer
Canadian Embassy
501 Pennsylvania Ave., NW
Washington, D.C. 20001
202/682-1740, fax: 202/682-7792

COLLABORATING ECONOMISTS

Sudip Chattopadhyay
Assistant Professor
San Francisco State University
1600 Holloway Avenue
San Francisco, California 94132

Alan Krupnick
Resources for the Future

Daniel McGrath
Illinois-Indiana Sea Grant
College of Urban Planning and
  Public Affairs
University of Illinois at Chicago
412 S. Peoria Street, Suite 400
Chicago 60607
312/355-1276
dmcgrath@uic.edu

PARTICIPANTS OF THE GREAT LAKES ECONOMIC VALUATION STAKEHOLDER'S FORUM

Don Arcuri
Ohio Lake Erie Foundation

Ron Baba
Oneida Tribe of Indians of Wisconsin,
Ecosystem Planning and Protection

Thomas Baldini
International Joint Commission

Jeanette Ball
City of Toledo, Division of
Environmental Services

Scott Bernstein
Center for Neighborhood Technology

Lee Botts
Great Lakes citizen

Werner Braun
Dow Chemical Company

James Bredin
Michigan Department of Environmental
Quality, Office of the Great Lakes

Tim Brown
Delta Institute

Kelly Burch
Pennsylvania Department of
Environmental Protection, Office of the
Great Lakes

Jeff Busch
Ohio Lake Erie Office

Dave Cowgill
U.S. Environmental Protection Agency,
Great Lakes National Program Office

Roger Crawford
Outboard Marine Corporation

Cameron Davis
Lake Michigan Foundation

William Desvousges
observer, Triangle Economic Research

Mike Donahue
Great Lakes Commission

Emily Green
Sierra Club

John Hartig
International Joint Commission

Greg Hill
Wisconsin Department of Natural
Resources

John Jackson
Great Lakes United

Sara Johnson
River Alliance of Wisconsin

Julia Klee
Joyce Foundation

Gerrit Knaap
University of Illinois at Urbana-Champaign, Department of Urban and Regional Planning

Merrill Leffler
observer, Maryland Sea Grant

Julie Letterhos
Ohio Environmental Protection Agency, Division of Surface Water

Percy Magee
USDA_NRCS, Ohio Lake Eria Office

Bill Majewski
St. Louis River Area of Concern

Daniel McGrath
Illinois-Indiana Sea Grant

Tracey Mehan
Michigan Department of Environmental Quality, Office of the Great Lakes

Jan Miller
U.S. Army Corps of Engineers

Nancy Milton
Great Lakes Science Center

Mary Mulligan
City of Gary, Department of Planning and Community Development

Diana Olinger
National Oceanic and Atmospheric Administration, Coastal Programs Division

Benjamin Perry
observer, American Rivers

Mary Powers
Kalamazoo River Area of Concern

Terry Quinney
Ontario Federation of Anglers and Hunters

Mike Ryan
Northwest Indiana Steelheaders

Sue Senecah
Office of New York State Senator Maziarz, New York Coalition of Great Lakes Legislators

Ray Skelton
Seaway Port Authority of Duluth

Dan Thomas
Great Lakes Sport Fishing Council

Geoffrey Thornburn
International Joint Commission

Marc Tuchman
U.S. Environmental Protection Agency, Great Lakes National Program Offce

The project team also thanks the following people:

Sudip Chattopadhyay
Kansas State University, Manhattan

Hyma Gollamundi
Portfolio Management Modeling

Sara Gottlieb
New Mexico Natural Heritage Program

Jon Jensen
George Gund Foundation

Alan Krupnick
Resources for the Future

Daniel McGrath
University of Illinois at Chicago, Great Cities Institute

Jon Rausch
The Ohio State University, Department of Agricultural Economics

Donald Scavia
National Oceanic and Atmospheric Administration, Coastal Ocean Program Sediment Priority Action Committee of the Great Lakes Water Quality Board

David Cowgill
U.S. EPA, Great Lakes National Program
Office

Frank Estabrooks
New York Department of Environmental
Conservation

Kelly Burch
Pennsylvania Department of
Environmental Resources

Greg Hill
Wisconsin Department of Natural
Resources

Julie Letterhos
Ohio Environmental Protection Agency

Jan Miller
U.S. Army Corp of Engineers

Tracy Mehan
Michigan Department of Environmental
Quality

Marc Tuchman
U.S. EPA, Great Lakes National Program
Office

Gail Krantzberg
Ontario Ministry of Environment and
Energy

Simon Llewellyn
Environment Canada

Ian Orchard
Environment Canada

Griff Sherbin
Environment Canada

Michael Zarull
Canada Centre for Inland Waters,
National Water Research Institute

PROJECT MANAGERS

Allegra Cangelosi
Senior Policy Analyst
Northeast-Midwest Institute
218 D St SE
Washington, DC 20003
202/544-5200, fax: 202/544-0043
acangelo@nemw.org

Patricia Cicero
Northeast-Midwest Institute
1996-1998
Carrie Selberg
Northeast-Midwest Institute
1999-2000

Jessica Taverna
Research Assistant
Northeast-Midwest Institute
218 D St SE
Washington, DC 20003
202/544-5200, fax: 202/544-0043
jtaverna@nemw.org

Rodney Weiher
Chief Economist
Policy and Strategic Planning
National Oceanic & Atmospheric Admin.
Department of Commerce
14th & Constitution Ave., NW, Room 6117
Washington, DC 20230
202/482-0636, fax: 202/501-3024
rodney.f.weiher@noaa.gov

Excerpt from Restoration and Compensation Determination Plan: Lower Fox River/Green Bay Natural Resource Damage Assessment[25]

1. INTRODUCTION AND SUMMARY

1.1 Introduction

The Department of the Interior (Department) acting through the U.S. Fish and Wildlife Service (the Service), the National Oceanic and Atmospheric Administration (NOAA) of the Department of Commerce, the Menominee Indian Tribe of Wisconsin (MITW), the Oneida Tribe of Indians of Wisconsin (OTIW), the Michigan Attorney General, and the Little Traverse Bay Bands of Odawa Indians (collectively, the Co-trustees)[26] are conducting an assessment of natural resource damages (known as a natural resource damage assessment, or NRDA, that have resulted from releases of PCBs to the lower Fox River/Green Bay ecosystem. Section 107 of the Comprehensive Environmental Response, Compensation and Liability Act (CERCLA, more commonly known as the federal "Superfund" law) [42 U.S.C. § 9607], Section 311 of the Federal Water Pollution Control Act (CWA, commonly known as the Clean Water Act) [33 U.S.C. § 1321], and the National Oil and Hazardous Substances Pollution Contingency Plan (NCP) [40 CFR Part 300] provide authority to the Co-trustees to seek such damages.

[25] *Prepared for U.S. Fish and Wildlife Service, U.S. Department of the Interior, U.S. Department of Justice, Oneida Tribe of Indians of Wisconsin, Menominee Tribe of Indians of Wisconsin, National Oceanic and Atmospheric Administration, Little Traverse Bay Bands of Odawa Indians, and Michigan Attorney General. Prepared by Stratus Consulting, November 2000.*

[26] *These agencies are referred to as natural resource "Co-trustees" because they have agreed to work together to perform a single, comprehensive, joint natural resource damage assessment with the aim of restoring natural resources that have been injured as a result of releases of PCBs. The Wisconsin Department of Natural Resouces (WDNR) declined a 1993 invitation to conduct a joint NRDA and entered into an agreement in 1997 to conduct a separate assessment led by the Fox River Group (FRG) of paper mills. However, in 2000 the WDNR entered a joint assessment plan addendum with the Co-trustees designed to merge compatible parts of the FRG-led NRDA with the Co-trustees NRDA, and WDNR subsequently has endorsed parts of the Co-trustees NRDA (U.S. FWS, 2000; WDNR, 2000). The Co-trustees have also invited other state and tribal agencies in Michigan to join the Fox River and Green Bay NRDA because much of Green Bay is in Michigan waters, Fox River PCBs contaminate natural resources that routinely cross between Wisconsin and Michigan, and many opportunities for environmental restoration in and around Green Bay are in Michigan.*

The Co-trustees' NRDA follows an administrative process that is outlined in federal regulations at 43 CFR Part 11 (Department regulations). The objective of this NRDA process is to compensate the public, through environmental restoration, for losses to natural resources that have been caused by releases of PCBs into the environment. The results of this administrative process are contained in a series of planning and decision documents that have been published for public review. The Department completed a Preassessment Screen and Determination in May 1994 (U.S. FWS, 1994), which concluded that there was sufficient information to proceed with an NRDA for the Lower Fox River and Green Bay Environment. In August 1996, the Co-trustees published for public comment an assessment plan (U.S. FWS and Hagler Bailly Consulting, 1996) for the Lower Fix River and Green Bay Environment. This plan provided information on which natural resources would be assessed for injuries, the Co-trustees authority for conducting the assessment, and coordination among Co-trustees. In addition, the assessment plan confirmed water, sediment, fish, and wildlife exposure to PCBs, discussed the recovery period for natural resources exposed to PCBs, and outlined pathway and injury assessment approaches, damage determination methodologies, and quality assurance measures. The Co-trustees published for public comment three addenda to the assessment plan. The first (U.S. FWS and Hagler Bailly Services, 1997) outlined additional approaches that the Co-trustees would use, including additional detail on injury studies of walleye, waterfowl, tree swallows, and Forster's terns; assessment of transportation service interruptions due to injured sediments; and assessment of injuries and damages specific to the Oneida Tribe. The second addendum (U.S. FWS and Hagler Bailly Services, 1998) was an initial restoration and compensation determination plan (iRCDP), which provided an overview of the restoration planning and damage determination process. In particular, the iRCDP described criteria for determining project acceptability, project focus, project implementation, and project benefits; the process for ranking and scaling projects (including the total value equivalency economic assessment); and the process and methodologies for determining compensable values, including the recreational fishing damages economic assessment. The third addendum (U.S. FWS, 2000) set forth a process that could result in a unified NRDA acceptable to both the Co-trustees and the WDNR.

In addition to these planning and decision documents, specific results and findings of the Co-trustees NRDA were published for public review in a series of reports addressing PCB transport pathways, natural resource injuries, and economic damage determinations (U.S. FWS and Stratus Consulting, 1998, 1999a, 1999b, 1999c, 1999d, 1999f).

This Restoration and Compensation Determination Plan (RCDP) represents the next phase of the NRDA process. In it, the Co-trustees present their planned approach for restoring injured natural resources and compensating the public for losses caused by the releases of PCBs. As such, the RCDP ties together the Co-trustees' previous injury determinations, completes the economic valuation of damages, and presents an evaluation of the type and scale of environmental restoration required to make the public whole. The public is afforded an opportunity to comment on the RCDP, and the Co-trustees will respond to those comments in the Report of Assessment.[27]

In addition to providing for the recovery of natural resource damages, the Superfund Law provides for cleanup of the environment by federal and state response agencies in order to address ongoing risks to human health and the environment. The U.S. Environmental Protection Agency (EPA) has proposed the site for inclusion on the National Priorities List (NPL) of Superfund sires, and EPA and WDNR currently are performing a Remedial Investigation/Feasibility Study (RI/FS) to evaluate possible cleanup activities. The culmination of this ongoing process will be the publication of a Record of Decision (ROD) by EPA in which the EPA's decision regarding remedial actions for the site will be documented.

As described in the Co-trustees iRCDP (U.S. FWS and Hagler Bailly Services, 1998), final assessment of natural resource damages is dependent on the results of the RI/FS process because the potential for restoration and the nature and extent of future damages will depend on the extent of PCB cleanup undertaken by the response agencies. Therefore, the final natural resource damage claim will be calculated after EPA has issued the ROD for the site. After publication of the ROD, the Co-trustees will issue a report of assessment [43 CFR § 11.90] that will make any necessary updates to previous determinations, will summarize and respond to comments provided on the assessment plan and addenda, and will result in a claim, on behalf of the public, for a sum certain, which is a definitive damage claim.[28] Once a damages award has been determined, the Co-trustees will develop a detailed restoration plan (the post-award restoration plan) for public comment that will provide a detailed description of the Co-trustees' restoration measures, including descriptions of the specific projects that will be undertaken to restore, rehabilitate, replace, or acquire natural resources and thereby compensate the public for harm caused by PCBs.

The RCDP is organized as follows: the remainder of Chapter 1 represents a summary of the Co-trustees' Restoration and Compensation Determination Plan. Chapter 2 represents a summary of the Co-trustees' determination and quantification of injuries to natural resources in the Lower Fox River/Green Bay ecosystem. Chapter 3 describes the

---

[27] *If, as a result of public comments, the Co-trustees make substantive changes to their restoration and compensation approach, the RCDP may be revised and finalized in a subsequent public release document.*

[28] *A final damage claim for the Fox River/Green Bay site cannot be completed until EPA and WDNR's response actions have been selected because of the relationship between the extent of site cleanup undertaken by the response agencies and total natural resource damages. As was discussed in the iRCDP, the quicker and more complete the remedy or cleanup, the less the total harm to the environment that must be addressed through restoration. At sites like the Lower Fox River and Green Bay Environment, where decades of harm have already occurred and where even the best available remedies will not compensate the public for past harm, restoration activities are necessary to compensate the public for losses incurred. In addition, even the most aggressive cleanup in the river cannot prevent further harm in Green Bay, where most of the PCBs released by Fox River paper mills now reside, and injuries will continue in the Fox River for some time in the future. The claim for damages therefore will require evaluation of the extent and timing of site cleanup and the rate of recovery of natural resources to baseline conditions.*

Co-trustees' selected restoration and compensation determination approach. Chapter 4 provides a summary of the Co-trustees' planning and coordination activities. Finally, detailed descriptions of key elements of the Co-trustees' restoration and compensation determination are provided in technical appendices to this RCDP.

1.2.1 Summary of Co-Trustees' RCDP for the Lower Fox River/Green Bay NRDA

The Co-trustees' natural resource damage assessment includes three primary elements: injury determination, injury quantification, and damage determination [43 CFR § 11.60(b)]. The Co-trustees have previously completed the first two elements, which yielded the following determinations for the Fox River/Green Bay natural resource damage assessment: PCB Pathway Determination (August 1999), Injuries to Surface Water Resources (November 1999), Injuries to Fishery Resources (November 1999), and Injuries to Avian Resources (May 1999).

This RCDP, along with the iRCDP published in September 1998 and the Recreational Fishing Damages Determination published in November 1999, describes the activities that constitute the third element of the assessment—damage determination. Under the Department's regulations, damage determination included four primary trustee activities: development of a reasonable number of possible alternatives for restoration, rehabilitation, replacement, and/or acquisition of equivalent resources; selection of the most appropriate alternative; identification of methods for estimating the costs of the restoration alternative selected; and identification of methods for determining the compensable value of the services lost to the public associated with the selected alternative [43 CFR §§11.80, 11.82-11.83]. These activities serve as a blueprint for producing the final natural resource damage claim, which comprises the cost of restoration to baseline of the natural resources and the services they provide, the compensable value of services lost until baseline is achieved, and the Co-trustees' reasonable assessment costs [42 U.S.C. § 9607(a)(4)(C), 43 CFR § 11.80(b)].

To select a preferred restoration alternative, the Co-trustees compiled and analyzed a list of more than 600 potential projects, in light of the factors set out in 43 CFR § 11.82(d) and decision-making criteria published in the iRCDP. In addition, the Co-trustees conducted a total value equivalency study (Appendix A) to help determine the types and scale of restoration projects that would be necessary to restore the natural resources to baseline, as measured by the value of the services they provide, and to compensate for any ongoing and future losses of services. CERCLA prohibits natural resource trustees from any double recovery for natural resource damages [42 U.S.C. § 9607(f)(I)]. To avoid double counting between the value of restoration projects and compensable values measured in the recreational fishing study, the Co-trustees propose to use the recreational fishing study for past damages only, and costs of restoration for future damages only.

In selecting their preferred restoration alternative, the Co-trustees rejected the no-action/natural recovery alternative. Under this alternative, no further actions would be taken to restore natural resources. In addition, the Co-trustees rejects a PCB removal alternative because PCB removal is currently being evaluated by EPA and WDNR as part of the ongoing RI/FS.

Instead, the Co-trustees' preferred restoration alternative focuses on performing resource-based restoration actions to improve the environmental health of the Lower Fox River and Green Bay Environment and thereby compensate for losses resulting from PCB injuries. The Co-trustees' restoration plan for the NRDA will involve a mix of actions designed to provide ecological and social benefits. A central element of the Co-trustees' restoration approach is ensuring that the restoration addresses the full geographical and ecological scope of the injuries to natural resources. Therefore, in developing their final restoration plan, the Co-trustees will ensure that restoration activities:

- Address the entire Lower Fox River and Green Bay Environment, from Little Lake Butte des Mortes in the south to the Bays des Noc in the north
- Encompass the unique range of habitats in the Green Bay region, including the aquatic habitat of the bay itself, the coastal wetlands on the west shore, the rich riverine habitats that connect to the bay, and the valuable ecological habitats of the Door Peninsula and the Bays des Noc
- Provide for long-term recovery, protection, and enhancement of the unique natural resource endowment of the Lower Fox River and Green Bay Environment
- Consider human uses of the natural environment to provide for ongoing and long-term active and passive uses of Green Bay natural resources.

The specific restoration actions that constitute the Co-trustees' preferred alternative include wetland preservation, wetland restoration, and reduction of nonpoint source runoff loads into the bay from cropland through conservation tillage and installation of vegetated buffer strips along streams. These actions will provide valuable environmental benefits that will compensate for the injuries caused by PCBs:

- Wetlands provide valuable habitat for many fish and bird species. They are highly productive areas, and help reduce wave erosion, contain nonpoint source runoff, and recycle nutrients. Many fish species of Green Bay rely on coastal wetlands for breeding and rearing, including yellow perch, northern pike, and largemouth bass, as well as shiners and minnows, which are essential prey items for many birds and larger fish. Many bird species also rely on wetlands for breeding and feeding, such as herons, rails, eagles, and terns. Coastal, riparian, and near-shore wetlands historically were an integral component of the habitat and wildlife diversity of the Green

Bay area. However, most of the wetlands around Green Bay have been drained or filled, making preserving the remaining wetlands an important priority. Actions to preserve and restore wetlands thus can improve the environmental quality of the Lower Fox River and Green Bay Environment to compensate for the ecological and human use of service losses caused by PCB injuries.

■ Nonpoint source runoff pollution into Green Bay can stimulate the growth of blue-green algae, which causes the periodic algae blooms in inner Green Bay. The blue-green algae also contribute to low oxygen conditions (when the algae die), making the water less habitable for some native fish species and more hospitable to species such as carp, which can survive in low-oxygen waters. Blue-green algae contribute little to the aquatic food chain of the bay, and can release a chemical when they die that can irritate people's skin and eyes on contact. The decreased light penetration in the bay caused by runoff limits the growth of submerged aquatic vegetation that provides important habitat for fish and waterfowl, and can also reduce the feeding success of sight-feeding fish such as sport fish like walleye and northern pike. Reducing nonpoint source runoff pollution can improve the quality of the Lower Fox River and green bay Environment, thereby compensating for the decrease in environmental quality caused by PCBs.

■ Runoff control through vegetated buffer strips and conservation tillage practices also provides some habitat services for wildlife. The streambank stabilization caused by the roots of the vegetation used in buffer strips helps to maintain stream geometry, thereby enhancing neighboring stream habitat for fish and macroinvertebrates. The vegetative cover of the buffer strip can provide wildlife nesting and feeding habitat, and can serve as connecting corridors that enable wildlife to move safely from one habitat to another. Conservation tillage can provide cover for birds and small mammals and higher quality habitat for soil invertebrates (which, in turn, are fed upon by small mammals and birds).

In addition, the Co-trustees also included consideration of improvements to existing recreational facility improvements as a component of the restoration. The scale of the environmental restoration projects necessary to compensate the public for injuries to natural resources of the river and bay was determined through a total value equivalency study. The value to the public of the improvement in the environment that will be attained through wetland preservation, wetland restoration, and nonpoint source pollution reductions is balanced with the value of the resources and services lost to the public because of the PCB injuries.

Table 1.1 summarizes the past compensable values (from the recreational fishing damages assessment) and the estimated costs of restoration to address present and future PCB injuries. The restoration costs shown in Table 1.1 are illustrative only, for the amount of restoration required depends on the level of PCB cleanup that will be conducted by the response agencies. In addition, different possible mixes of restoration projects are possible, and the composition of the mix affects the total restoration cost. The Co-trustees prefer a mixture of projects types so that the full range of ecological service types lost because of PCB injuries are restored and the public's full values and attitudes toward restoration of the Lower Fox River and Green Bay Environment resources are adequately addressed. Furthermore, a mix of project types allows for the flexibility necessary to actually implement a restoration plan. The final mix of restoration projects will be determined in the Co-trustees' post-award restoration plan.

Table 1.1.
POTENTIAL DAMAGES UNDER DIFFERENT REMEDIATION SCENARIOS[a]
(MILLIONS OF DOLLARS, 2000 PRESENT VALUE)

Remediation Scenario	Past interim damages (recreational fishing losses)	Present and future damages (restoration costs)[b]	Total
Intensive PCB cleanup (baseline achieved in 20 years)	$65	$111-191	$176-256
Intermediate PCB cleanup (baseline achieved in 40 years)	$65	$158-268	$223-333

[a] *Table does not include the reasonable and necessary costs of conducting the assessment, which will be included in the final claim.*

[b] *Values are from illustrative mixes of restoration project types and are not intended to necessarily represent the costs that will be used in the final claim. See section 3.2.9.*